WOME

on WORK,

Love,

Children

& LIFE

Also by Peggy Orenstein

SchoolGirls: Young Women, Self-Esteem, and the Confidence Gap

WOMEN

on WORK,

Love,

Children

& LIFE

PEGGY ORENSTEIN

PIATKUS

Published in the UK in 2000 by
Judy Piatkus (Publishers) Limited
5 Windmill Street
London W1T 2JA

e-mail info@piatkus.co.uk

For the latest news and information on all our titles,
visit our website at www,.piatkus.co.uk

First published as *Flux* in the USA in 2000
by Doubleday, a division of Random House Inc.

The moral right of the author has been asserted

A catalogue record for this book is available
from the British Library

ISBN 0 7499 2104 4

Printed and bound in Great Britain by
Mackays of Chatham plc, Chatham, Kent

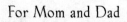
For Mom and Dad

Acknowledgments

Women's lives, as I have discovered, rarely run smooth, and my own has been no exception. The writing of this book coincided with the most challenging period of my life, and I am deeply grateful to those who helped me through not only professionally but personally.

Thanks especially to my editor, Deb Futter, who has been a guiding light throughout my reporting and writing as well as a true friend, more concerned about my well-being than about any publishing deadline. Sandra Dijkstra, my agent, encouraged me to pursue and develop the germ of the idea that became this book.

A network of women across the country helped me arrange the group interviews that formed the core of my reporting, Since some of them are pseudonymously in the book, I will not name them, but thank you all. Thanks, too, to Heather Larsen for transcribing thousands of pages of conversation.

For their advice and counsel at various points during my research, thanks to Joan Jacobs Brumberg, Laura Carstensen, Shirley Feldman, Jane Hamilton, Ravenna Helson, Hazel Markus, Christina Maslach, Phyllis Moen, Philip Morgan, Rachel Rosenfeld, Lillian Rubin, Deb Tolman, and Marilyn Yalom.

A million thanks to my family and devoted friends for their love and patience: to Beatsy, Mel, David, Leslie, John Orenstein (and all the kids!), my "legal eagle" Debbie Orenstein, Rosy Okazaki, the Hamilton and Kawafuchi clans, Hannah and Diane Okazaki, and May Yamamoto, as well as to Barbara Lee Swaiman, Ruth Halpern,

Acknowledgments

Eva and Elly Eilenberg, Peg-bo Edersheim-Kalb, Scott Kalb, Connie Mathiessen, David Weir, David Fallek, Neal Karlen, Susannah Grant, Catherine Taylor, Richard Milner, Robert Washington, John McCormick, Larry Brown, Elly Eisenberg, Jay Martel, Jane Gottesman, Ashley Craddock, Youseef and Kaela Elias, Rachel Silvers, Natalie Campagni Portis and the Cancer Cluster gang, Adam Moss, Doreen Weisenhaus, Lisa Cericola, Laurie Abraham, Diane Cardwell, Laura Marmor, Pat Towers, Beth Fouhy, Joe Marty, Veronica Chambers, Marcelle Karp, Mike Paterniti, Lisa Bain, Kerry Lauerman, Will Dana, Janet Pierson, Danny Sager, and the inimitable Cornelia Lauf. Special, incalculable thanks to Sara Corbett, my ever-gentle reader.

My most profound gratitude goes to two people. Doug Foster is my editorial adviser and dear friend. I could not have written this book without him. And to my husband, Steven Okazaki: Thank you, darling, for cheering me through the rough spots, for your discerning editorial eye, and for your rabid insistence on vacations.

Finally, and most important, I would like to thank all the women who participated in interviews for this book for their candor, their courage, and their commitment to bettering women's lives.

Contents

Introduction:
Lives in Flux

I HADN'T COME TO KALAMAZOO, Michigan, looking for an epiphany, but that is where one found me. Perhaps it was being back in the Midwest, in the clear air, the clean thinking, the familiar topography of my youth. Maybe it was just one of those days when you hear an old question a new way, that quite suddenly shifts your perspective.

I had come to Michigan to talk about teenage girls' declining self-esteem, something I'd done many times since writing *SchoolGirls*, a book that explored the forces that distort young women's self-image and undermine their dreams. I was speaking at a small college on an icy night, and I didn't expect much of a turnout. But when I arrived, the auditorium was packed with parents, teachers, community workers, and students, some sitting cross-legged in the aisles or leaning against the back wall. When I was through, a small platinum-blond woman in her mid-twenties raised her hand. She identified herself as a graduate student in psychology. "It's still so amazing to me that when so much has changed, when we have so many more choices now than we've ever had, girls still go through this," she said.

I'd heard versions of that comment before: from a single thirty-eight-year-old tobacco executive in New York; from a married twenty-seven-year-old social worker in San Diego; from a forty-year-old mother of two daughters in Texas; from white women, black women, Asian women, Latinas. I gave my stock reply: I shrugged my shoulders, offered a wry smile, and said, "Well, you know, it's not like we adult women have it all figured out, is it?" The audience chuckled, and the discussion moved on.

But I didn't. For the first time since I'd begun lecturing across the country a year before, my flip response began to nag at me. I knew it was inadequate. Teenage girls weren't the only ones laboring under the burden of double messages—that much was clear from the evening's knowing laughter. I felt troubled by how blithely we brushed off the connection between the crisis of female adolescence and the contradictions we face as adult women. How could we change the social forces that squelch the hopes of so many girls if we minimize their impact in our own lives?

After that night I focused more intently on my discussions with adult women, listening in the way I'd learned to listen to girls. I began paying attention to a conflicted voice that on the one hand spoke proudly about independence and professional success and on the other fretted over its potential price. In a series of conversations over the next few months, women expressed confusion, even betrayal, over a clash of expectations imposed both from without—from parents, spouses, employers, other women—and from within.

The women I spoke with, who were in their twenties, thirties, and early forties, had, like me, been girls during the heyday of the women's movement. Our identities were formed in a crucible of change; by the time we became adults, sexual norms, marital patterns, relationships with family, and career expectations—the warp and woof of what it meant to be female—had undergone a radical transformation. Like girls today, we had been told we could "be whatever we wanted to be." That message, while well intentioned, ignored the very real obstacles that would block our paths and sometimes set us up, as adults, to blame ourselves when we failed to overcome them. By the late 1980s, that confusion—combined with rollbacks in the gains women made in the workforce, politics, and reproductive rights—resulted in the pronouncement that we "could not have it all" and should stop trying to do so.

Ten years later that backlash has turned to whiplash as both strains of thought duke it out. *The Wall Street Journal* announces "Male Professions Are Much Less So," but *The New York Times* counters, "Equality Eludes Many Women in Law Firms." *Elle* trumpets, "A New Generation of Women Are Examining the Realities of Wedded Life—and They're Not Thrilled with the Result." But how could that be if, according to *Redbook*, "Marriage Is Hot Again"? the Minneapolis *Star Tribune* insists that "Disenchanted Women Give Up Careers to Stay Home," yet, according to *The Wall Street Journal*, "Women Indicate Satisfaction with Role of Big Breadwinner." In separate issues, *Mademoiselle* proclaims both that women are "Single and Loving It" and "I Couldn't Stand Being Single." And while according to the *San Francisco Chronicle*, women who aren't mothers have "No Children, No Regrets," the *Los Angeles Times* warns, "They Wanted It All. Now Some Women Are Finding They've Lost Something Precious—Motherhood."[1]

Hollywood does its part by projecting this cultural schizophrenia at the local megaplex: The early nineties brought *Thelma & Louise*, in which two women who bust loose from female stereotypes are eventually forced to commit suicide. A few years later in *The American President*, Annette Bening knew better. Critic Frank Rich pointed out that as the androgynously named lobbyist Sydney Wade, she was the prototypical media image of a single, successful thirtysomething woman: She may have been a Washington player, but she was ever-glamorous (Annette in Armani!), suitably feminine despite her "mannish" job, and willing to chuck it all for the right guy.[2] Meanwhile, television has offered up its own, if equally confused, heroines: There's Ally McBeal, who listens to her roommate's astute rant that "society drills it into us that women should be married, society drills it into us that smart people should have careers, society drills it into us that women should have children and mothers should stay at home with their children, and society condemns the working mother who doesn't stay at home," then proclaims, "If women really wanted to change it, they could. *I plan to change it.* I just want to get married first." And on *Caroline in the City* Lea Thompson ponders a marriage proposal this way: "I envision myself in a house in Connecticut, driving the three kids to soccer. I don't know if it's a dream come true or my worst nightmare."

THIS IS THE condition we find ourselves in at the turn of the century—a state of flux. Old patterns and expectations have broken down, but new ideas seem fragmentary, unrealistic, and often contradictory. Even the statistics confuse. By the late 1990s, 77 percent of married women with school-age children were in the workforce and 48 percent provided half or more of their family's income. Still, the wage gap between women and men barely budged during the last decade, and women's earnings remain just 74 percent of men's. Women comprised 27 percent of lawyers, although just 13 percent of law partners; 48 percent of managers, but just 3 percent of top earners; 43 percent of tenure track professors, although just 26 percent of those with tenure.[3] As their economic power has grown, women now marry later, have fewer children, and are more likely than ever to remain single or childless.[4] Yet they're also more likely than men to end their lives in poverty. What statistics can't tell us, however, is how real women actually navigate those contradictions, how they perceive their opportunities and constraints in the personal and public realms, how they approach dilemmas involving ambition, sexuality, economic self-sufficiency, partnering, and childbearing in the wake of monumental but incomplete change. Individual stories can provide that deeper understanding. In the mirror of others' experience, women can gain insight into how we all might live fuller lives.

I HAD PERSONAL reasons for talking with women about the themes of their lives. I was hoping, through my work, to find answers for myself. When I started my reporting, I was thirty-four years old, agonizing over a decision newly familiar to women my age: whether or not to have a child. But, I realized, my own state of flux had begun long ago, and it had touched all aspects of my life. Like the women I interviewed, as well as those disjointed Hollywood heroines, I had long vacillated between two visions of womanhood, each posing a conflict between relationships and the self. There was the Good Woman, who earns approval by giving to those around her at the expense of her own needs, and there was the New Woman, who pursues her own desires but risks ending up alone.

To me, the Good Woman was my mother. Unlike the frustrated housewife-moms of many of the women I spoke with, she loved being a caretaker. She raised my two brothers and me, nursed her parents in their old age, and still keeps in touch with a broad network of family and friends, remembering birthdays, anniversaries, deaths, and other milestones. The New Woman was me. By the late 1970s, when I was a teenager, girls were expected to stake our identity on achievement instead of on family roles. We were, as sociologist Ruth Sidel has said, the New American Dreamers, convinced that we had no limitations.[5] As much as I loved my mom, I knew I didn't want to be like her. In fact, I quickly came to see anything that smacked of conventional feminine behavior—from motherhood to female-dominated professions—as retrograde, a threat to my newfound selfhood, unthinkable.

Yet, even then, even as I began to dream about being a journalist (I fancied myself a fifteen-year-old Ellen Goodman), it was clear that something was amiss. In the fall of my junior year of high school I was diagnosed with an eating disorder. I still don't know exactly why it happened. Perhaps I believed that being thinner would attract boys, or maybe it was just the opposite: I was trying to keep the confusion of sexuality at bay. I may have been aping unrealistic media images of women, or honing my physical self to conform to the world of men I strove to enter. Individually, each of those explanations seems both plausible and insufficient; together they speak to a profound ambivalence, an unresolved tension about female identity that went far beyond my own case: It continues to permeate the culture, and women's psyches, to this day.[6]

After stumbling in my teens, I put my faith firmly in the manifest destiny of the New Woman, trusting self-fulfillment to lead to a gratifying life. I moved to New York after college and took a job doing scut work at a magazine. A friend of a friend was vacating an apartment in the West Village. At forty, she had become engaged and believed that the apartment had brought her luck. She wanted to pass on its magic to some other bereft single woman. Marriage? No way. But for a rent-stabilized one-bedroom, I lied, telling her I was desperate to catch a man. That summer I juggled two relationships: with a motorcycle-riding French waiter and a criminal defense attorney who was in town for a few months from San Francisco. This, I thought, was the life: I was moving up the masthead at the magazine, had two boyfriends, a great apartment, what else could a girl ask for?

A few years later, though, something inside me began to shift. I was, by then, twenty-seven, the senior editor of a start-up magazine. Sometimes, after weeks of twelve-hour days, I'd wonder if I'd made a mistake. Was this the life I wanted to live? I began to question whether my focus on career would keep me from finding lasting love. The infamous Harvard marriage study—which said that women who were not wed by thirty were doomed to be married only to their work—had just been released, and though I dismissed it as junk science, it was a direct hit on my secret fears.

Around that time I was offered a position at a political magazine in San Francisco, where the criminal defense lawyer had returned.

He seemed like the kind of guy I ought to marry, although he was in less of a hurry to formalize our relationship than I was. I grabbed the opportunity, letting my heart—or, more accurately, my fears about my heart—make the decision. At work I wrote articles as the resident feminist. In the new desperation I felt in my private life, however, I began measuring my worth through my boyfriend's eyes, and our relationship became the fulcrum of my self-esteem. Slowly, I became unable to articulate my emotional or sexual needs, afraid that if I asserted myself he would leave me. Sometimes I didn't even recognize myself. I stayed with him too long, and I stayed with my next boyfriend too long too, out of a fear of being alone. Why should that have been such a frightening prospect? I was supporting myself, had plenty of friends, a thriving career. But I felt untethered. Old friends were pairing off. Positive images of single women—the Mary Richardses and Anne Maries of my youth who had flourished without husbands—had disappeared to be replaced by the bunny-boiling harridan from *Fatal Attraction*. I was far from home, in a big city among people who were as unmoored and transient as I was. I felt like no one would notice if I just disappeared.

I decided to give relationships a rest for a while, and when I met Steven Okazaki, an independent filmmaker, I told him flatly that I wasn't interested in commitment. Maybe that's what allowed me to be a little more assertive with him, a little more myself within the relationship. As we began to fall in love—discovering shared values and passions—the feeling of being me didn't go away, it was just enhanced. Now, though, after four years of marriage, I found myself at yet another crossroads that seemed to demand a choice between opposing visions of myself as a person, as a woman. I wanted the richness of motherhood in my life but worried over its costs. I could almost hear the traditionalist in me clucking, "You can't have it all," and it infuriated me. Why couldn't I? Why couldn't any of us?

SO, BEGINNING IN 1996, I spent four years interviewing women across the country, both alone and in small groups, to get a sense of the key pressures they faced. I spoke with over two hundred women between the ages of twenty-five and forty-five, women who are in what psychologist Daniel Levinson defines as "early adulthood"—the time when one sets up one's career, makes decisions about love, sex, marriage, childbearing.[7] I asked for volunteers for my interviews when I gave talks, I attended meetings of women's professional associations, advertised in community newsletters and on e-mail lists. I even corralled women in restaurants and on airplanes. It was not a scientific process—sociologists call it the "snowball" method—but it yielded broad results: The groups I convened spanned ethnic, regional, religious, and racial lines. They included women who were single, divorced, married, and lesbian; women with and without children; working, stay-at-home, and single mothers as well as women trying to become pregnant on their own; women in elite, previously male-dominated professions such as law, medicine, and finance, as well as those in more conventionally feminine fields such as teaching, clerical work, and nursing.

Most but not all of the women I interviewed had graduated from college, which was significant. A college education is crucial to the architecture of a female self: Women with BAs report a greater sense of agency and enhanced feelings of potential than less educated women,[8] and I wanted to talk to those who believed they had options. All the women were currently in the broad swath considered middle class—the group Gail Sheehy has called "pacesetters"[9]—although many were raised in blue-collar homes or in poverty. They had grown up all over the country, but at the time of our interviews lived on the East and West coasts or in the Midwest: in New York City and its suburbs, the Washington, D.C., area, Philadelphia, Minneapolis, Chicago, Los Angeles, Portland, the San Francisco Bay Area, and rural South Dakota. Because they shared a great deal about their private lives, I have changed their names and, when they requested it, omitted those of the companies where they worked.

Initially I met with groups of four or five women in living rooms and offices. Our conversations typically lasted three hours and spanned a wide range of topics: how, as adolescents, the women imagined their lives would unfold; what they had learned from their mothers' experiences; their sexual histories and levels of current satisfaction; how their career aspirations changed over time; their evolving expectations regarding relationships, marriage, and motherhood; what they'd learned about managing conflicting demands and choices. With the age young women marry at an all-time high, more of them than ever expect to remain single through their twenties and even well into their thirties, establishing their careers and exploring multiple relationships.[10] I wondered whether this new period of self-discovery, formerly enjoyed only by men, had instilled in them a greater sense of sexual entitlement than women felt in the past. I wondered, too, whether they believed they would be treated equally to men in the workforce, and how nascent ideas about marriage and motherhood affected their career expectations. Did young women fear that traditional roles would derail them from other goals? Did they see commitment as a trap or a challenge? Was there a point when they felt they "should" marry, that they "should" have children—and how were they responding to such pressures? How did they feel about remaining single indefinitely?

As women moved into and through their thirties, I wondered how they resolved the dilemmas of family life and nurturing. How did women, especially those who had achieved success in their professions, make decisions about partnering and marriage? How did they make the choice to have children? What encouraged couples to remain childless? Why were increasing numbers of accomplished women leaving the workforce when they became mothers?[11] How were working mothers balancing the demands of careers and parenting while staying romantically connected to their husbands (who were also juggling several roles)? What forces conspired—whether women worked outside the home or not—against true co-parenting? How did the rising numbers of women who are unmarried and childless combat social pressure, creating feminine identities separate from traditional roles?

I hoped that my conversations with the oldest among the women—those who had already navigated these conflicts—would be particularly revealing. What had they learned that might help younger women better understand their alternatives and make choices more freely? What did they wish they'd known ten or twenty years before? What did they see as the next set of challenges they faced? And perhaps most important, could their experience help others think more expansively about how to approach their own "early adulthood"?

I was often stunned by the raw candor my questions inspired. Over dinner with a group of women in Philadelphia, a forty-three-year-old foundation director described her divorce, after fifteen years, from the man she'd thought of as her best friend. Suddenly a stay-at-home mom who was happily married began to cry. "That gets me where I live," she explained, "because I realize that as happy as we are now, that's no guarantee." Often the women joked that the interviews felt like therapy. One found the courage to change careers after we met; another made a decision to marry; a third sat down to talk to her husband about the ways their relationship had drifted since their children were born; two more decided to have children. A few times groups of total strangers made arrangements to meet again, reminding me of stories I'd heard about consciousness-raising groups in the early days of the women's movement. This emotional intensity sometimes surprised me, until I realized how isolated women can be in their feelings of guilt and confusion, how rarely they take the opportunity to talk honestly to one another, especially across lines of experience and age. This book intends to encourage that discussion, to break through the barriers we so often feel in the presence of other women whose choices in life have differed from our own.

The group interviews were invaluable in defining the commonalties of women's experience, and they anchor the opening chapter of each of this book's sections. Those are followed by a series of in-depth profiles, showing how individual women grapple with a particular set of pressures and how they seek solutions. These portraits are neither representative nor comprehensive: I selected women who I felt had valuable stories to tell, whose experiences might be particularly useful to readers in trying to assess their own options. Sometimes their circumstances are extreme, but extreme circumstances can sharpen our understanding of the choices in more moderate lives. I spent days at a time with each subject, observing her at work, at home, with friends. I interviewed husbands, boyfriends, employers, sisters, and mothers. The women I profiled each allowed me such intimate access for the same reason. As Denise Littleton, forty-one, a corporate vice president and mother of two girls, put it, "I hope someone else can benefit from the lessons of my life."

Through these many discussions, I began to understand better the nature of women's dilemmas: the competing personal, political, and social forces that put us, over and over again, in excruciating positions demanding painful trade-offs. *Flux* is a result of my inquiries, an exploration of the limits women still face in this era of half-change, as well as the often ingenious ways they've discovered to push back. I hope, for young women who are just beginning their journey into adulthood, it will prove a useful tool in assembling your own lives. For those further along the path, I hope that, as they did for me, the voices of the women who speak so candidly in these pages will both challenge and affirm your own experience, encouraging you both to reflect back on your choices and to consider the ongoing possibilities for change. For all my readers, I hope *Flux* will expand the way you think about women's—and men's—lives in ways that are creative and that can contribute to lasting change for us as well as the next generation: I hope that it will inspire you in the search for a more satisfied life.

Part I

The Promise

Chapter 1

Anything Is Possible

Erin Wilson kicks off her sensible low-heeled pumps and stretches her legs. At twenty-four, Erin is a junior account manager at a large New York City advertising agency in whose conference room we are sitting. She has jaw-length wheat-colored hair, which she absently tucks behind her ears whenever she starts a thought, and is dressed conservatively in a short-sleeved yellow sweater, a dark pleated skirt, and nylons. She is one of five young women—including a social worker, a budding playwright, a finance associate, and an administrative assistant in an architecture firm—who have agreed to meet me here tonight for an evening of frank conversation and soggy deli sandwiches. She leans back in her chair as she speaks, expanding into the space around her as if to physically illustrate her point: that she, like many young women today, feels her potential is limitless. "When my mother graduated from college, the only careers that she thought were available to her were teaching, nursing, and maybe being a flight attendant," she explains. "For me the world is totally open. If I want to run a company, I can do that. If I want to stay home, I can do that. If I want to work in a corporation, if I want to be an entrepreneur—I can do anything that I want to do."

Jennifer Lyle, twenty-five, au courant in a beige sundress and small oval glasses, her blond hair long on the top and shaved up the back, bobs her head in agreement. "My mom has told me, 'God, you are so independent. I would never have done what you've done at your age.' I've lived in Europe, I moved to New York. She went from college straight to getting married to my father. She interviewed for a job once, and when they asked her what her biggest accomplishment was, she said, 'raising my three children.' There are just more options for us now."

My Mother Is *Not* Myself

Daughters are notoriously unreliable narrators of their mothers' lives, but their beliefs about the previous generation of women—and in particular its deficiencies—are the backdrop against which they measure their own greater expectations. If their mothers were thwarted by circumstance (although, the truth is, Erin's mother went back to graduate school when Erin was thirteen and became a successful architect), today's young women feel redeemed by possibility. Feminism has been passed down to them as an ethic of personal potential. They were weaned on the mantra "you can be anything you want to be." "My parents told me I could be president of the United States," said a twenty-seven-year-old district attorney in Chicago. "My parents always said I could do whatever the hell I wanted to do," proclaimed a twenty-five-year-old website designer in San Francisco. They graduated from college feeling entitled to the same opportunities as their male classmates. Nothing about their lives felt predetermined; marriage and motherhood seemed one among a menu of options rather than inevitabilities. Even the most conservative among them expects to take advantage of this period of unencumbered time, until recently enjoyed solely by men, in which to live independently, explore career opportunities, enjoy friends and lovers, establish the self.

But talk a little longer, cut a little deeper, and these same confident young women express something else too—an anxiety about the consequences of their new freedom. A few days after my conversation with Erin and Jennifer, I sit across town in another conference room, of a publishing house, with a different group of twentysomething women. All are ambitious, have come to the City to pursue their chosen careers. Leslie Elder, twenty-nine, who works in finance, wears a business suit and carries a briefcase. Claire Ricci, twenty-eight, an assistant editor at the publishing company, has accessorized her outfit with ice blue nail polish and eye shadow to match. Like Erin and Jennifer, these young women believe that the essential difference between their mothers' generation and theirs is the wide range of "choices" they have. "But it's kind of a double-edged sword," says Abbey Green, twenty-six, who recently moved here from Houston to work in sales. "The good thing about being able to do anything is that you can, but you could also be overwhelmed by the buffet style. There's so much to choose from that you could be totally paralyzed by it."

"Yes!" exclaims Claire. "I've got this absolute phobia about looking back and thinking, 'Shit, I picked the wrong one.' Like, I don't want to be married now, I don't want to have a baby now, but I don't want to be eight years down the road thinking, *I blew it! I had every choice in the world, I could've done anything, been anyone, gone anywhere, and somehow I still managed to be thirty-six going 'I didn't get what I wanted!'* "

"You know," says Leslie, "sometimes I wonder if we'd be happier living in a society where there weren't so many choices."

Among young women like these I found a longing, not so much for an oppressive past as for a guide to a murky future, a road map to contemporary female life. They may have more opportunity in terms of self-expression, lifestyle, and financial gain than women of any previous era. They may have never known a time when it was legal to discriminate against women in education and employment or illegal to get an abortion. In college at least half of their classmates were female; for those who have gone on to law school, medical school, or for graduate degrees in such fields as journalism and psychology, the same is true. Yet, beneath their boundless optimism lies a sneaking suspicion that the rhetoric of "choices" is in part a con job, disguising impossible dilemmas as matters of personal preference. As these young women look forward, they see "choices" threatening to morph into cruel trade-offs: double binds, which, along with their own subtly dual expectations have already influenced their decisions regarding ambition, sex, love, marriage, and motherhood—and could ultimately trap them in the narrow roles they're expected to escape.

Talking Gloria Steinem, Thinking Carol Brady

If for previous generations the "feminine mystique" surrounding marriage and motherhood was the trap, the solution for today's young women—and the object lesson drilled into their heads—is financial independence, or, as Erin Wilson puts it, "The message I got was be able to support yourself no matter what." Like "you can be anything you want to be," "financial independence" is an appealing buzz phrase but oddly only half absorbed. Many of the young women I interviewed thought of economic self-sufficiency as precisely that: supporting them*selves*, not a family, which is a peculiar blind spot in a world where dual-earner couples and single mothers are now the norm. They spoke of the work world primarily as a means to identity, to self-fulfillment and avoiding the predestined fate of women in earlier generations. Salary and economic advancement were often secondary—I wondered how, over time, that would affect their progress in the workplace.

According to sociologist Anne Machung, who interviewed seniors on six college campuses about their expectations for career and family, young women and young men typically perceive their career paths differently. Machung found that men, for the most part, considered work as a way to earn money. They were more likely than women to pursue fields that would lead to well-paying jobs, were more conscious of entry level salaries, and were more likely to have specific titles and job structures in mind as they approached graduation.

Women, meanwhile, saw work more as a vehicle of personal satisfaction. They, too, planned ambitious careers (although they tended to be hazier about specifics, such as salary), but, unlike the men, they reflexively factored inequality into their futures: They assumed that they would move in and out of the workforce and that family responsibilities would limit both their advancement and earning potential—but not their husbands'. Seven out of ten said, once married, they expected their spouses' jobs to take priority. So, well before they enter the adult world (and, perhaps, long before they'd entered college) young women were making decisions that would virtually assure that their careers would be secondary to men's and that their incomes would be lower—decisions that would, in the future, profoundly affect both their options and their leverage in organizing their family lives. They would be able to support themselves, but, truly, only themselves. As Machung wrote, they were "talking 'career,' but thinking, 'job.' "[1]

"IT'S BEEN ON my mind a lot lately that I should be more successful than I am," says Lauren Miller, who grimaces each time she's reminded that her thirtieth birthday is next month. Lauren is chatting over pizza with two friends in San Francisco's South of Market district.

Hers is an artsy, socially conscious group: Lauren works as an editor for an on-line magazine. Melody Yun, twenty-nine, dressed in a leather jacket and black bell bottoms, is a fund-raiser for a nonprofit organization. Becky Schumacher, thirty-one, is an independent filmmaker who just quit her day job to finish a documentary on body image that she's been filming for five years. Lauren and Melody are single; Becky lives with her boyfriend. "Recently I went back East for a family reunion," Lauren continues. "I looked around the room and noticed all my male cousins and my brothers have really good jobs and really good salaries. And none of the women do. There's one cousin, we were born six weeks apart. He has a condo in Boston, he's made it financially. I started wondering, 'What is it?' Because we grew up with the same kind of parents, very similar in their mind-set. And I realized that all the men had *envisioned* themselves in those places. I think I took my career less seriously. In the back of my mind I was thinking, 'I can't get too high up, I can't have too much responsibility, because then what happens if I want to take a couple years off and have kids?' "

"Well, I never expected to get married or have kids," says Melody, "I still don't. But that idea of entitlement"—she pauses, her brow furrowing—"I really feel like men have this innate belief that things are going to happen for them, and that gives them confidence, and then things *do* happen for them."

"It's like guys have some 'thing' we don't have," Becky adds. It's not that she has ever felt overtly discriminated against, she says, she just has a sense that men get better mentoring, develop a stronger sense of vision about the future.

Lauren sighs, pushing her pizza crusts around her plate. "I know what you mean," she agrees, "but I end up feeling kind of sorry for men too. I mean, we think *we're* so pressured. They have to become something and make all this money, and they just accept that and do it. At least we've allowed ourselves self-expression. We could choose careers that are meaningful to us. We didn't have to choose based on money."

"But I wonder," Becky counters, "if your only pressure is to satisfy for your own interests, is that enough to push you to the kind of success that knowing you'll have to provide for a family might?"

Listening to these young women, I remembered debating my own career choice in the years after graduating college: My two older brothers, who are both talented writers and musicians, had already become lawyers, probably not a profession they would have chosen if they hadn't believed they would be providing most of their families' incomes one day. My parents pushed them firmly in that direction, but when I refused to take the LSATs, saying I was going to be a writer, they let it go. I knew the latitude wasn't based so much on faith in my talent as on a kind of sexism: I could pursue passion rather than prudence, freedom rather than responsibility, because I was female, because, like Machung's college seniors, my parents believed my income would be secondary and that writing was the sort of thing you could do part-time after you had children. If I'd stopped to examine it, I suspect I would've found that deep down I operated under the same assumptions. Fifteen years later my brothers earn more money than I do, but, as it turns out, my income is just as integral to my family's economic survival. Yet I enjoy my work more. So, which path was wiser? Going for the money or going for the heart?

Meaningful Work vs. Getting Paid

Even women who believe they've made their decisions may change their minds after facing the realities of the workplace. In college Jennifer Lyle and Erin Wilson believed that entering a highly paid male-dominated profession was the ultimate expression of women's new opportunities. Erin majored in women's studies with an emphasis on gender dynamics in corporate life. Jennifer majored in finance so she'd have some credibility on the job market. Both joined investment banking firms after graduation, but their capitalist-meets-feminist mind-set didn't prepare them for the isolation and hostility they found when they got there. "It wasn't like anything obvious was said, but there were all these little things that made you feel unwelcome," says Jennifer. "The men would all go golfing together, or they'd all go out to lunch and never ask us. And you had this feeling that you couldn't speak out in meetings, like your opinions wouldn't be respected."

Jennifer lasted two years. Erin quit within six months. "There were five women bankers in my firm," she says. "Everyone else was a secretary. And I was like, 'I am going to be a role model, and I'm going to work my way up and change the system.' I felt like I got smacked in the face. I had no idea how hard it would be. I had to really examine why I was doing it. You've got to work in a business like that because you actually enjoy the work, not because you want to make it better for women coming up or to prove to men that you can be just as good."

"I'm a strong woman," Jennifer adds. "I could play along with the boys. But I felt like I was giving up so much of myself. I decided I can make more of a difference at a battered women's shelter than I would in a corporation."

Young women who try out and subsequently reject elite professions described the atmosphere as too soul-corroding to endure, requiring them to put on a false self each morning along with their business suits, a self they felt was essentially male. Anthropologist Patricia McBroom calls it "putting on the mask."[2] Whether they walked away from such jobs, like Erin and Jennifer, or remained committed to pushing their way to the upper tiers, they felt that the only way to make it was to compromise their personal lives. "If you look up and you see what is going on at the top, the female executives are thrice divorced," says Mira Brodie, twenty-six, a junior executive at a Fortune 500 company who was part of Erin's and Jennifer's interview group. "Some have never been married. They have no children." She shrugs. "You have to be aware of that going in. Then you can choose to get on the track or you choose not to."

Mira's assessment of the corporate world is pretty accurate: Although the statistics are slippery—studies based on job title alone are more sanguine than those based on salary—top-ranking women executives are significantly more likely than other women to be divorced, widowed, never married, and childless (ninety-five percent of men in one survey, by contrast, were married with children, and three quarters had stay-at-home wives).[3] The women I spoke with seem to accept the stark terms of female success among the elite as a matter of "choices," but how liberating is it, really, to work under the same gray flannel constraints as men—without even the comfort and satisfaction of a home life?

Some young women react to this bind with an abrupt about-face in attitude. One pregnant twenty-five-year-old investment analyst in New York, for instance, was about to quit her job. To her, staying at home with a child feels like a rebellion, an assertion of femininity in the face of women who, she believes, have sacrificed too much for their careers. "The senior women at my bank are very disappointed in me," she says. "These are very hard-core women who are still single and I think they're bitter toward people like me who fall off the beauti-ful career track that they've laid out for us."

Young women may dream of power, prestige, and financial security, but often, like Jennifer, they feel more authentic pursuing the helping professions: "meaningful" careers such as social work or teaching, which allow them to incorporate values traditionally ascribed to women. Yet, women who enter those fields—or "glamour" jobs such as publishing and working in the arts—often trade away status and money. Claire Ricci, who was among the women I spoke with in the publishing house conference room in Manhattan, earns $22,000 as an assistant editor, which, in New York City, barely allows her to pay the rent; she's taken a second job, as a paralegal, to make ends meet. "I always thought I would be totally capable of taking care of myself, that I would never need any extra income from the hubby side. But the fact that I've chosen *this* profession—whoo!"—she laughs—"how do I think I'm going to do that? Anyone can see the numbers are not work-ing out. This was not part of my plan: I was supposed to maintain my independence and never need a husband."

Across the country in San Francisco, Melody Yun, a fund-raiser for a nonprofit foundation, is also reevaluating. "All my friends who were doing cool work are suddenly going back to get their MBAs," she says, "I'm beginning to wonder if I should too." Melody says she was adamant about doing socially responsible work when she gradu-ated college, but now she's looking ahead, realizing the limits of the lifestyle she's chosen. "At my salary, I'll never be able to do certain things, like buy a house, and that's frightening. But it's also confusing: Doing good work has been such a big part of who I am, and now I find that maybe it's not so important. It leaves me scrambling for something else to make up my identity."

Young women who enter male-defined fields worry about alienation; those who enter traditionally female domains fret about financial dependence. Both groups of women wonder about the impact of their current professional choices on their future personal lives, and those concerns gnaw at their aspirations. They were asking questions that would resurface powerfully, later, among women who were ten or twenty years their senior: about the unique costs to women of ambition and power; about how hard they were willing to push—and how much they expected to sacrifice—to make change; about potential alternatives to conventional paths; about the definition of professional success and their freedom, really, to pursue it.

The Pleasure Gap

"Okay," I say, smiling at the five women assembled in the publishing company conference room. We've talked about their mothers, their jobs, their hopes. "Let's talk about sex." For the first time in three hours, the group falls silent. I can hear the buzz of the fluorescent lights and the sound of the janitor banging wastebaskets down the hall. The women look around at one another. I wait, curious to hear how the mix of entitlement and confusion they feel in their professional lives plays out in the realm of the intimate. Do they feel as confident in pursuing their desires as they do their ambitions? Can they bring their new assertiveness into the bedroom, and if not, why not?

Abbey Green, a tall, wispy woman with a pixie haircut, breaks the silence. "Well," she says, "I think the most important thing in sex is to ask for what you want—but most of the women I know still can't do it."

"I can't," admits Tracy, a twenty-seven-year-old publicist who moved to New York from Virginia two years ago. "I can't ask for what I want. And if we're being honest here, I don't even always make men wear condoms. . . ."

"Me neither," interrupts Leslie. "And the next day I think, 'I can't believe I did it.' We're talking a smart, educated woman. I know better."

Tracy nods in Leslie's direction. "I call it lack of confrontation skills," she says. "You just let it go because it's easier. And it's not just about sex, it affects other parts of my life, like asking for a raise or whatever; anything where you have to ask for what you want."

Just as they recognize their right to equality in the workplace but can't always achieve it, young women like Tracy and Leslie feel an entitlement to sexual pleasure on which they can't convince themselves to act. It's the dirty little secret of a generation: They had sex earlier than their mothers did, have had more partners and are more likely to initiate encounters, yet more experience and freer license haven't necessarily translated into greater enjoyment. Most young women are profoundly alienated from their bodies at sexual initiation; they're rarely privy to adequate information, and less than half have masturbated.[4] The women I met had often rushed into intercourse in their early teens, not out of desire, but to unburden themselves of virginity, to dispel the mystery, to be the first among their friends to "do it." Whatever gauzy, Fabio-induced fantasies they had about the first time were usually numbed out with drugs or alcohol; the reality was, at best, disappointing, at worst, coerced or forced. According to a 1994 National Opinion Research Center poll, a full quarter of American women did not want to have sex the first time,[5] and writer Karen Bouris found that only a handful of the rest enjoyed it.[6] "At fourteen you were too young to get any pleasure out of sex," remembers a twenty-five-year-old law student in Philadelphia. "It wasn't going to be the beautiful extension of your relationship that you have with your fourteen-year-old-boyfriend. It was just about being cool, like drinking and smoking."

The women I spoke with who reported a positive early experience had usually made a conscious decision to have sex, generally within a trusted relationship.[7] Jaws dropped among a group of medical students in Philadelphia when one announced that she'd had her first orgasm with a partner at sixteen ("he was *Swedish*," she explained half apologetically). But for most, the incentive was pressure—either from the boys they dated or from girlfriends—a need to feel wanted, fear of abandonment, or the rush of power they felt in evoking male desire. And even when it was disappointing, they went right on doing it. "I had sex for five years before one of my girlfriends told me it could feel good," recalls a twenty-seven-year-old teacher in San Francisco who lost her virginity at fifteen. "Before that sex just felt compulsory, I was doing it for the guy."

After a series of group interviews in eight cities, I began to realize that the awkwardness generated by my questions about sex was not simply about modesty: It was also a reflection of insecurity, confusion, even pain. By the time they were in their mid-twenties, most of the women I met had been sexually active for a decade; it wasn't easy to admit that they were still grappling with basic issues of sexual self-determination, especially after they'd spoken with such authority about their choices and opportunities in other areas of their lives. Yet, according to sociologist Marcia Douglass and anthropologist Lisa Douglass (authors of the aptly titled *Are We Having Fun Yet?*), less than a third of women experience orgasm regularly in sexual encounters, while seventy-five percent of men do.[8] That pleasure gap says something profound about women's deepest feelings of legitimacy, the license to, as Abbey puts it, "ask for what you want," and expect to get it. Will a woman who suppresses her needs during sex be able to assert them in other realms of her life? Can someone who sacrifices her own satisfaction because, as Tracy says, "it's just easier," form truly equal relationships outside the bedroom? Germaine Greer once wrote that women's freedom is contingent on a positive definition of female sexuality.[9] By that measure, not nearly as much has changed for young women as they would like to believe.

When young women had taken control of their sexual pleasure—whether in a relationship or outside one—they saw it as part of a larger quest for autonomy. Abbey Green, in New York, talks about "working really hard" to get to know her body. "It's absolutely key to esteem issues for me," she says. "If you're comfortable with your body, you're comfortable with yourself. If you feel like you deserve all this pleasure in bed, you start to feel like you deserve it other places too." A few weeks later, Melissa, thirty, a blond, fresh-scrubbed lawyer from South Dakota, echoes that sentiment. "My aunt is a sex researcher," she says. "When I was twenty, she sent me a vibrator for my birthday. That really broadened my horizons. I've developed a really healthy respect for female orgasm: It makes me feel more control in the rest of my life to feel that control and pleasure in my body. But I do wish my aunt hadn't waited. I wish she would've told me at sixteen, 'This is your G-spot. It's okay to masturbate. You should learn how to feel good during sex. It's an important part of being a woman.' " As I continued my interviews, I thought a lot about Melissa and her aunt. I wondered what it would've been like for these young women if as teenagers they'd had someone older with whom to talk honestly about sex. For that matter, I wondered what it would be like for them now.

Is "We" the End of "Me"?

"I have trouble having both a career and a boyfriend," says Julie Rubacky, twenty-five. Julie is a recent transplant to Los Angeles from Seattle, a solid, pragmatic woman with short, brown hair and large dark eyes. She is sitting in a friend's kitchen with several other women, none of whom grew up in L.A., all of whom are the young, single, career-oriented sort that tends to migrate to big cities during or after college. Tania, twenty-six, whose hennaed hair is the color of a cherry lollipop, is in the MBA program at UCLA. Meghan, twenty-seven, an actress, is tall and blond with fashionably nerdy black-framed glasses. Earlier in their conversation Julie said she would like to be a successful television producer, get married, and have a child all in just under five years, by the time she's thirty. For the moment, however, a career and a boyfriend would suffice. The trouble is, the two seem mutually exclusive. "My goal right now is to learn how to do my work and then to be in a relationship," she says, "to get that whole balance thing going. So far it hasn't worked very well."

Establishing "balance" in a relationship—learning to be involved without submerging oneself, to pursue goals unrelated to love without sacrificing it—is the first challenge young women face on their way to the bigger negotiations of marriage and motherhood. They may be told they have unlimited potential, but they've also been trained from an early age to put male needs and desires before their own. Some women described their relationships as a home base of acceptance from which to venture out and explore the self. Others felt decidedly mixed. Even as they sought out the euphoria of love and connection, they spoke repeatedly of their fear of "losing themselves," of being unable, in a relationship, to hang on to the authentic, autonomous woman who knows what she wants and is willing to pursue it. Those who had big dreams for their careers, especially, feared that relationships with men would leach their personal power and distract them from other goals. As professionals, they felt strong and independent. In romance, they felt vulnerable to relationships that undermined their strength. As Tania puts it, a boyfriend could "knock you off your center."

"It's like you wrap yourself around a guy," she says, pretending to drape her arms around a man, lean her head on his shoulder, and look up adoringly while the other women laugh in recognition. She lets her arms drop to her sides. "Then all your energy goes into how he feels about you, why he hasn't called, when you're going to sleep with him, blah, blah, blah. And you lose track of what you want to do with your own life, where you're going. A lot of my friends have gotten sucked into very obsessive thoughts about guys that have led them in the wrong direction.

"I have to admit though," she adds, picking at a glitter-polished fingernail, "if I had to pick the super career or the super relationship by age thirty, I'd pick the super relationship."

I ask her why she thinks she'd have to choose. She sighs. "I don't know," she says, "but it feels that way. You know rationally it's not true, and yet it's there."

"Well, I definitely have that problem with balance," Meghan declares. "I kind of see relationships as all or nothing, and if I'm involved with someone, I'm *really* involved. Otherwise, what's the point?" Meghan's career is important to her though, so, to get some traction in it, she says she's made a categorical decision to avoid relationships entirely. At first she describes this as a luxury, an opportunity to focus completely on herself. "I can't even fathom having a relationship right now, and I love that," she enthuses. "I love what I'm doing and I really believe in my work. I cherish the time to myself. So I'm not questioning it." Yet in the very next sentence, that's exactly what she does. "But I do wonder," she continues. "I'm missing my tenth high school reunion this year and a friend's wedding back east. I wonder if ten years from now I'm going to be missing my kid's field day. I mean, if I even get to that point."

The other women nod sympathetically. "It's weird," Meghan adds. "I feel like I'm making decisions now, even though they're on a minor level, that maybe in ten years will be . . ." She trails off, the energy draining from her voice. "Sometimes," she concludes, "it just feels like there's a lot more at stake than it appears."

What's "at stake," Meghan implies, is the possibility that she'll pay for her current priorities later on with a stunted personal life. Like Tania, she suspects that the "super career" could preclude the "super relationship," that ambition and romance are incompatible: One requires the assertion of self and one encourages the suppression of it. Not only can't Meghan integrate both, she doesn't feel she has enough time to try. The fallout for women like her is a constant second-guessing of priorities: How can they confidently pursue either a career or a relationship in a satisfying way?

Listening to Meghan, I remembered a conversation I'd had a month earlier with Jodi, a twenty-nine-year-old paralegal in Minneapolis who had just begun dating after a self-imposed three-year hiatus. "I wanted to get my act together, to figure out why I would lose myself in relationships," she'd told me over beers in her apartment. Jodi was sitting cross-legged on her futon couch. She had wide blue eyes, a nimbus of long, curly hair, and was dressed in shorts and a T-shirt. "I would just set aside what was important to me, the things I normally do, to do what was important to whoever my boyfriend was. I would go out because they wanted to go out. I would have sex because they wanted to have sex. And I felt guilty about it, because I was cheating them as well as myself."

I asked what three years of solitude had taught her. "I don't know," she moaned, grinning sheepishly. "I guess it was important to have their approval, but why? Why did I feel that by speaking up and saying what I wanted I would damage my relationships?" Jodi considered her own question briefly, then shrugged. "Maybe I'm afraid that I'm too independent. Or maybe I'm not independent enough." She broke off again, leaned her head back on the couch, and stared at the ceiling. "Maybe I'm just too picky and I'm going to end up alone," she continued more to herself than to me, "and I don't want to be alone."

Marriage Panic

Of the dueling fears expressed by young women—"losing" oneself versus being by oneself—the fear of being "alone" (that is, without a male partner) was by far the more potent, particularly as they rounded the bend toward thirty. That may be a residual effect of the now-debunked "man shortage" of the 1980s.[10] Or it may be a contemporary spin on what psychologist Daniel Levinson called the "thirty transition": an urgent need to reassess one's life that is a natural part of adult development.[11] While both men and women experience thirty as a turning point, only women channel it into a panic about marriage. (Levinson, incidentally, found that women who take a more conventional route, focusing on relationships over career, were just as likely to feel off track at thirty: Unfulfilled in their domestic roles, they were searching for something to fill the void.[12])

Since the early 1980s, the age of first marriage for both women and men has been rising rapidly,[13] and a poll in *Jane* magazine found that eighty-two percent of readers believed a woman "doesn't need to get married or have kids to live a full and rewarding life."[14] That sounds like progress, and every woman I spoke with agreed—but only in theory. When I ask the young, ambitious women I meet in the New York publishing firm—the ones who'd been so vocal about their myriad possibilities—how they would feel about being unmarried at forty, they look horrified.

"That's just not an option," Leslie says with a little frisson.

"Do we have to have this conversation?" Tracy says, grimacing. "I don't want to think about it."

Abbey goes so far as to rap her knuckles against the table. "God forbid," she says, shaking her head. "God forbid."

At first the eagerness of most young women to wed surprised me. Roughly half of those I interviewed had seen their parents divorce; some had so many half siblings, stepsiblings and former stepsiblings that they had to draw explanatory diagrams, and most of the rest described their parents' marriages as unhappy. Their own relationships with men had also often proved disappointing. Still, they hadn't lost faith in the idea of good marriages, and they fully expected their own unions to last. Even women whose parents had divorced dismissed the possibility for themselves: They believed that because they would wed later, had more experience with relationships, and were better judges of character, they would do better. "I have no doubts for two reasons," says Lauren in San Francisco, whose parents split up when she was in ninth grade. "One is, I've seen many examples of really good marriages: friends, my brother, my cousin. And the other is I know myself and how I relate to people. I think marriage would suit me very well."

"You know, you all talk about marriage like it's for life," points out Tania, surrounded by friends in Los Angeles. "But, honestly, everyone, well not everyone, but fifty percent of people, get divorced. So how permanent an idea is it, really? I know for me, I'd like it to be, but"—she waggles her hand in the air and squints into the middle distance—"I do have some sort of vague life plan involving, perhaps, two husbands." The other women were quick to disagree—"I feel like once you make that decision, you're in," says Meghan as the others nod. "I'd rather not get married than think about getting divorced." I found myself intrigued by Tania's suggestion, though, even if it was made mostly in jest. Maybe she was right; clinging to the happily-ever-after ideal may keep women from imagining more realistic (and potentially more joyful) alternatives.

That's not to say that young women were dewy-eyed about what, over the long haul, marriage would provide. As psychologist Lillian Rubin has observed, today's young people approach marriage with a unique combination of inflated expectations and utter cynicism.[15] Often, the women I spoke with careened between those extremes. "Ultimately, marriage is a choice," proclaims Julie. "It's unrealistic to expect that you'll look at your husband after twenty years and say 'You are the most fabulous person.' "

"That's what I want!" says Tania, waving a hand in the air. "I want fabulous!"

Julie rolls her eyes. "What you can expect after twenty years," she continued, "is respect. You respect that person, and you like them and, hopefully, you love them. But I don't think you can say 'this is a fabulous person' after twenty years, because there is no fabulous." It's hard to imagine that either woman's vision can be sustained: One relies on romantic illusion, the other seems joyless, reducing marriage to an endurance contest.

Often, for the women I spoke with, marriage seemed a means to an end: They wanted children, and virtually all of them thought single motherhood was too hard. Even the notion of marriage as an economic necessity, which feminism aimed to obliterate, endures, particularly among those who were in female-dominated professions. "When I was young I didn't want to be married," says a twenty-seven-year-old event planner in Minneapolis. "Maybe it was because of my parents' divorce: I was afraid my husband would leave me. But now I think it would not only be nice to have somebody to share my life with, it would be nice to have two incomes. It would make my life much easier financially. It would be nice to be able to buy a house. Maybe it's stupid, but I don't think I'd like doing that on my own."

That last comment may reveal the main reason that the dream

of a lifelong marriage persists: It promises a hedge against isolation, an anchor of intimacy in a confusing world. The fear of being "alone," which one might have expected these independent-minded young women to have conquered, seems to have, instead, intensified, in part because they often live thousands of miles from home. Rather than developing solid multigenerational communities that might broaden their conception of satisfying relationships, they live among an ever-shifting constellation of friends and roommates who move away without warning or pair off and leave them behind. Marriage rather than a romantic proposition may be a way to assure an ally, someone with whom to establish roots. "For a long time, my network of friends made up for not having a relationship," says one woman in San Francisco. "We all moved in together after college and adhered to this communalism idea. But now it's like, 'Well, sorry, I'm getting married! Bye-bye!' It changes things. It creates a division among your friends where there didn't used to be one. I never wanted to get married myself, and I'd like to be more satisfied than I actually am with being single. And I used to be more sincerely satisfied. But now I feel pressures I never thought I'd feel: that I should be in a relationship, and what's wrong with me if I'm not. Things that I never questioned before. I never thought I'd feel this way. It's frightening."

"I Want to Have Kids; I Just Don't Want Them in My Life"

Nowhere do the potential trade-offs between individual growth and its cost weigh on young women more heavily or make them feel more precarious in their choices than when the conversation turns to motherhood. Jennifer, the twenty-four-year-old social worker in New York, sums it up when she says with no hint of irony, "I want to have kids, I just don't want them in my life."

Nearly all the young women I spoke with believed that having a child "too soon" would be a disaster: It would cut short their quest for identity and destroy their career prospects. "Having a baby before you reach the vice-president level is death," explained a twenty-six-year-old advertising account executive in Chicago. Over and over young women cite their social and physiological freedom to defer motherhood as the essential difference between their generation and their mothers', the key to realizing their personal potential. Still, although the ability to control their fertility has been transformative for women, it hasn't freed them from reproductive pressure. Young women—nearly all of whom say they want to have children—still feel held hostage, but now, instead of by accidental pregnancy, it's by the fear that they will wait "too long." But the line between what they describe as "too soon" and "too late" is very fine indeed; walking it is made more perilous by a constant flow of distorted information which, once again, intensifies as they close in on thirty (it is no accident that that's the age women are most likely to enter therapy).[16] "I feel a lot of pressure about not having kids too late," says Julie in Los Angeles, who is twenty-six and single. "And my mother is Miss Be-Sure-to-Have-a-Baby-Before-You're-Thirty, Because-That's-When-You-Get-Too-Old-and-If-You-Can't-Have-a-Child-You'll-Be-So-Devastated. It makes me furious when she says that, but then, I also sometimes think she's right."

A few weeks later, over drinks at her friend's apartment in Minneapolis, a twenty-nine-year-old legal secretary confides, "It freaks me out to read that if you don't have a baby by the time you're thirty-five, you have this big chance of getting cancer." Later still, in the New York publishing company conference room, Leslie Elder, also twenty-nine, confesses that she burst into tears over an *Atlantic Monthly* article that warned that women's fertility declines in their thirties. And in San Francisco, Melody Yun, who is also twenty-nine and said repeatedly that she didn't even want to have children, was nonetheless shaken by an article in *Harper's*: "It was written by this guy whose wife didn't want to have kids, then she changed her mind at thirty-nine," she says. "It was all about what they went through to have a child. I never would've thought an article like that would've affected me. But I read it and thought, 'Wow. That could be me in ten years.' "

"I know what you mean," says Lauren, who is on the cusp of thirty. "It's like our bodies are punishing us for our choices."

Like the "man shortage" of the 1980s, the current panic induced by the "fertility crisis" seems designed to drive straight to young women's biggest fears: that the price of freedom is isolation, that a woman who doesn't give in to conventional roles by the Big Three-O will be denied. While the man shortage was a sham, this new assault is not as easily dismissed: A third of women over thirty-five will have difficulty conceiving.[17] Even so, infertility, let alone cancer, is not as inevitable as young women have been led to believe (and, in reality, the male partner is as likely to be the cause). Despite the fact that more people are seeking treatment, infertility rates have actually dropped since the 1980s, indicating that couples are anticipating problems they may not have. Meanwhile, the only group among which infertility has jumped is women in their twenties who have unprotected sex and, unknowingly, contract chlamydia or genital warts.[18] Perhaps, then, instead of wringing their hands over how their age and professional choices affect childbearing, young women should focus on their own reluctance to demand that their lovers wear condoms and their inability to articulate their needs.

Some of the young women said that they would rather not have children at all than wait until they were thirty-five. Considering that none of them was married and all were between twenty-four and thirty-one years old, the pressure they were under was extreme—so extreme that it left no time to think through whether motherhood was really for them. "I'll tell you what that pressure makes me feel," says Melody, who had said she didn't want children. "I feel like I have to meet someone now, because you want to date for a couple of years before you get engaged, and then you don't want to just get married and have babies right away, you want to have a married life first. So, suddenly every date counts, and you think, 'I can't waste time with you because you're not a keeper.' I say I don't want to have kids, but that's because I know I still can. I have that option. But I feel like I'd better decide damned soon, because I won't have it much longer."

Becky nods. "I wouldn't have children after thirty-five," she

says. I point out that she is already thirty-one. "Thank you for reminding me," she replies acidly, and begins ticking off her to-do list on her
fingers. "That means I need to finish the documentary I'm working on,
make my first feature film, and produce another feature film within
three years." She folds her arms across her chest. "That's the kind of
pressure it puts *me* under."

Among women who have entered fields that remain male-
defined, the stress is especially acute. After her disastrous foray into
investment banking, Erin, in New York, says she was determined to
pick a profession that would be conducive both to high achievement
and motherhood. Her own mother hadn't pursued a career until Erin
was a teenager, so she wasn't much of a guide. "She never really talked
to me about how hard it would be to balance everything," Erin explains. "To be honest, I don't think she knew. She was a teacher before
she got married. Then she stayed home with us for thirteen years, and
then she started her career. It was different for her."

If her mother couldn't advise her, Erin figured, she'd find someone who could. So, for six months she conducted informational interviews with female executives in New York about their career choices. It
was, she says, a disheartening experience. She ended up feeling that,
sure, she could "be anything"—she could pursue the same opportunities as men—as long as she didn't have children. "My plan was, I was
going to cruise right to the top," she says, "and I'd be so successful
that they would make an exception for me. They would let me keep my
job three days a week and let me have this balance. But I found out
that is not reality. So I have this feeling of, 'Oh, my God, do I have to
make a choice? Why can't I have both things?' I see the women at my
advertising agency who have made it. They are not having kids until
they are forty, or they have a full-time nanny. More and more I see
women just leave. And I wonder, how am I going to be able to accept
staying home, spending time with the kids, and not making it to that
next level? Is that going to be good enough for me?"

What About the Men?

Young women like to talk about an ideal world. In an ideal world they could be anything they wanted to be without being limited by sex. In an ideal world their husbands would be eternally and unconditionally loving and nurturing. And in an ideal world childcare would be a joint responsibility. "It would be like, 'I'll pick them up today you pick them up tomorrow,'" says a twenty-seven-year-old nurse in Minneapolis. "In an ideal world everything would be shared." When pressed for details about how they imagine childcare working on this decidedly non-ideal planet, however, women revealed that they expected—and often even wanted—the responsibility to fall squarely on themselves. Often, in a single interview, the same woman expressed contradictory ideas about how she anticipated combining providing for her children and nurturing. "I liked having my mom at home," said a twenty-eight-year-old social worker, also in Minneapolis. "I'd want to be home too when I have kids." An hour later, though, she mused, "If I didn't work, I'd go crazy. If I had to stay home with kids, I don't know what would happen to me." And later still she said, "Being the breadwinner would be way too much pressure. I'd rather be the one staying home."

Other women, particularly those with high career aspirations, hoped that by the time they have children, the problem will magically disappear. "With the modem and the fax machine, there's no real reason you need to spend eight hours in the office," says Claire Ricci, the twenty-eight-year-old assistant editor in New York. "So there's this glimmer of hope that I'm going to be able to work at home and not have to completely take a step back and say, 'Okay, I'm going to be on the B team of editors instead of the A team, because I want to be a mother. I have my fingers crossed."

The idea that "balance" is specifically a woman's problem is even reinforced by those purporting to offer solutions. In Philadelphia, a second-year medical student gathers five friends in her living room for me to interview. They are all agonizing over how to get through their residencies and establish their practices while simultaneously trying to find a loving man and start a family. More to the point, they resent that their male classmates aren't twisting from the same rope. Just before our interview, they'd attended an event, which some of them had organized, designed to help them: a panel in which women in different specialties discussed how they'd met the challenge of mixing work and family. "How many men came to the session?" I ask. They look blank. "Did they have their own panel in which male doctors advised them on how to be good fathers and good physicians?" I continue, "Or don't they expect to have to be both?"

As it turned out, not only didn't it occur to the organizers of the panels to include their male classmates—"They wouldn't have shown up anyway," one says—the women didn't really want them to attend. In the end, they believe that it is their role to make personal sacrifices for their families despite the fact that men want children just as much.[19] "I feel like a big hypocrite for saying this," admits Shay Thomas, a twenty-four-year-old African American woman with a heart-shaped face surrounded by dozens of tiny braids. "I say I'm pissed off that the men aren't thinking about it, but the truth is, I don't imagine my husband going through the same struggles, thinking about working part-time and all. I think of it as being my choice."

Gayle, twenty-five, who plans on being an obstetrician, agrees: She wants her husband to "help" with childrearing but doesn't really expect him to be an equal partner, let alone a primary caretaker. "I don't want anyone taking care of my child but me," she says. "It might be wrong for me to feel this way and it might be something that society has done, but at that panel there was a woman surgeon who really put herself first, before her children, and I looked down on her for that. I thought that she was not being a good mother. Whether that's wrong or whether it's right, I don't know. But that's how I felt."

"Well, I want a guy to be grappling with those issues too," says Ruth, a twenty-six-year-old Dominican woman who was a second-year student. "I want someone who will acknowledge that we are both going to have to make sacrifices and cut down on hours if we have a child. And it's hard, because a lot of men aren't like that. Or if they are, people think they're less than a man because they aren't ambitious.

It's just so frustrating: We want to be able to pursue our careers, but then we look down on the men who say, 'Well, you go do your thing, and I'd like to stay home.' "

Ruth is right: Despite their contemporary career ambitions, for most women I talked to, traditional motherhood—in which they are the primary caretaker—remained central to their core conception of self. In her interviews with a racially diverse group of women in their twenties, sociologist Kim DaCosta found that the traditional mother's role has actually supplanted marriage as a source of romantic fantasy for many young single women. Instead of the disparity between the ideal and the actual that they anticipated in their relationships with men, women expected motherhood to be exactly as they imagined it: a source of self-nurturance, permanence, and unconditional love—all the things they doubted they could, in reality, find with a man. Very few mentioned the difficulties that can arise in relationships with children. Some even saw traditional motherhood as a form of "feminist self-sacrifice," imbuing it with qualities of independence and self-reliance, which, taken to their extreme, would make it a solo pursuit. By envisioning motherhood as such a powerful extension of the self, however, young women risk damage to their relationships with their future husbands and children, as well as to their own financial well-being.[20]

Most of the women I spoke with had developed a kind of amalgam of old and new expectations, a hybrid that even they knew was insupportable, if not downright hypocritical. "What I was going to say in jest, but what I sometimes feel, which scares me, is that there is a lot of validity to what your mother says, 'You have to marry a doctor,' " says Melody Yun. "If I want to have kids, the reality is I have to find someone who will support me and be the one who works. Or maybe I'd do something half time, or dabble in whatever I find fulfilling, but I don't think a career will be my priority. I know that sounds very retro because you'd expect me to say, 'Oh, it will be a complete partnership and he'll invest as much in childrearing as I will.' I do have certain expectations for that, but I don't have very high expectations of my potential to be a major breadwinner. In my field I won't command a high salary." Melody pauses and grins sheepishly. "In my most idealized vision," she says, "we'd have an equal partnership where he brings home all the money and also does half the childrearing."

In their professional lives, their personal lives, and their dreams of the future, young women face a series of interlocking dilemmas, a dizzying combination of external obstacles and internal contradictions that push them simultaneously toward autonomy and dependence, modernity and tradition—that leaves them hovering in a state of flux. They are encouraged toward economic self-sufficiency yet are subtly pressured to "choose" lower paying, more flexible professions that would accommodate conventional motherhood. They learn from a young age to be assertive professionally yet not to express their desires in their relationships with men. They hold out an ideal of shared parenting but anticipate inequality. As Ann Machung has observed, it appears that beneath their New Woman personae, today's young women may largely be replicating their mothers' lives.[21]

While the pressures young women experienced were similar, the way they responded to them could be very different. To truly understand the conflicts that young women face, I needed to go deeper into everyday life to see how individuals negotiated today's set of choices and paradoxes. I chose three women I'd met in the groups on whom to focus further. Mira Brodie, the associate in Finance at a Fortune 500 company, is at one end of the spectrum, willing to defer or relinquish a personal life for professional success. Abbey Green, a sales rep for a comic book company, puts her faith in women's traditional strengths as the key to advancement. Shay Thomas, a medical student, is engaged in a double negotiation, as a woman and an African American in an elite profession. As they set their courses into adulthood, all three women are framing questions about feminine identity, ambition, and relationships; and, in their own ways, all three are seeking the answers.

Chapter 2

The High-Potential Female

MIRA BRODIE TALKS ABOUT corporate America as if it were a geographical place. And in that parallel country she has been officially designated a "high-potential female." "I was actually called that to my face," she says, rolling her eyes. "I was like, 'Oh, great! An HPF'—it makes me sound like a calculator." Which, if one's definition includes a person who engages in calculation, who plots how she and other women can ride that HPF status to the upper tiers of the company, pretty much fits.

At twenty-six, Mira is tall and athletic with black hair that grazes her jaw, light golden skin (inherited from her Indian mother), and a smattering of freckles (the legacy of her Scottish father). Her face is classic: high cheekbones, aquiline nose, full lips. When she meets me at her office, the New York headquarters of an insurance and financial services conglomerate, she's wearing a casual tweed pants suit, the result of a newly relaxed dress code. "When I first got here, although women could, technically, wear pants, it was not recommended, career-wise," she says. Also frowned upon were obvious makeup and long hair. Mira points to her head. "There are rules in corporate America. You have to have corporate hair."

On the way back to her desk, Mira stops to chat with a colleague whom she describes as her "office spouse"—"you know," she explains, "the person you complain to about work and have lunch with and pick hair off his clothes without asking." She sweeps by her secretary and into her office, a glorified cubicle in the company's finance division. According to another of corporate America's unwritten bylaws, her seniority entitles her to an office with a window—*one* window she emphasizes—but since her department is about to move to another floor, she hasn't bothered staking her rightful claim. Instead, she's made her space homey with pictures of friends and a modest snow dome collection, including the Eiffel Tower, the Golden Gate Bridge, and a can of Spam. There's a pizza menu tacked to the wall for late-night dinners: Mira complains that she's jumped from a size six to a ten during her team's current eighteen-month project, selling off a billion-dollar portfolio of credit card loans, on which she puts in as many as one hundred hours a week. There's also a Dilbert cartoon in which, while interviewing a woman for a job, he asks about her long-range goals. "I'd have your job in six months," she snaps. "In a year you'd be working for me, you big pile of dinosaur dung." Mira smiles at the comic, mentioning that two people mailed it to her when it ran.

I first met Mira among a group of young professional women I interviewed in New York City who were on the board of a nonprofit women's advocacy organization. During that discussion, Mira made no secret of her ambition. "I want to be a vice president in corporate America by the time I'm thirty," she said. "Will I be married by then? Probably not. Will I have children at some point? Maybe not. To have dreamy ideals like 'I can do it all'—it's just not going to happen. If you look up at the top, all the female executives are thrice divorced. Some have never been married, most have no children. Some are happy. Some aren't. But I'm committed to it. You choose to get on the track, or you choose not to. And I have chosen to get on."

There were two other women present—also, no doubt, high-potential females—who had recently dropped off "the track" to take more conventionally feminine jobs. They seemed unnerved by Mira's detachment, by her willingness to sacrifice her personal life in the pursuit of power and money. When the first, who had once planned to be a CEO by her thirtieth birthday, wondered how she would combine her own aspirations with a desire to have children, Mira shrugged. "Your career will suffer," she said simply. "I think you realize that."

"Right," the woman said, nodding and looking down at her hands.

"I think I could have made it," said the second, who had quit her job at an investment bank and was now applying to graduate school in social work. "But I felt like I was giving up so much of myself. I can make much more of a statement in social work."

Mira disagreed. Her mother runs a nonprofit social services agency, and she considered similar work but decided against it. "You need to be in a position of power to make real change," she said, "and corporate America is never going to improve until there is a quorum of senior women. Women have a responsibility to play by the boys' rules until there are enough of us at the top so that we can change them. That's my whole thing about being in corporate America as opposed to social work."

Looking back on that discussion, Mira speculates that those other women may not have been temperamentally suited to the challenge. She pulls a folder out from beneath a Minnie Mouse pencil and hands it to me. This, she says, will explain why she's ready to take it on. Inside are the results of a California Psychological Inventory test that Mira took through the company's human resources department to help evaluate her strengths and weaknesses as a leader. "See here," she says, pointing to a graph. "I'm way above the norm on aggressiveness and assertiveness. I'm in the last little skinny piece of the curve." She moves her finger over a few inches. "And then here, on the 'feminine' characteristics, I'm way below the norm.

"When they first told me that, I just roared," she continues. "I was like, 'this is so true!' But then I thought about what it meant. I suspect I get more feedback about not listening because women are supposed to listen, that's the stereotype. I'm not saying I don't need to temper myself—I should, just like all male managers should—but I *do* think that I got more of that type of feedback than they do because I'm a woman."

Surprised that anyone is still measuring "feminine characteristics," I ask what that means to her. "Girlie stuff," she says, shrugging. "Pink things, frilly things . . ." She trails off, waving her hand dismissively. "I don't really think of it as relevant to me," she continues. "Do I wear perfume? Yeah. Do I wear makeup? Yeah. But I don't necessarily consider those things feminine. I just have fewer nurturing qualities than people expect." She pauses a moment. "And you wonder, what are the implications of that, in terms of how comfortable or uncomfortable people are with me?"

I glance down at the test results and notice that feminine is defined as "sympathetic," "nurturant," and "sensitive to others and to criticism," while masculine is "decisive" "action oriented," and "direct in communications." Despite recent claims about the importance of "soft skills" and "EQ" in the new economy, Mira thinks it's still difficult to vault up the corporate hierarchy with a feminine personality as it's defined here.[1] In fact, in her book *The Third Sex*, anthropologist Patricia McBroom found that high-achieving corporate women often expressed a conflict between "being feminine"—which they associated with maternity and gentleness but also with weakness—and "being a woman," which connoted power, assertiveness, and professionalism. Women who viewed femininity negatively weren't necessarily less happy than those who saw it positively, but it affected their perception of their personal and professional choices, making them less likely to marry and have children or, as they rose to power, to identify with women who did.[2] I wondered, then, not only about how rejecting "feminine" traits affected others' perceptions of Mira, but how it affects her vision of herself, her view of intimate relationships, her perception of her female colleagues, and the nature of the change she wants to make for corporate women.

Good Girls and Little Womyn

"There were times in my childhood that were really happy-go-lucky," says Mira. "I have some great photos." It is Saturday afternoon and Mira, fresh from a shower, is sprawled across her bed with a towel wrapped around her head, dressed in sweat pants and a Wellesley College lacrosse team T-shirt. Outside this room, the rest of her apartment is replete with bouquets of dried flowers, kitschy animal figurines, and a plaque that reads A HUG IS A GREAT GIFT: ONE SIZE FITS ALL AND IT'S EASY TO EXCHANGE. Those things, Mira informs me dryly, all belong to her roommate, who holds the lease. "Would I decorate a place like this?" she sneers. "Please!"

Perhaps not so overtly. But in a subtler fashion her bedroom has many of the feminine touches Mira claims to eschew: a scented pomander dangles amid the clutter of CDs and photographs, and her tastefully muted flowered sheets are set off by an array of perfectly contrasting throw pillows. But then, Mira seems easily able to hold on to conflicting realities about her life. Even as she remembers, for instance, that "my parents just loved me to death and always told me I could do anything, be anything, gave me every support that I needed," she also recalls a darker truth: Her father's fortunes went up and down, and he occasionally hit her mother, who, when Mira was eight, left him for another woman. "She had so much hostility toward him," Mira explains. "And he had a lot of hostility toward her, because when you live in a small town and your wife leaves you to go live with a woman, that's not okay.

"But I didn't know anything about any of that when I was

little," she continues. "I don't think I realized that Liz was my mother's girlfriend for years. And with my father"—she glances over at a framed photograph of him, handsome as a movie star, which she's almost completely obscured with toiletries—"well, there is not a lot I can do about it now. I mean, he should be held accountable for those things he did, but you can't really continue to hold that against someone and have an ongoing relationship with them. At least I can't."

After the divorce, Mira's mother declined alimony, so Mira says, "we were piss poor for a while," which may account for her current belief that she'll need to earn $200,000 a year to be comfortable. They moved so often that she can keep track of the years only by recalling the names of her school-bus drivers. Still, she insists, "I was the most secure, happy little child in the world." It would've been different, she suspects, if she'd had a brother, a boy onto whom her father might have showered attention. But as an only child, she felt her parents, whatever their personal problems, continued to project all their hopes and dreams onto her. Mira's experience is not unusual: Perhaps because of that extra encouragement, women who are only or eldest children tend to excel beyond others in elite fields.[3] "It was like all their eggs were in one basket," she says, "and they wanted their little basket to go as far as it could. It didn't matter that I was female."

Mira pulls out a photo album from high school and begins to flip through it. She stops at a picture of herself with a group of friends taken during her senior year, her hair poufed in defiance of the laws of gravity around her baby-fat face. "This is my big-haired cheerleader phase," she says, tracing the photograph with her finger. "I wore lipstick and saddle shoes with bells on them and got up at six every day to curl my hair." She glances up, incredulous. "I used to curl my hair just to go to the corner deli."

She looks back at the photograph, at her broadly grinning friends. Here is her first boyfriend, Stuart, who went on to Virginia Military Institute. And her best friend, Allie, who came back after her freshman year of college as "the sorority girl from hell." "It was awful," Mira remembers. "I was like, 'Okay, where is the Allie that used to have a brain in her head?' I had absolutely nothing to say to her."

At Wellesley College Mira found a different kind of sisterhood. Living among 2,300 women, the big-haired cheerleader who dreamed of marrying her high school boyfriend was, she jokes, quickly replaced by a "womyn with a 'y' ": a serious, self-determining student who was passionate about competing on the school's lacrosse team. For the first time, she encountered openly gay women, and came to accept homosexuality beyond the single case of her mother. Many young women I spoke with believed gay friends had been vital to their personal growth in college, much the way some whites in their parents' generation reflected back on befriending people of a different race. Gay friends, they said, challenged the norms they'd grown up with, inspiring them to rethink gender roles and expectations.

Most also developed a new feminist consciousness in college, grounded in abortion rights—and for Mira that came "not a moment too soon." By the time she became accidentally pregnant in the spring of her freshman year, she had become staunchly pro-choice. Her decision to abort, along with her tolerance of homosexuality (and a brief refusal to shave her armpits), strained her relationship with her conservative VMI beau and, ultimately, severed the last ties to her former self. "Had I gotten pregnant a year before, would I have been more inclined to say 'Maybe we should get married and raise a family?' " Mira says. "It's possible. I may have been quietly pro-choice. But by the time I was a sophomore, I was marching on Washington. My boyfriend and I had broken up. I was much more self-actualized."

Over the next two years Mira jettisoned her plans to become a social worker and, after uninspiring summer internships with a probation department and a disability law center, ruled out psychology and legal services as well. Instead, she decided to use her economics major to interview with corporate recruiters. She could keep up her philanthropic work as a volunteer, she reasoned. Besides, if she had learned one thing from her childhood, it was that "I don't plan on marrying my lifestyle. I plan to make it for myself." She chose her current employer in part because its representatives stressed the importance of a balanced life. "The whole idea that someone actually cared that I had a life outside of work was very attractive," she recalls. "It was totally different than the investment bank guys who were like, 'You don't have a problem working 120 hours a week, do you?'"

These days, however, she often does work nearly that much. "That's all sort of fallen by the wayside," she admits. "It didn't start out that way, but my second project was selling off one of the company's subsidiaries. It was really intense, really focused. and I started thinking, 'Hmmm, maybe I am really good at this. Maybe I really like this. And maybe I have to pay my dues and work really hard when I'm young. That's just the price you pay to work in this field.'"

One of the Guys

Today was supposed to be a big day in corporate America. Mira was poised for a conference call that would advance the billion-dollar deal to sell off a credit card loan portfolio that her team has been working on for a year and a half. "It's normal to me to work with huge amounts of money," she says. "To me a billion dollars . . ." She waves her hand in the air. This is the stuff Mira lives for: the challenge of the deal, the psychology of negotiation, the intellectual satisfaction of working out an agreement that sticks. "Admittedly, it doesn't have a lot of redeeming social value," she says, "but it's stimulating—I learn new things all the time—and it's really, really fun. Also, it pays well, and when you get that fat paycheck, *then* you can do something redeeming with it." As it turns out, though, the day is a bust: A guy named Owens didn't finish his paperwork, and without it, everything stalls. Mira picks at her nails furiously when Owens puts her on hold. "This is why you were passed over for a promotion," she grumbles to dead air. "This is why you're not a managing director."

Mira makes a round of calls to bankers, lawyers, and colleagues to postpone the meeting, explaining repeatedly that the glitch is not her fault. When she suggests rescheduling at three o'clock on Friday, one of them begins to argue with her. She holds firm. "If my boss said, 'We are having a four-hour conference call on Friday afternoon,' they would think, 'What an asshole,' but they wouldn't actually challenge him," she complains after hanging up. "I've got two factors working against me. They can't believe this junior person is telling them what they have to do. And then there is the female factor: 'I shouldn't have to take orders from her.' "

Getting used to the male culture of corporate America was an adjustment for Mira. There is only a handful of women at her level or above in her division, and, way at the top, a lone female senior manager. Mira has developed little tricks to fit in with the guys: As she gets dressed in the morning, she watches CNN to catch the college sports scores so she can participate in Monday morning quarterbacking. "I can't tell you who won the World Series in 1988," she says, "but if there's a Notre Dame game on Sunday, I know that on Monday they'll all be like, 'Hey, Randy, you guys looked like shit out there,' so I want to be able to do that too."

Sometimes, Mira says, being female can even be an advantage: Higher-ups tend to remember her and, when she's on a conference call, no one ever has to ask who's speaking. Mira's current boss has said that if anyone could shatter the glass ceiling, it would be Mira. She tells me this with pride, but adds, "That's also proof positive that it still exists." She's heard that at a recent meeting of senior managers, one executive supposedly said, "All of our clients are white, male CFOs, so why shouldn't our staff mirror that?" There are also rumors of hushed-up incidents of sexual harassment, of office affairs between senior men and entry-level women, and male managers wondering aloud why women with high-earning husbands "need" to be working.

Mira is a pragmatic woman. She was aware from the outset that she would face resistance and sexism from some men on the job. But, especially after her happy college experience, she was unprepared for the problems she's encountered with other women. "The biggest conflict for me is with other female professionals and secretaries," Mira says. "There is a very different dynamic going on when you're a woman too. Like, I have to befriend my secretary and ask about her weekend and tell her how nice she looks to get her to do stuff for me that I feel she should be doing anyway. And it's a fine line because I don't want to be stereotyped as someone who's hanging out with the wrong people."

The wrong people? "If you're a woman, you have to be careful," she says. "They always think you're a secretary."

Mira once read that there are four images projected onto successful women in corporate life, none of which is flattering. "You can be seen as the power-hungry bitch, the kid sister, the vamp, or—" She pauses, searching her memory. "Maybe the mother? I can't remember. Anyway, I'm the power-hungry bitch. People think that I'm unapproachable. I don't exude those 'Come on in, hang out' vibes. I look busy. I *am* busy. I don't want to be bothered."

Mira is so insistent on portraying herself as aggressive, as the embodiment of ambition gone wild, I begin to think she protests too much. Although it's clear, since they don't speak except when necessary, that there's some antagonism between her and her secretary, for the most part Mira's self-image is contradicted by her actual behavior: by the concern she expresses over her "office spouse's" love life, by her admission that she's the one who makes sure everyone eats dinner at late-night conferences—even by her Minnie Mouse pencil. When a colleague on her deal calls to check in, Mira's voice shifts from its usual confident timbre to something softer: not flirtatious exactly, but a little sweeter, a little more, well, feminine. "I will bring that in only for the people that I'm friendly with," she explains later when I point it out. "But in general I'm not very friendly. If someone finds that offensive in a woman, I don't care. I don't have time to change."

SINCE BUSINESS IS shot for the day, we head over to lunch in the cafeteria, where Mira uses my presence as an occasion to chat up Paula Keyes, the female member of her division's senior management team, whom she's cultivating as a mentor. "Even at her level, it doesn't go away though," Mira told me earlier. "Everything she does is still perceived in the context of her being a woman."

Paula has regulation chin-length hair, highlighted blond. She wears a navy jacket with a chiffon scarf knotted around her neck and red lipstick. She has a distinctly girlish smile, which seems incongruous—although pleasantly so—with her businesslike manner. She looks to be in her mid-forties, although she won't reveal her age. "I've noticed that women who think about the fact that they are women have a harder time," she tells Mira. "They expect more obstacles against them and so they see more. And most don't succeed. The ones who do don't think of themselves as women first."

On the other hand, she cautions, the worst career strategy a woman can employ is to try to be like men. "Some women try to take everything that's feminine in them and erase it," Paula says. "Or they'll swear a lot. Men recognize women who are doing that and they don't like it. If they're going to deal with a woman, they want her to *be* a woman. They may be uncomfortable with you being there at all, but it's worse if you pretend to be a man."

Mira nods, but she looks uncertain. By advising her to be at once conscious and unconscious that she is female, Paula has struck at the heart of the corporate double bind: Women who are perceived as stereotypically feminine are considered ineffectual, but those who are seen as too masculine are considered to be overly aggressive.[4]

"Do people expect you to be more mellow as a woman?" Mira asks.

"I mainly get that from other women," Paula says. "At first they were pleased when I started managing. But I didn't do it like some of them thought I should. I managed like men, who are more like I am and not like they are. So they didn't like it." Paula's experience is not uncommon: Highly assertive women tend to be perceived more positively by men, perhaps because, as they rise in the ranks, they identify less with other women.[5] For instance, when a woman became CEO of Ogilvy & Mather, an advertising agency, she prohibited anyone who worked part-time from becoming a senior partner in the firm, infuriating working mothers.[6]

"You know," Paula says, "sometimes women think there are sacrifices in this field because you're a woman, but they don't see that there are just sacrifices because that's what it takes to succeed.

There are just realities—if you have a senior position, you cannot have flextime."

Mira seems pensive as we walk back to her office. "Paula's more 'I played by the rules, I did it on my own, and you can too.' " she says. "But I feel like it's beholden upon women of my generation to look up and say, 'Okay, there is one of me up there at the top. What are we going to do to change that?' And not just what am I going to do. Because I think I can probably get myself there. But that's not really going to help change the face of corporate America. That's just going to be me taking over for Paula when she retires, and it will still be eight men and one woman."

It is unclear, however, with which other women Mira plans to join forces, or precisely for whom she expects to advocate. She has, for instance, declined invitations to women's networking groups. "They're all mid-level managers and I already know I'm going further than that. I need to deal with the top. Like, how do you get there?" She admits that despite her good intentions, she's done very little herself so far to agitate for change for women within the company. "You don't have the luxury of thinking about that as much as you would like to," she says, "because work is work, and if you get off it, that's not good for you. You really need to look out for yourself. And in doing so, you kind of lose that sense of 'I would like to do the following things to change this company.'

"So, I think it has to be more about people like Paula mentoring younger women and not being as much 'I got here, you can get here,' " she continues. To a certain extent, she is right: Although women are less likely to have mentors than men, when they do, those relationships have an even bigger impact on their careers.[7] It's one of a series of strategies that have been found to enhance the success rate of young women in corporations. Others include participating early on in a high-visibility assignment, behaving entrepreneurially within a company, and displaying a range of skills.[8] By those measures Mira's prospects look good. But one of the most important tactics—adopting and promoting the values of the corporate culture—may be more problematic. Is it possible to embrace the very values she wants to change?

"I don't know," she says. "I hope my desire to change corporate America won't become less as I move up." We walk in silence for a moment. "But I think part of what needs to happen is just time too," she adds. "People are going to need to come into contact with more than one or two powerful women in their lives to really break that stereotype down."

If I Change My Mind, I'll Become a First-Grade Teacher

"Would you like Diet Coke or fat Coke?" Mira sings out from her kitchen. It is Super Bowl Sunday and she has invited a few friends over to watch the game. I choose the skinny stuff, and as she pours it, she mentions that she's been worrying lately about her parents' finances. "I just loaned my father money for his back property taxes," she explains. "They don't have a plugged nickel between them. Maybe it's because I'm an only child, but I feel a real responsibility to make sure they'll be okay financially. It's a real stressor."

Charlie Hess, Mira's boyfriend, a lanky twenty-seven-year-old with sandy hair and a goatee, is sitting in the living room, looking glum. So far only women have shown up to the party, and they seem more interested in the ads than in the game. Mira is the only other person who knows the names of the players, but she jumps up every few minutes to refill glasses and plates or bustle around the kitchen, washing dishes. She's prepared an effete spread, with baked brie, homemade guacamole, and low-fat potato chips. Charlie focuses on his contribution—a bottle of hot sauce whose sales gimmick requires the buyer to sign a release absolving the company of damages—which is the most self-consciously macho item on the table. "You think you're a man until you try some of this," he says, "then you find out you're not."

He pours a drop onto a cracker. "That's hot!" he whoops, sticking his tongue out, eyes and nose watering. "Did you see the size of the drop that I ate?" Mira takes a bite of the cracker and does not re-act. "It's hot"—she shrugs—"but it's not *tasty* hot, so what's the point, exactly?"

Charlie falls back into his sulk, wondering out loud whether he might be happier with Mira's male neighbors, who would better appre-ciate both the game and the hot sauce. He doesn't follow through on the threat but remains in a funk through most of the evening, needling Mira when she says that generally she'd rather "do stuff" than watch television. "As long as you don't *relax*," he says with a tight smile. "Oh, no, we couldn't do *that*."

Charlie was having an off night, Mira tells me later, but that crack wasn't unusual. She considers his occasional cracks about her drive or her salary—which, at $120,000 including bonus, is double what he makes as a middle manager in a health care company—as a nearly inevitable feature of her relationships with men. "Find-ing someone who can handle someone as independent as I am, and who can deal with my income and the level of authority I have, is tough," she says. "Like, at work, all the men in my program who are married are with first-grade teachers. If I ever change my mind, I will just go become a first-grade teacher. I'll be married inside of six months."

For Mira, "first-grade teacher" is a catchall for women who've chosen a more conventionally feminine path. "It's women who will eventually have kids and stay home for five or six years. Then they'll sub part-time. The balance of power is clearly with the man." I ask Mira if she would ever consider marrying the male version of a "first-grade teacher" herself, a man who would be willing to offer what soci-ologist Arlie Hochschild calls "backstage" support for her career.[9] That way she could have the same advantages as the men around her. She shakes her head and responds that it just doesn't work that way. Men, she says, are threatened by women who make more money than they do: Charlie recently told her flat-out to stop paying for dinner so often because it hurt his ego. Anyway, as someone who values ambition, and is herself disinterested in traditionally feminine roles, she's not sure that she is willing to "marry down." "I have issues with people who aren't ambitious enough to want to make more than $35,000 a year," she says. "I don't think I'll be super comfortable with that lifestyle in my business."

So, I ask, where does that leave her? "Talking with all of those guys I work with and trying to avoid their wives like the plague," she says, shrugging. "That's why I'm going to be thirty-five and single."

Mira tends to talk about relationships as another arena in which to assert or relinquish autonomy, to acquiesce to the traditionally feminine or transcend it: She describes her ideal mate as someone "who does his own thing," and says that marriage would involve "putting the unit ahead of the individual." She guards against the potential of commitment to impede her career, and defies me, given the statistics, to tell her she's wrong. Yet she's also aware that relationships provide her with something essential: her main counterweight to work, an essential source of rejuvenation and pleasure. When I ask her what she loves to do with Charlie, she describes lolling in bed all day on weekends, eating strawberries with cream and making love. She and her previous boyfriend, Josh, with whom she lived for three years, cooked dinner together most nights. She broke up with him, in part, to work her hundred-plus-hour weeks. She's unsure, without the balancing factor of a live-in partner, what would inspire a shift back to a more reasonable schedule, but given how entangled her life became with Josh's, she's not willing to move in with someone again unless she thinks she's getting married.

Shortly after splitting up with Josh, Mira did, for a time, feel as if she'd lost her footing. An office romance with a man who'd been a close friend fizzled; a college pal who was living with her for the summer moved on; and the intensity of her new workload was overwhelming. "I felt like I was falling off the peak," she recalls. "I didn't feel good about anything and there was nothing to balance that. So, I went into therapy. We talk about a lot of things: about corporate America, and trade-offs, and what I really want out of life, and if that's okay. Like, if I said to my boss, 'I don't want to have a conference call this Saturday because Charlie and I were supposed to spend the whole day together,' would that be okay?' " Well, I ask, would it? Mira shakes her head. "For me it wouldn't," she says. "Because there is this hierarchy of things, and there's a big gray area in which you have to weigh 'What have I done lately, and what's coming up, and which of these things is really more important to me?' "

MBA, not MRS.

The next time I see Mira, nine months later, she has just entered the MBA program at Columbia University. She'd decided that a business degree would make her more competitive as her career progressed, give her more options. In a few more years, she figured, it would be too late to take the time out for school. Her boss had agreed, and recommended that the company sponsor Mira's education, which means it will pay her tuition if she returns (if not, whomever she signs on with when she graduates will defray the costs through extra bonuses). Just before she left, Mira sat down for a candid conversation with her boss, one she believes could've jeopardized her future if his respect for her were any less strong. "I told him rather bluntly that it's hard to attract women and retain them in this environment," she said. "Finance is a real boys' club—there's not one good example of women's career advancement there. It was a risky thing to do, because my boss advocated very hard to get me sponsored for school. But he listened. And he's a good guy: He tries to make it better on a case-by-case basis. He'd do it for me. But I'm not sure he's so principled that he's going to fight for all women. That would be a really hard situation on him."

Her relationship with Charlie is still meandering along, Mira says, its somewhat tense status unchanged. She's living uptown now, in a small studio on the fourth floor of a walk-up near campus with heavy bars on the back window to keep out intruders. It's a little grim, but convenient, and for two years Mira says she can tolerate it. The only other significant change is her hair, which now brushes her shoulders: Since she's in school, she figures it's her last chance to grow it out.

We walk a few blocks up Broadway, the grimy storefronts giving way to the university's neat brick buildings, through the gated entrance to the campus and into the business school. In the library, students sit at rows of tables, studying together over laptop computers. Columbia has the largest female enrollment among the top business schools—thirty-five percent, Mira reports. She's become involved in the school's formidable women's organization, which, among other things, strengthens ties between students and alums, and she plans to run for office in it. Still, she says, her female classmates have so far proved somewhat disappointing. "Frankly," she says dryly, "I think some of them are a little more interested in their MRS. degree than their MBAs."

We join Mira's friend Felicia Jonas, who looks younger than twenty-six, with her large, luminous blue eyes, chubby cheeks, and bangs. Felicia worked in public relations for a medical devices company in Boston before deciding she needed to learn more about the "quantitative side" of business. She's also contemplating marriage to her longtime boyfriend; although it won't influence her decision, she worries that being married might be a liability on the job market. "If a man is married, employers feel like he's settled down and will be committed," she says, "but there's some ambiguity about women. They're not sure if you're just looking for a job for a year or two before you get pregnant." Some women she knows have actually slipped off their wedding bands before going into an interview, a small act of deceit that she, too, has considered.[10]

"I think that's less of a problem for us though," Mira says. "You're not going to go $80,000 into the hole for an MBA just to work for a year and quit. But it is a double standard. They figure if you're a married woman, you won't travel or take out-of-town assignments." At the same time, when Mira recently talked to an executive who had lectured one of her classes, the woman advised her to marry before she graduated or risk never having the time to find a husband.

If wearing a ring to an interview is imprudent, though, asking about maternity leave seems downright foolhardy, even to Felicia, who already knows she wants to have children. "I don't want them to think I'm not serious," she explains. "I'd try to research it quietly, so they wouldn't know." Perhaps she's right, and recruiters would blackball her if she were blatant about so feminine a concern, regardless of its importance to her long-term prospects with the company: After all, as recently as 1996, a survey of literature on women in corporations found that those with children were seen by their superiors as lacking commitment.[11] The truth is, Felicia's not so sure herself that achievement and children mix. Both she and Mira feel disappointed by what they've seen among corporate women who have become mothers. Felicia had two different supervisors who cut back to three days a week after their maternity leaves; even then, they left promptly at five while she toiled on until eight or nine at night. Mira, meanwhile, worked with a lawyer who, because she had a one-year-old, kept regular hours and refused to take calls on nights or weekends. "Theoretically I am supposed to support the notion of balance and working women having a family," Mira says. "So, I surprised myself when I resented it. She truly slowed the pace of our deal. It was a hard realization for me."

Felicia nods. "They make a personal decision, and that's fine," she says, "but when you think about it from the position of the company, the quality of the work suffers and that makes me sick."

"It makes you sick?" I repeat.

"Yes," she says, "because that's what I'll have to do. Or I'll have to step away from work for six years. And I feel bitter about it. I wanted to have a role model, I wanted mentoring." She shakes her head. "There were no women mentors. No one had time for it."

"In my office there was a woman who just had a kid and my sense is she'll sacrifice the kid for her career." Mira says this without indicating whether or not she believes this is commendable, although it's clear that in the dichotomous thinking of power versus femininity, she believes that's the only other option. "I think that when you're used to sacrificing your personal life like we are, you just keep on doing that even after you have kids. It's a more male attitude, like being the dad in that 1950s *Leave It to Beaver* way."

Felicia looks thoughtful. "But I don't want to do that either," she says. "And if I have kids—you notice I don't say *when* even though I said before that I want them—I may not be so interested in work.

I wouldn't quit my job, but I wonder a lot about things like job sharing." She shakes her head and laughs, blushing. "I feel like I'm being contradictory."

Later, Mira says: "She is living in la-la land, thinking, 'It'll all work out when the time comes.' I suspect she'll end up giving up working and do it fairly easily. I don't think she'll become a permashopper/tennis player though. I see her contributing to her community. Unlike some women here."

Even as they protest them, both Felicia and Mira have absorbed the lessons of the male culture in the workplace, and, in their own ways, both are trying to duck the penalties being female can bring. By hiding her wedding ring or pretending she's not interested in maternity leave, Felicia may be able to compete with the men around her on their terms for a little while longer, but she's also reinforcing the very dynamics she fears: that betraying signs of femininity is a form of weakness, that motherhood is not part of the employment benefits package, that it is incompatible with professional power.

Mira is more extreme in her views, and, as a result, less conflicted. If need be, she plans to avoid the obstacles of the feminine by simply rejecting marriage and motherhood. Certainly, there are many paths to a satisfied life, and marriage and children offer no guarantee of happiness. Still, as anthropologist Patricia McBroom has pointed out, forfeiting a family life as a condition of success is not only an unfair demand (and one made almost exclusively of women—and priests), but is qualitatively different from a free choice to remain single or childless.[12]

Few women would weigh those trade-offs the way Mira does. And who knows? She may weigh them differently herself someday—even she can't say for sure. Given her intelligence and determination, she'll doubtless achieve whatever she chooses to, but I wonder: In doing so, will she truly break new ground for women or simply reaffirm the limitations? How much will she reshape corporate life and how much will it reshape her?

Before Mira heads off to class, I ask her one more question: What, to her mind, would constitute a satisfying life? "Oh," she says, smiling, "all of the things we've been talking about. A great partner who is really, really, really smart and independent and who does a lot of charity stuff. Ideally I'd like to have a job where I have a lot of responsibility, whether that's working for a big corporation or for myself. And while I might work a lot of hours a week, when I'm not working, I'd be doing something I really enjoy. I don't know if that will be hanging out with a guy, or having a kid, or traveling, or just hanging out with good girlfriends. But I think if you find work satisfying enough, the personal side of the balance sheet just looks different."

Chapter 3

Searching for Superheroines

I STEP OFF THE ELEVATOR at the DC Comics offices and straight into Gotham City. The Batman distress signal is projected against one wall of the reception area and, along another, there's a mural of an urban skyline, painted in postnuclear ocher, purple, and orange. A full-scale model of the Caped Crusader himself lurks in a corner; not far away, there's a life-size figure of Michelle Pfeiffer in full Catwoman regalia. I half expect the receptionist to be in costume, but she turns out to be merely another of the familiar, bored-looking mortals who hold such posts all over New York. "You get used to it," she says when I comment on the decor.

But Abbey Green will never get used to it. "The first time I came here I couldn't believe it!" she enthuses when she comes out to greet me. "This is American mythology. We don't have Mt. Olympus. We have Metropolis. Comics and jazz are America's only indigenous art forms. And I want to be *the one* responsible for making comic books as acceptable a medium as television or movies."

Abbey, twenty-six, is a tall, willowy woman with dark hair shorn a half inch from her head, wide hazel eyes, and a resplendent smile. An amateur artist herself, working at a major comic book publisher has been her long-held dream. She moved to Manhattan—a place she can barely tolerate—from her native Houston eighteen months earlier expressly to work for DC. The company appealed to her because, in addition to the standard ten-year-old-boy fare, it dabbles in graphic novels and published the hit fantasy series *The Sandman,* which has a significant following among women in their twenties. Abbey's own office is a shrine to all-girl comics, decorated with posters of Supergirl, Tank Girl, and a character called Anima, whose slogan is "There's a new grrrl in town." The images inspire her, she says, certainly more than the poster we pass a few minutes later in hall, of a bosomy cartoon Catwoman in thigh-high boots, a whip dangling from her arm. "If she were real," Abbey observes wryly, "she'd probably fall over with those breasts. I believe in the First Amendment, but I do not always approve of the rendition of women here."

Lately, there's more and more that Abbey disapproves of about DC. Despite her devotion to the product, she's grown frustrated with the company's sales strategy, which she considers masculine and outmoded. Like Mira Brodie, Abbey brought up her ideas about "masculine" and "feminine" traits early in our conversations, and I was similarly curious about how they influenced her relationships, her sense of self, and her career expectations. Like Mira, she hoped not only to succeed personally in her field but to advance the position of women in general. Beyond that, though, their visions diverge. Abbey identifies her "feminine" characteristics—which she describes as sensitivity, nurturing, cooperation, sexuality—as a special source of power,

innate to women: If used creatively, she believes, they can revolution-
ize how business is done. There are many who agree with her, who
celebrate "women's style of management" as the wave of the future.[1]
It's an intriguing idea, but I find myself wondering about the potential
danger of linking specific qualities and characteristics to one's sex.

As we head toward the elevator, Abbey says that someday she'd
like to start her own company based on what she calls a "feminine
model": She would handpick her staff, even the secretaries, whom she
considers the most important part of an organization. There would be
on-site childcare, and family commitments would be actively accommodated. She even imagines offering monthly sick days for women
who suffer from PMS. "The feminine model is a holistic approach to
employees, to an industry, to a customer-client relationship," she explains. "It's getting people what they need. It's a little like being a parent." We take a long last look at Gotham as the elevator door closes. "I
see being feminine as a strength," she continues. "Even now, as a sales
rep, I know more about my clients, all of whom are men, than any of
the guys I work with do. I send them birthday cards, and I ask how
their wives are. I want to know about their lives. And I want them to
know that I have a life too."

Model Women

On a Saturday night Abbey and I are eating burritos at a makeshift
dining room table in her apartment in Park Slope, Brooklyn. It's post-
student digs: a dingy, rambling space with a futon couch and a couple
of battered chairs. Abbey's personal touch is evident in the framed
page from a vintage *Archie* comic book displayed on one wall. Her
roommate, Leila, a friend from Houston, has just gone out for the
evening with her fiancé, leaving Abbey and me alone to talk. "My
roommate is one of my idols," Abbey says. "She is one of the most outstanding women I've ever met. She was at the top of her class in law
school—the most driven, most directed feminist I've ever known. But
now she's in love. Last night she told me, 'All I want to do is be Mike's

wife. I don't want to go to school, I don't want to go to work, I don't want to wear a suit ever again. I just want to be Mike's wife.' " Abbey shakes her head, looking at the spot where Leila had been standing a few moments before. "So here's my idol, and it's all in the balance, everything, every career goal she ever had. It's been horrible." A few minutes later Abbey mentions that her supervisor, whom she thinks of as a mentor, is about to go on maternity leave and may not return, and I comment that two important role models seem about to abandon her. Without warning Abbey starts to cry. "It's true," she says, sniffling. "You're absolutely right."

Other women—friends, relatives, employers—have been essential to how Abbey constructs her own identity, how she sifts through her conception of what it means to be female. She's particularly eager to find mentors whose balance between personal and professional responsibilities could serve as a model, but, as for other young women I spoke with, they've been hard to come by. Each time one falls short taps an earlier, far more profound loss: When Abbey was twelve, her eighteen-year-old sister died suddenly of leukemia. Up until then Abbey had a happy family: Her father was a history professor; her mother, a housewife and the emotional center of the home. As a small child she remembers feeling safe and well loved. In the years after their tragedy, though, her home life unraveled. Her father spent long hours at work and said little. Her mother, grieving and sedated, couldn't muster the resources to tend to her youngest child. "She just checked out," Abbey remembers. "She was basically catatonic."

Although she describes her relationship with her mother now as "unusually close," and her anger has resolved itself, Abbey felt abandoned throughout her teens. "I didn't have a mother during my most important years," she says. "My childhood friends would tell you, 'Abbey was always the most popular, the funniest, the this, the that.' Well, that was a huge act. I was just trying to preserve some semblance of normalcy because it was so unbearable at home. She wasn't there for me. I have had to find mentors and role models, women who were not my mother."

While Abbey's circumstances may be extreme, the yearning for someone who could act as a guide to contemporary womanhood, who could help them navigate its confusing crosscurrents, was typical of the young women I spoke with. Absent a range of images and icons—or, as Abbey might put it, without a culture of female superheroes—it is more difficult to make choices that would allow for a freer, more authentic life. "I'm not committed to the idea that other women are so important to me just because of my past," Abbey says, still dabbing her eyes with a tissue. "I think it's also a sign of the times we live in. We're all searching for role models."

Body and Soul

Abbey rolls up her pant leg to show me her sculpted calf muscles. For the past year she's been training for a marathon, although, she says, the preparation has meant more to her than actually entering a competition. Her exercise regimen has changed her relationship to her body, and, for the first time, has made her feel "marketably attractive." Throughout her teens and into her twenties, Abbey says, her self-image was abysmal. In high school she may have been popular with friends, but she was unconventional-looking, "a toothpick," an "ugly duckling" without a pair of de rigueur designer jeans to her name; she was not, she says tersely, the type boys noticed. Perhaps if she'd had a strong female figure in her life, she says, someone whom she could talk to, she would've been less vulnerable to seeking confirmation in male eyes. As it was, like so many girls, she pursued boys' attention desperately and was often unable to distinguish between healthy connections and destructive ones. During her fourteenth summer Abbey snuck off for secret makeout sessions with a twenty-two-year-old camp counselor who made her feel womanly, special—although, she learned later, she was just one of a string of underage girls with whom he was involved. Their liaisons lasted until Abbey was sixteen (he was twenty-four), when, without her consent, he had intercourse with her. "He absolutely just put his penis inside me and then came on my stomach," she remembers. "There was no dialogue at all."

Abbey still can't decide whether she was raped. "I went with him willingly," she says. "So his defense was clear, more clear than mine. Also, in my little group of friends it was like whoever lost their virginity first won. So in my warped teenage way I felt sort of special because I was in the club. I'd had sex, even though this was no kind of sexual experience you would ever want to have."

Beyond basic plumbing, Abbey says, no one ever talked to her about sex; certainly no one mentioned pleasure. Even during college at Tufts, where she felt academically self-assured and buoyed by a burgeoning feminist consciousness, she continued to feel undeserving in her interactions with men. Her sexual encounters were mostly brief—she calls them "repeat one-night stands"—and left her feeling ill used. "There I was," she remembers, "an educated, upper-middle-class white woman who has it going on and knows all this stuff except for how to have a good sexual experience."

Was it her negative first time—something she shares with as many as two thirds of women[2]—that made her undervalue her own happiness, or was that first time itself in part a result of a culture that disconnects girls from their bodies and their needs? "I don't know," Abbey says. "But growing up, there is no education telling girls, 'This should be a pleasure thing, not just a service thing.' There is no one saying, 'Dear heterosexual girl, P.S., are you getting love in ways that are supportive to you emotionally and physically?' No one ever asked me that. I didn't know that you *could* ask that.

"If I had daughters, I would spell out the facts of life for them about sexuality and sensuality at a very early age," she continues. "I would tell them sexuality is key to esteem issues. I'd even encourage them to masturbate."

It has taken Abbey years of conscious effort—"a self-confidence that goes above and beyond"—to learn about her body, about what feels good and what doesn't, and to expect that both her desire and her emotions will be respected. Working out, developing a more expansive definition of beauty, has helped her gain some of that confidence. Attaining her initial round of professional goals, supporting herself, and building a life in a new city have helped too. But the real turning point, she says, came a year ago, when she broke up with a man she'd been dating because he was taking her for granted, a man whom she describes as being "everything I thought I could never have: gorgeous, a lawyer, a frat boy, a sports fan—just this total hunk dude." Her parents happened to be in town when she ended the relationship. When she went to their hotel to let them know what she'd done, her mother hugged and comforted her. Then her father told her to put on her running shoes.

"When my ex-boyfriend and I would exercise together, he would always make a point to be one step ahead of me," she explains. "He always had to win. That was part of how I knew I had to end it. But when I went out with my father, he ran right next to me for three miles. Then the whole way back he ran a few steps behind, saying, 'You have to beat yourself, not me. Unless you beat yourself, you will never get better.' "

Abbey nods at the memory. "What more support could you possibly ask for?" she says. "First he's by my side, and then he's behind me—figuratively and literally. I mean, how beautiful is that? I never would have been involved with that guy in the first place if all of my relationships had mirrored that beautiful moment of running with my father."

Why, I ask, do you think they haven't? She shakes her head and says, "I wish I knew. My parents love and support each other, but they have a relationship of a different age. I don't know why there is this chasm. Maybe it's because of my first experience. Except that lots of women who didn't have that kind of first experience still feel the way I did."

Abbey looks thoughtful for a moment, then brightens. "But now I am involved with such a loving guy and I think that's a credit to my own self-development." Jeremy Gordon, she tells me, treats her "like the rare jewel that I always thought maybe I was, you know? He believes in me. He gives me emotional support. He's just so *there*. I never had that before. I didn't think it was possible." She believes it took the epiphany she had with her father, as well as walking away from her "ideal" man, to feel she deserves this level of respect. "It took the Abbey of last summer to appreciate it," she says, referring to when she and Jeremy started dating. "Not the Abbey of last winter or even last spring. It was like I had become a different person."

A Roomful of Excellent Women

Abbey pulls some of her own cartoons out of a folder. They are whimsical, short strips about postcollege life, gen-X style: the transition from café habitué to would-be business mogul; life from the perspective of the corporate cubicle; a cartoon reminding sexually active women to tell their partners "no glove, no love." Abbey has always been artistic, known as the girl who could draw anything. After college she even published several issues of her own all-comics newspaper in Houston. It was there that she discovered her true gift was for business. She was a good artist, she says, flipping through the sheaf of her work, but she was an even better boss. To her surprise, people looked to her for leadership, and she excelled at organizing and sales. "I stepped up out of that female role of needing guidance myself and into managing, and I loved it."

Abbey hoped to refine those skills at DC, to learn from the best. When, after six months as an assistant, she was assigned to a team that was revamping the company's direct sales policy, she thought she'd found her niche. She was especially pleased that her new boss was a woman—the one who is currently about to go on maternity leave. "She and I would have these long, idealistic conversations about developing a feminine, organic sales model," she says, "about this utopian office in which everyone works to their strengths, and we don't just plug people in and make them fit a job." Inspired by those talks, Abbey geared up for a revolution. But when management announced the final sales plan, nothing had been changed: The "feminine model" had been rejected. "I have nothing but good feelings toward my boss," Abbey says. "She's a great manager, an incredible motivator, but she's a dreamer. And I was naive. They weren't interested in our vision. I don't think she knew how to pitch it. And I didn't know how to sell it myself."

Abbey still believes in her vision, but implementing new ideas at a major corporation, particularly as a young woman, wasn't going to be as easy as she'd hoped. Discouraged, she renewed her search for women whose experience she could adapt to her own situation. She attended a networking session for women who'd graduated from Tufts. One by one the older women in the group, who were in their mid-forties, stood up and described their career paths. One worked in the cosmetics industry. Another had found success on Wall Street. A third was a psychology professor at Columbia. Each woman, Abbey says, was more inspiring than the last, and when they were done, and everyone was chatting informally over coffee and dessert, several honed in on her. "I told them what I did and they said, '*Comics?* Girl, what are you doing with your life? You have got to go further.' " Abbey explained that this was what she'd always wanted to do, but they didn't want to hear it. "They were almost saying right out 'That's not good enough. You—*you*—have to be a symbol for your generation, because you can.' "

On the subway ride home Abbey began thinking. Maybe they were right: She was earning only $29,000 a year at DC with no promise of a future. And yet she still wasn't willing to give up her dream. For weeks she weighed her options, then, summoning up her courage, she put her job on the line. "Look," Abbey told her supervisor, "you know I love what I do, but I'm being stifled here." Although she didn't say it out loud, she was also thinking, "And a room full of excellent women just told me that I'm better than this."

Her boss listened patiently, nodding her head in agreement. Her response: "You're right, I think we *are* stifled."

Abbey looks down, disheartened. "She couldn't help me," she says. "And it was a blow, because she's my friend and my role model— I adore her. But even she recognizes that she can't give me any more here." Maybe her expectations were too high when she came to DC, Abbey says, maybe she was unrealistic about how much she could accomplish—after all, this was her first real job. Although it's been painful, she's learned a lot about the benefits and limits of mentoring, about what she values in an employer, about the sort of corporate environment in which she might thrive, and the kind in which she can't.

"Those women I met woke me up," she says. "I feel like I have options. I still think I could turn this place around if someone could point me in the right direction. But as enthusiastic as I am about comics, I'll leave if I have to. And that makes me feel a little invincible: I know there's something else out there for me."

Husband Material

Jeremy Gordon, Abbey's boyfriend, looks stiff and irritable when the three of us meet at an Upper West Side restaurant for dinner. He is a husky man in his early thirties, with dirty-blond hair and glasses, wearing a flannel shirt and corduroys. His eyes project a kindness but also a wariness, which may be circumstantial: Jeremy is convinced, Abbey tells me, that I'm going to "blame something on him." When he begins to relax, though, his affection for Abbey becomes obvious. He kisses her on the cheek and occasionally gives her a smooch on the lips. He rubs her short hair like she's a puppy and she looks back at him with adoring cocker-spaniel eyes. This is the guy she'd told me about, the cuddly fellow who sends her erotic e-mail at work.

Jeremy is an art director, also at DC, and although he's not too concerned about it, Abbey has been scrupulous about hiding their affair in the office. His last girlfriend worked at the company too, and their breakup was a source of hot gossip in Abbey's marketing meetings. "I don't want to be the topic of conversation like that," she says.

"Legitimate," Jeremy says. "But for the record, that wouldn't happen in one of our meetings. That may be the difference between having a staff that's male dominated versus one like yours, where there's women."

Abbey bristles slightly. "What does that mean?" she says. "And what about your meetings? You guys are always talk about bazooms."

"Yeah," he concedes, "but we're talking about *Catwoman!*"

Abbey picks up her menu and scrutinizes it, unwilling to argue. Jeremy comments that Abbey is almost never willing to confront him when she's upset. "She has such a hard time saying what she feels that it's actually taken me a while to believe that something she says is honest," he says.

"I try to preserve people's feelings," Abbey explains. "But Jeremy is teaching me to stand up for myself. Like at work, he's always telling me I should just go in and tell them to fuck off." She gazes at him fondly. "That's so male," she continues, "but, you know, when I've done it, when I've said what I mean, I've found it liberating. Like today, for the first time I asked a real straightforward question in a meeting. Usually I write them down and think about whether it's worth it, because the vice president belittles you for asking questions. So I am taking Jeremy's advice and allowing confrontation in my life. And they don't all end badly."

In the spirit of the moment I bring up a topic I know is touchy: Abbey is thinking about going to graduate school in the fall, and most of her applications are to schools outside New York. "Can I ask what you think will happen to the two of you next year?" I say.

Abbey looks down. Jeremy colors and looks straight into my eyes.

"No," he says.

LATER, BACK AT her apartment, Abbey tells me that she's tired of not addressing the future with Jeremy, but she's afraid that if she brings it up, she'll be forced to end their relationship. Given the limits of her job, Abbey expects to leave New York within a year, either to go to graduate school or to return to Houston, and there are no real jobs for Jeremy outside the city. "I have such strong feelings of tenderness and love toward him, but I feel like my career and my life are just really taking off," Abbey says. "Maybe it's just bad timing: I feel like I'm a little more important than our relationship right now. I have plans that don't include him that I have to be true to."

For Jeremy, though, nothing is more important than his relationship with Abbey. He's said that if she wants him to, he'll move, he'll give up his job, he'll even change careers if it means staying together. And when he says that, Abbey has to face an uncomfortable truth. "Maybe I don't want to be committed to Jeremy," she says, "and maybe that's what I'm afraid of. That's what I'm not ready to say." Jeremy makes her feel good, Abbey says, and his devotion has made her confidence in her romantic appeal soar. She adores him: He's a "wonderful guy," an "outstanding sweetheart," and yet when she imagines a husband, she pictures someone who is "more excellent" than she is. "I want to be with someone who is always pushing themselves to be better," Abbey says, "self-improvement, emotionally, physically, and mentally as a full-time job."

Jeremy, for all his loving qualities, just isn't that guy. His style is a little coarse for Abbey, a tad unsophisticated. There's something else too: In what Abbey sheepishly calls a "real feminist turn of the screw"—especially given that he's in the industry to which she is so committed—she's uncomfortable with his limited earning potential. "I'm a professional woman," she says, "and I plan to stay a professional woman. But somewhere in my unconscious, I have to admit, I thought that when I settled down and had kids, I wouldn't have to work. I mean, I couldn't imagine not working but . . .

"Jeremy and I go round and round about it," she continues. "He says, 'Why would you like for me to be economically dependable?' And I don't know, but I would. I don't know where it comes from. A storybook? White America? My parents? They've asked about his future very plainly. I have had to explain to them that what he does is a viable profession. I've tried to convince them and tried to convince myself."

Listening to Abbey, I find myself agreeing with Jeremy. Why *does* she need him to be the provider? I ask. If she wants to accomplish all she says she does, if she wants professional entitlement and equality with men at work, isn't it inconsistent to demand that her mate excel beyond her? What's more, it may backfire. As writer Rhona Mahony found in her study of the economics of marriage and family life, women who "marry up" for emotional insurance guarantee that they'll be the ones to put extra time into childcare at the expense of their careers.[3] That hardly jibes with Abbey's grand plans. How can she seek equality in the workplace while looking for a fallback based on inequality in the home? How can she realize her "feminine model" of power in the professional world without challenging men's family roles?

"Believe me, I've grappled with that," Abbey says, looking miserable. She's been surprised herself by this internal contradiction, by how deep her core traditionalism runs. Certainly, her parents raised her to be independent and accomplished. Yet, at the same time, they've fueled her concern about Jeremy's future. Abbey's mother, who started a successful publicity business in her fifties, often encourages Abbey to come home and take over—but makes it clear that she expects it to be a secondary income. "I have these arguments with them all the time: 'Mom, Dad, if you just wanted me to get married, why did you raise me to be so excellent, why did you let me have the freedoms that put me in an intellectual class where I won't want to be just a wife?' "

Sometimes, she says, she does fantasize about marrying Jeremy. She imagines the two of them having children: He would become a househusband and she would earn their keep with her newly gotten MBA. In the end, though, it's not a dream she wants to pursue. "I'm just not that progressive," she says flatly. "And, to be honest, the responsibility scares me." Abbey rubs her hand across her buzz cut. Even if she could make that leap, she says, Jeremy still might not be the right guy for her. Her friends think she's already decided to end it, but she says that's not true. "I really like him," she says. "And it's worth it to me to feel this good with someone even if we are doomed to break up. But now that I believe in myself so much more romantically, I wonder if I could have more. It's like, this feels really good, but could it feel better?"

A COUPLE OF months later, when I'm back in California, Abbey calls to tell me she's broken up with Jeremy. She felt too guilty about being involved with someone who loved her so much when she knew, deep down, she would never marry him. It wasn't easy to explain to him why things wouldn't work out: After all, she wasn't exactly unhappy, she just thought she could be happier with someone else. "I ended up having to be painfully honest and mean," she says, "I said, 'I'm not inspired by you. Don't you think I deserve to be inspired?' " They're still

traveling together for work, though, which has, at times, been excruciating. "Now I understand why people say, 'Don't go out with someone
you work with,' " she says.

Meanwhile, she's given notice at DC, although she's not
sure what she'll do next—she's taken the entrance exam for business
school but isn't convinced that she'll score well enough to make it into
one of her top choices. Recently, to get some other ideas, she attended
a panel on women in business sponsored by New York University. All
of the women there had sprinted up the corporate ladder until they'd
had children. Then, Abbey says, "they faced all these hard choices. All
the ones who were mothers ended up leaving whatever corporation
they worked for and went on to do consulting and they're now doing
fabulously well.

"It was disappointing that they couldn't make it in corporations
and have kids," she continues, "but that's why I feel so strongly about
this feminine workplace model, with childcare at the office and more
communication and responsibility between women. The workplace is
hungry for it. I hope I'm not being naive, but I want to be in a position
someday to make these decisions. Maybe someone like me . . ." Her
voice trails off, then comes back more assured. "I want to be a role
model."

Chapter 4

One Woman, Two Worlds

My Best Friend When I was yay high was a white girl," muses Gayle Webb, placing one hand against her waist, at a child's height. "But as we grew older, you just"—she flips her palm over, turning the gesture into a shrug—"it's like, you separate."

Gayle is twenty-four, a second-year medical student at the University of Pennsylvania. She's a slim, long-legged woman with hair that cascades in rippling curls to her shoulders: It's no surprise when, during our conversation, she alludes to dating professional athletes, or lets it slip that she was asked to star in a Dark and Lovely hair relaxer commercial. She is one of six women gathered this September afternoon at Shay Thomas's apartment in West Philadelphia. Shay herself is twenty-five; her round face, with its deeply etched dimples and golden eyes, is surrounded by dozens of tiny braids. I'd asked her to assemble a group of her black medical-school classmates for me to interview, but at the last minute she felt that would seem "weird" with a white reporter. So, she threw in two white friends—another medical student and a law student—who sit together on one side of the room, saying little. Listening to Gayle, though, Stephanie, twenty-seven, nods. "That's right," she agrees, "it happened in middle school. Eighth grade."

"I had this white friend when I was little," says Nicole, twenty-four, who grew up in Atlanta. "She still e-mails me, and I *never* write her back. And I feel so awful, but we're in totally different worlds. It's like I've come into my blackness, almost."

With the exception of Gayle, who went to Spellman, the black women in this room attended similar, overwhelmingly white colleges: Brown, Cornell, the University of Georgia. Shay went to an almost exclusively white prep school as well, and there are only fifteen black students in their class at Penn. Given that background, it would seem they would have plenty in common with white girls.

"And I do feel a sisterhood," Shay says. "I definitely do, especially professionally."

"That's true," says Ruth, twenty-six. Ruth is lighter skinned than the other three, the product of a racially mixed Dominican family. She wears wire-rimmed glasses and has wound her hair into a bun. "But at the end of the day, I still think we're looked upon differently. The problem society has with being female is that family gets in the way: Women want to take maternity leave and go to PTA meetings, all that business. That's a totally different concept than being black. It's like we're not supposed to be here. We're dumber. We have less class. We're inferior.

"So, yes," Ruth continues, glancing over at the white women, "I feel a sisterhood. Yes, we're all women. But the end of the day"—she turns back toward her friends and shakes her head in a gesture both matter-of-fact and angry—"we're black."

Young, Gifted, and Black

A few months later Shay Thomas meets me across the street from the university for an evening on the town: She's dressed for the occasion in an Indian print shirt, jeans, and mules so high, they force her to take tiny, tottering steps. Her nose is pierced with a delicate silver ball and, since I last saw her, she's had her braids coiled into elaborate thick knobs all over her head. So far, she says, none of her supervisors at the VA hospital, where she's doing a two-month rotation in internal medicine, has hassled her about the new 'do, "but the patients are mostly black men, and their daughters are always in there saying"—she puts a little attitude in her posture, changes the timbre and accent of her voice, touches my arm—" 'ooo, girl, your hair is *sharp*! Where did you get it done? How much did it cost? How long did it take?' "

We hop in her leased Jetta and drive toward a café in Rittenhouse Square, one of the poshest neighborhoods in the city. I get the feeling that she thinks it's a place I'd like. "We don't go here too much," she admits, fiddling with the radio dial. She settles on a favorite hip-hop song, bumps the music up to full volume, and begins moving to the beat in the driver's seat, making any further attempt at conversation impossible until we arrive at our destination: Xando, a noisy café and bar that's been skimming off some of the Starbucks crowd. On a Thursday evening it's packed with people in their mid-twenties: graduate students, newly minted professionals, young men and women with upwardly mobile dreams. On one hand, as a medical student on a rare night off, Shay fits right in, sipping her grande double mocha. On the other hand, looking around at the all-white faces, she is constantly reminded that she is a long way from home.

"You know," she says as we settle in with our drinks, "if you asked ninety percent of Americans how they grew up, they'd say middle class. And I would too. But if I was going to be honest"—she frowns, jutting out her lower out lip—"I didn't live in like a 'hood or anything, but it *was* an all-black neighborhood and it was a block away from a ghetto. No one would say 'Your neighborhood was a nice neighborhood.' It was lower working-class. But there wasn't anyone selling drugs on the corner. People were trying to be positive."

If the white women I spoke with were the beneficiaries of the fight for women's professional rights, Shay is the product of a different sort of dream. Unlike the mothers of many of the white women, Shay's wasn't a frustrated housewife forced to trade in other aspirations for domesticity; nor did she return to graduate school when the kids were older or launch a successful business later in life. She was, until she died earlier this year of breast cancer, a postal clerk. She brought in the family's steady income: Shay's father worked at an automotive factory and was, for a time, unemployed. The Thomases looked to the promise of the civil rights movement, not feminism, to fulfill their hopes for their only child, and to them that meant providing her with the best education money could buy—a white education. Every day, from the time she was in third grade, Shay rode the city bus forty-five minutes from her home in Detroit's inner city to a prep school in one of its swankiest suburbs. She did well there—she was valedictorian of her graduating class—and was friendly enough with her white classmates: She studied with them, sometimes even ate lunch with them. She didn't feel alienated exactly, but she always felt apart. When I ask her if she keeps up with any of her eighteen classmates, she shakes her head. But when I ask what happened to the kids in her neighborhood, she rattles off a litany of who is working and who is on welfare, who has had kids and who's in jail; she exchanges regular e-mails with a nurse and a bookkeeper who, like her, have moved away; she even knows that there's only one other woman she grew up with, the older sister of a friend, who is in graduate school, studying communications at Eastern Michigan University. "I may have known the kids I went to school with from the time we were seven," she explains. "But friendshipwise, my *real* life was always once I got home, with my black friends."

In some ways Shay's dilemma is not so different from Mira's or

Abbey's. They all wrestle with what it means to be female in arenas that are still defined and run by men. And like them, the higher Shay climbs, the fewer people like herself she encounters, and the greater the pressure to relinquish a core part of herself. But for her, role models are even more scarce, the inner conflicts even more profound. Despite the gains of affirmative action, African American women remain severely underrepresented in managerial positions compared to white women, and are concentrated in the three lowest paying industries.[1] Fewer than four percent of doctors are black, fewer than three percent of lawyers, and fewer than seven percent of college professors.[2] Shay had only one other black classmate in high school. Stanford, where she went to college, was about eight percent black, and of the fourteen other black students in her medical school class, nearly all are foreign born or the children of immigrants, as were Ruth and Nicole from our original interview group. Young African Americans like Shay, who are groomed for mainstream achievement, are tacitly taught that the white world and the values associated with it represent success. But if that's true, where does that leave Shay's "real" life? How much of the world she grew up in is she willing to leave behind in order to succeed? And who will she become if she does? In *Children of the Dream: The Psychology of Black Success*, psychologist Craig Polite and journalist Audrey Edwards explore the contradictions that confront the emerging black middle class. "The aim is to be an exception," they write. "But to be an exception means that a stereotype has been accepted as the standard of measure, and it is this acceptance of the stereotype that both propels black success and dislocates it."[3]

Like Mira and Abbey, Shay frequently compares herself to other women, but instead of focusing on femininity or ambition, her continuum measures black authenticity: Where she places herself on it is key to her sense of identity. She brings up friends at college who were in Jack and Jill, an invitation-only black youth group Shay calls "hoity-toity," a mirroring of whites' preoccupation with class. She wonders what it means that Ruth is in her second relationship in a row with a white man. She mentions another black classmate who is mentoring a teenage girl in the ghetto but is afraid to go to her house. "Most of the black women here see themselves as that W.E.B. Du Bois talented tenth. And I feel like I'm part of that, but I kind of turn my nose up at it too. Because that other thing, that's also part of me: It's part of my background and part of who I consider myself to be."

Shay lights a cigarette and cocks her head, thinking. "I do feel like I live in two worlds," she says. "But don't most people? I mean, don't you think most people have two selves like that?"

Golden Opportunities
and Pink-Collar Dreams

Shay and I stroll through campus during a break from her rounds at the VA hospital, where she's spent much of the morning trying to schedule dialysis treatments for an indigent diabetic who's about to be released. We turn onto tree-lined Locust Walk. The sun dapples the brick and stone buildings. Late summer cicadas buzz above us. Students ride by on junky, three-speed bicycles. Shay stands out in her official doctor's mufti: blue scrubs and running shoes. "I'm examining my first HIV patient later," she says. "I'm really nervous about it. They tell you to just assume everyone has a blood-borne infection and observe universal precautions, and HIV shouldn't be different, but it feels that way. They don't make medical students draw blood if we're not comfortable, but you have to do a rectal and a genital. So, there are bodily fluids involved."

Shay chose Penn over Washington University and Michigan not so much for the quality of its medical school—although it's one of the best—as for its prestigious MBA program. The truth is, she says, she doesn't really want to be a doctor; she's not sure she ever did. "You have to jump on the medicine track early," she explains. "There's a big math-science triage point in about eighth grade, and if you're still doing well after that, people are like, 'engineering, biology, medicine.' You're just on the track. You *can* do it, so you do."

And then there is her dad. Despite his own college degree, earned at a community college—which Shay describes as a "sham" school—he reads at only about a sixth-grade level. To have a daughter who's a doctor "feels like an achievement to him," she says. "It means the world. And he wanted it for me so much." Her closest female cousins bask in Shay's success too. Single mothers who live from paycheck to paycheck, they went out and bought her fifteen rolls of toilet paper last time they visited so she could save her own money. She is, clearly, the pride of the family. "But it *is* a lot of pressure on someone too," she adds.

Of course, Shay says, she's not here just for other people—that wouldn't be enough to sustain her through years of grueling course work—there's something deep within that drives her as well. She wants to have the degree, something no one can ever take away from her, showing that she is capable of the rigorous training, the sleep deprivation, the massive amount of memorization required to be a doctor. "Medical school," she says, "is like a hurdle I have to get over to prove something to someone, although I don't know who."

We sit on a bench kittycorner from a cast-iron statue of Benjamin Franklin leaning on a cane, reading *Poor Richard's Almanack*. Shay sighs. "Sometimes I think after this I want to go on to Wharton, get my MBA, and be the head of the World Health Organization. And sometimes I think, no, I don't, I just want to be a nurse. If I had to do it over . . ." She trails off, then swivels around to face me. "You know, there's nothing wrong with being a nurse or a secretary," she says, "a nine-to-five, stable job. I'd have a nice little salary, respectable, but have my free time."

I'm surprised to hear Shay say this, and I tell her so. I can understand deciding against medicine, but she is an intellectually gifted woman. Could a pink-collar job really be enough for her? "I really believe that it could," she says. "I really do."

We sit in silence for a moment, and Shay opens a book to brush up on the treatment of hepatitis for a class she's attending in about an hour. If she were someone else, I might speculate that her fantasy was about a nostalgia for simplified feminine roles, or a way to question the terms of success in formerly male-dominated fields. And to an extent that could be true. But with Shay I suspect her ambivalence about success involves race and class as much as gender—including, perhaps, her desire to exceed her community without leaving it behind, her struggle to redefine her own sense of place and home.

"You know," she says, looking up from her book, "sometimes I think, I'm going to Wharton, and I'm going to get my MBA and I'm going to run Aetna U.S. Healthcare and I'm going to make $250,000 and I'm going to have this kind of car and all of that. And then I think, 'What do I want all that for?' Part of me thinks I am *entitled* to make $150,000 before I'm thirty-five. And I will if I go that route. And that's not pipe-dreaming either. That's not an unrealistic expectation for myself."

What would be the downside of doing that? "My life would be all about working," she says glumly. "That, and I might not ever really fit in.

"I feel like I've lost something," she continues. "I lost what people back home have: being able to come home after work, stopping over at your grandma's house, stopping over to see your nephew, stopping to pick up your niece. Catching a movie with my girls. Kicking it at home, where you know people, where you go get something to eat if you feel like getting something to eat and you don't call it brunch. Maybe that's what life is about: laying back, kicking, relaxing, having kids, not caring whether you work for the biggest corporation."

She leans her head back, looking at the sky. "Maybe."

I ask her what she really thinks she'll do. "I think I'll get the MBA," she says. "I think I'll do medical consulting or work for some-place like the Red Cross."

What about being a secretary or a nurse? Shay looks sad. "I'm never going to do it," she says, gazing into the distance, "it's just a dream."

From Where I Sit

On our way to the University Medical Center, where the class on hepa-titis is meeting, we bump into Shay's friends Bethany and Lily, who are sitting at an outdoor table, studying for their medical boards. "We are in Stressville," Lily moans as Shay pulls up a chair. Bethany is white with dishwater-blond hair pulled into a ponytail and a Peanuts T-shirt with "Lebanon" improbably emblazoned across the front. Lily is Asian American with short black hair, pointy features, and a laconic voice, which may simply be a reaction to too much studying. They are the two people Shay feels closest to at Penn, but since they live in the Center City neighborhood along with most of the white students, and she lives in largely black West Philly, they don't get together very often.

The three gossip about mutual friends, the medical boards, and Shay's resident, who is also Asian ("a sweet Asian guy on campus who I don't know?" Lily asks with interest). Bethany mentions Stephanie, who was in Shay's original interview group, and who is currently deciding on her specialty. "She's thinking about ER," Bethany says.

"What happened to surgery?" Lily asks.

Bethany shrugs. "She says she's got to think about the future and it may just be too much."

"I know," says Lily. "I keep telling her to go for it, to be a great female surgeon because we need more of them." She shakes her head. "But then I think, 'God, you don't want to put yourself through that.'"

The other women nod. "How old is Stephanie?" Shay asks.

"Twenty-eight," says Bethany.

Shay counts silently on her fingers. "So she'd be thirty-four by the time she was done with her training." She juts out her lip, considering. "That's fine. Except that she can't have kids during all that."

"Yeah," says Bethany, "but then, there's no guarantee she'll have kids if she *doesn't* become a surgeon. So if she's going to give up her life, it might as well be for something she loves." Bethany laughs. "Well, 'give up her life' might be a *little* dramatic."

"We all say, 'I want a life, a family, a marriage, a kid,'" Shay says, "but we have no man, so isn't all that a little abstract? Should you really make a choice based on that?"

Lily sighs. "That's why I chose radiology. For a life. And I don't even have a boyfriend."

As we head over to the medical school, Shay reflects that as thorny as the issues of sorting out family life and career are, she still feels more pressure as an African American in medical school than as a woman. "I don't feel like they question your competence as a woman," she says. "I kind of feel that they do question it racewise. But then, I don't know how real that perception is. I don't think it's possible for me to know purely in an objective way how real racism is, because I don't know what it's like to not be black and have people evaluate me."

SIXTEEN STUDENTS SHOW up to the class on hepatitis, tossing their stethoscopes jauntily over the backs of their chairs. With one exception, the students of color—five Asians of both sexes and two black women, including Shay—sit clustered together at one end of the large oval table. The resident running the session, an amiable white guy with a receding hairline, sits in the middle between two empty chairs. Typically, he quizzes each student in turn about which tests they would order if a patient presented with a particular set of symptoms and what they would conclude from the results, but today he breaks form and allows them to simply call out answers to his questions. After about fifteen minutes, I notice that he rarely looks toward our end of the table, that, in fact, he swivels his chair so his back is facing us, making it difficult for him to hear any responses. Over the course of the two-hour class, the people at the white end begin to dominate, while the students in our section pay less and less attention, after a few discouraging tries.

During a break Shay says, "I like the way he's running the class: I don't have to say anything if I don't want to."

"Well, I don't," snaps Rochelle, the other black woman in the room. "I'm like, 'Excuse me, why are you addressing only that end of the table?' "

"I noticed that," I say.

"I'm glad *someone* did," she huffs.

"And when you tried to answer . . ." I begin.

"He says"—Rochelle looks dismissively over her shoulder—" 'Right' and turns back to the other side of the table immediately."

"I saw that too" says an Asian woman who was sitting next to Rochelle.

"You did!" Rochelle says, triumphant. "I mean, is this guy going to be *evaluating* me?" She rolls her eyes.

"That was one of those times when you just don't know what's going on," Shay says later. "You wonder, was it us or was there something else behind it? Were we not being aggressive enough? Were we not shouting out the answers loudly enough? But, then, when Rochelle did shout out, he ignored her. So you have to wonder . . ." She shrugs. "You learn to ignore it, though, to put your head down and do what you have to do. Otherwise, you get too frustrated."

I nod at what Shay is saying, but I realize I'm only half listening. I'm looking at the notes I took during the class. Of all the students, I realize, three of the white women were the most assertive. I wonder, if I'd been following one of them instead of Shay, would I have even noticed the exclusion of the students of color? If I'd been following one of them, would I have come away with a different perspective of the class entirely, a sense of progress and accomplishment instead of unease?

Single Professional Black Female Seeks . . . Who?

At six o'clock Shay is done for the day. She's checked in on her patients—the diabetic, who is staying in the hospital for a few more days, and the man with HIV, who turns out to be a groggy fiftyish recovering heroin addict. As she walks down the dingy, antiseptic-scented corridor toward the elevator, she glances idly into a room and notices an old, grizzled African American man tied to his bed, struggling with his water cup. She's off duty, and he's not one of her patients, but she pops in and helps him anyway. "Thank you," he says as politely as if he were at a tea party, then adds, "You know, I'd appreciate it if you'd just cut these strings."

"Now, I can't do that," she says gently. Back in the hallway she chuckles to herself. " 'I'd appreciate it you'd just cut these strings,' " she repeats, shaking her head. "Those are *restraints*."

We leave the VA hospital and head back across campus to get a burrito for dinner. I mention that while our conversation has been about how Shay negotiates the demands of conflicting worlds, so far I've seen only one of them. She looks away, silent.

"Is it because you see me as part of this world?" I say.

She nods.

"I'm part of the Ivy League white world, so I can't cross over?"

She nods again. "It's not part of the rules, you know?" she says slowly. "I just can't . . . I'm sorry."

I ask if we can at least go to her apartment for the evening, but she again declines. "It's a mess," she says.

Sometime over dinner, at a Cal-Mex place swarming with graduate students, Shay must have had a change of heart, because she invites me home with her. As night begins to fall, we walk along Chestnut Street, which runs through the University City and on into West Philly. Within a few blocks, the number of white people drops off. Soon there are none at all. "I wanted to live somewhere where I'd see black faces on the street," Shay says. "It makes me feel comforted." After about a mile we turn down a side street: The gutter on the corner is filled with trash, but most of the homes, while old with sagging porches, are well cared for. Little kids play in the scraps of yard that front each row house. A group of boys hangs out on the curb, rapping along with a boom box. Old ladies sit on their stoops gossiping, waving, and wishing us a good evening as we walk by.

Shay wasn't kidding when she said her apartment was a mess. She's had only one day off in a month; between studying and working at the hospital, she hasn't had time to play Suzy Homemaker. Dishes are piled on the counter in the kitchen and overflowing from the sink. Medical journal articles and lecture notes are strewn on the floor, making a trail to the living room, which, since she seems to have pulled the batting out of the pillows on the couch, looks like it was caught in some crazy snowstorm. A box of Cap'n Crunch, two empty bags of Chee·tos, and coffee mugs filled with cigarette butts litter the floor of that room, along with six pairs of shoes, some nail polish remover, and various items of clothing. There are three books on her coffee table: *Diet for a Small Planet*, *The Reader* (a novel about the aftermath of the Holocaust), and *Breaking Ice*, an anthology of writing by African Americans. The centerpiece of the room is a large picture of her mom in an oval frame, perched on top of a small TV.

Shay starts tidying up just as the phone rings. For the next two hours it doesn't stop. She gabs with friends from medical school, friends from her past, people who are getting ahead and people who aren't. As she talks, her voice slides out of the clipped tone she uses at work and relaxes into a down-home drawl. "I can lay up on the phone all night," she tells me happily between calls, and she does, cleaning as she chats. By the time she finishes her final call, the living room is sparkling, the pillows restuffed and covered with a bright-patterned sheet.

The evening's big drama centers on Travis, the guy Shay has been dating for the past few weeks, who calls her from his car every few minutes trying to convince her to let him come over late tonight. She resists, since she has to be at the hospital at seven tomorrow for rounds, but he keeps pushing. The two met at a citywide monthly event called First Fridays, where single black professionals get together to mix, mingle, and, hopefully, to match. Like most of the men who attend, however, Travis is not actually a professional: He doesn't have a college degree, and Shay doesn't know exactly what he does at the office supplies company where he works. "He and his friends want to be a little 'bougie-bougie,'" she explains. "They don't think of themselves as street, roughneck dudes. He thinks of himself as halfway—" She stops, catching herself. "And he *is*," she continues. "I'm not saying that anything's wrong with him. I just want someone who's a little bit more . . ." She trails off, then backpedals again. "He's real sweet though. He's a very, very nice guy."

Shay tries to be diplomatic when she talks about Travis, she tries to be upbeat. But the truth is, her feelings about him hover somewhere between ambivalent and disappointed. "It would be easier if . . ." Trailing off again. Easier if what, I press. She sighs, lights a cigarette. "I mean, Travis doesn't have much conversation," she says. "Travis lives at home. Travis's biggest accomplishment is the purchase of his automobile. Travis loves to rip and run the streets. Travis has a kid. Travis is a very nice guy, but . . ." She takes a puff of her cigarette, exhales hard. "It's that *Ebony* magazine thing, girl. Yes, it is."

WHEN I FIRST interviewed Shay's friends, I'd brought up an article I'd read in *Ebony* chiding black professional women for their snobbery: If these highfalutin lady doctors and lawyers wanted to find a man, the magazine advised, they should stop insisting on a peer and look among the blue-collar set—at plumbers or mechanics.[4] I couldn't imagine seeing a similar piece in *Cosmo* or *Glamour*. In some ways it seemed a liberating, or at least liberated, notion: After all, male professionals have always married secretaries and nurses with no class qualms. The idea that a man ought to earn as much or more than his wife, to which both Abbey and Mira implicitly subscribed, is based on the assumption that he should still be the provider. And that in turn locks women into primary responsibility for the home. But in this case, the motivation for "marrying down" wasn't feminist idealism so much as desperation: If finding an intellectual and economic equal wasn't realistic, the magazine suggested, any man would be better than none.

The dearth of available professional black men was the hottest of hot-button issues among the women in the group and, perhaps, for good reason. The "man shortage" among whites may be a myth, but for black women it's quite real: African American women are approximately fifty percent more likely to graduate college than their male peers, and a disproportionate number of black men are indigent, incarcerated, or on drugs.[5] Partly because of that, the percentage of adult African American women who are unmarried tops forty percent.[6] As Debra Dickerson wrote in *The New Republic*, "Any black woman, especially one with a college education, knows she will not be outnumbered by black men *anywhere* unless she does community service at the city jail. In the African American dating game, men occupy the driver's seat, and they bloody well know it."[7] Call it the *Waiting to Exhale* syndrome: It's given rise to an industry of books that blame women for their single status, such as *How to Marry a Black Man* (by *Mrs.* de Jongh and *Mrs.* Catto-Louis), which explains that the reader has probably already met her ideal man, but "deep down inside, you believe that you don't deserve him."[8]

During her first week at Penn, when only two men showed up at a reception for new black medical students, Gayle's mother actually suggested she transfer. "I keep telling her, 'Mom, chill,'" she said. "I came here to *become* a doctor, not marry one." Still, Gayle frets that she'll never find an economically stable, intellectual equal to marry.

"And then," Nicole piped up, "you are pressed to find a man who is not just professional, not just wonderful and sweet, but has a sense of blackness."

I asked her what that meant exactly. "Someone who can put on some Timberlands on the weekend . . ." she started to say.

"Who was pissed off when Biggie Smalls and Tupac died," Shay chimed in.

"Yes," said Nicole, stomping a foot. "Thank you. Like a guy who just has a certain walk, and has that talk, and that 'Yeah, baby, whassup?' but yet can come out on a Monday morning in a Brooks Brothers suit and take care of business. Because it's not just enough to *be* black. You have to think black, walk black, talk black."

"But now think about the pressure you're putting on black men," sputtered Stephanie, who is white. "That's a lot of pressure for him to be able to do all of that."

"Well, I can," Nicole snapped. "I don't mean to be funny, but"—she gestured to the other women—"we do it. We do it every day."

"*And* raise babies, and hold the household together," Shay added.

"I know," said Stephanie, frowning, "I know, but . . ."

Were they asking too much? Nicole and Shay want their mates to straddle the same two worlds that they do, and to do it as gracefully—perhaps more gracefully. They want their husbands' "blackness" to enhance and reflect their own, their relationships to be a kind of cultural sanctuary in a world that questions their presence every day. If the challenge is to keep a connection to community—to language, to style, to custom—while striving for mainstream success, partnering with a man who retains his "blackness" may be the best way to reassure themselves they haven't assimilated too much. Yet it also creates tremendous strain. The danger, therapist Audrey B. Chapman suggests, is that black women (and men) will freight their relationships with unrealistic demands, wanting their partners to compensate for the rebuffs of society, for all that they feel entitled to but are still denied because of race.[9]

Months later, when we are alone in her apartment, I ask Shay to describe her ideal partner. "Oh," she says, smiling, "I already know him. He's so cool." She tells me about a man she met last year, a former L.A. gang member turned Wharton graduate student. He was exactly the combination of homeboy and buppie she dreamed of, but the timing wasn't right. "We kicked it for a while, but I was dating someone else at the time, and when it came down to deciding, when he said, 'Are you going to be with the next man or are you going to be with me,' I said I had to figure things out with the other guy." Looking back, she can't believe she let him go. Now he's a stockbroker working in New York, living with a girlfriend. I ask if Shay thinks she'll find someone else. "I hope so," she says in a mock-plaintive voice. "I hope there's some other little ex-gang member/stockbroker out there."

Shay's worlds clash more directly than either Mira's or Abbey's, but, like them, she faces a series of dilemmas in forging her identity at work and in intimate relationships. All three women wonder how they'll create a satisfying calibration of personal and professional life, how they'll resolve the tension between new opportunities for women and ongoing constraints—both internal and external. They look forward with excitement, and a bit of trepidation, to the next phase of their lives: When decisions about marriage and motherhood become more pressing, when past choices can have unforeseen consequences, when the challenges of our half-changed world can hit like a tidal wave.

Suddenly Shay looks melancholy. "I guess when it comes down to it, I see myself as single," she says. "Always single. One of my friends tells me, 'You're looking for Jesus.'" She laughs. "Well, maybe I am. But I just think I deserve it, you know? But you look at who's out there and it's frustrating. You say to yourself, 'As a single black professional woman I deserve *more* than this.' I always say, if I were a secretary, I'd be able to find a man much easier. Then maybe the Travises of the world would be good enough."

I tell her about the white women I talk to, and their fixation on "first-grade teachers," women who they think won't make nontraditional demands on a man. She seems surprised and pleased that white women have the same issues. "Do they?" she repeats several times. "Do they really, Peggy? Hmm!"

What's a Nice Doctor Like You . . .

On Saturday night Shay had planned on throwing a dinner party for Travis's birthday, with the secret agenda of putting her friends and his friends in a room to see if any sparks flew. But she's fed up: Travis stood her up last week, then called her the next night from his car. She suspected he was drunk and driving, which she thought was plain irresponsible—so she's going out for a drink with Nicole instead. They go to a neighborhood dive a block from her apartment, the kind of place with bars on the door, where the bouncer lets in only those he knows. He greets Shay and Nicole heartily. Inside, the bar is narrow and murky with cigarette smoke, with mirrors on the wall and old soul tunes playing on the jukebox.

"Look, Peggy," Shay says, pointing to two men sitting near the door, "you're not the only white person here." One of the men is middle-aged and mostly bald, his stomach hanging over his pants. The second has a greasy ponytail, an earring, and a missing tooth. I don't feel much kinship with either of them, but then, maybe Shay doesn't feel a connection to the other lone blacks in the all-white settings where she always finds herself. Or maybe she's just reassuring herself that it was okay to bring me here. We sit down and within minutes a man buys us a round of drinks. Then another does, then a third. Sometimes, Shay says, she doesn't pay for a single drink all night; the men don't seem to expect anything in return either, although they surely have their hopes.

A guy with a dashiki and dreadlocks strikes up a conversation with Nicole. Shay, meanwhile, has her eye on someone across the bar. He's wearing an aloha shirt and the kind of neatly trimmed beard that's fashionable among black men in Philadelphia. He's cute, if a little old for her, and she says she'd send him over a drink if she had the money. I offer to pay and she laughs, covering her face. A new song comes on the jukebox, and the friend of the man in the aloha shirt starts to dance in his chair, a little too intensely. "Look at him," Shay says, narrowing her eyes. "He's cracked up." She decides against sending the drink over.

Instead, we make small talk with Al, a baby-faced man in his forties who had bought our first round of drinks. He asks if Shay goes to school here, a question probably prompted by my presence. "She's a doctor," I interject, and Shay stiffens. We chat with Al a few more minutes. When he turns away, Shay whispers to me, "You told him I was a doctor! I don't usually tell people that."

I'm a little confused: I thought she'd be proud of being a doctor. I ask her what she normally says.

"I tell them I'm in nursing school, or I don't say what I do."

I ask her why not. "I don't know," she says, taking a swig of her beer. "Maybe it's just because I want to forget I'm a doctor for a while. Or maybe it's because people have expectations of doctors." Shay looks around the bar, at Al and his friends, who are watching sports TV, at the crackhead lost in his trance, at her neighbors drinking, flirting, and starting to dance in the narrow aisle. She turns back to me with a half-smile. "And they just don't include hanging out in a place like this."

Part II

The Crunch

Chapter 5

All at Once, All the Time

THE PHONE RINGS AND I feel my jaw clench. I'm sitting at my desk, surrounded by piles of transcripts, trying to gather my thoughts about the challenges women face as they move into their thirties. During the Promise years, women have a similar arc to their experience despite their different backgrounds. As they age, however, their lives diverge sharply and they can become critical toward those who choose different paths. It's hard to see the unifying patterns in lives that are so wildly disparate.

I pick up on the fourth ring. It's my friend Diane, a software developer who's hit it big in Silicon Valley. More than anything else, she now hopes to share her success with a husband and a child—or at least she thinks she does. She's been dating a man for the last year but can't quite decide whether to marry him. "Suddenly I feel like I'm recognizing the life I'd lose," she says. "I've been on my own a long time and I like it. I like being able to go out dancing, or be with my friends without having to accommodate to someone else's schedule. And I don't know: Would all that matter if he were the right person?"

We chew that over for a while, then say good-bye. Twenty minutes later the phone rings again, and I curse softly before picking up the receiver. "Oh, is this a bad time?" my friend Adrienne, who lives across the Bay in San Francisco, asks with a catch in her voice. My work can wait; after all, Adrienne put her career as a filmmaker on indefinite hold to be a full-time mom to her two sons. In her own way, she's feeling as pressured as Diane. "Sometimes I feel so isolated," she says, "just overwhelmed with the two kids and no one to help. Martin's job is so demanding. And my own work . . ." She trails off. We discuss carving out some time for herself, but she can't justify paying for childcare when she's not bringing in any money. She sighs. "I'm just feeling sorry for myself," she says. "I don't know why." We say good-bye and I glance at the clock. The day is more than half over and I've made no progress. Aside from the customary tension I feel about making deadlines, falling behind triggers my anxiety about deciding to have children: How can I even consider getting pregnant when I have this much work to do?

When the phone rings again, I let the machine answer. But it's a childhood friend in Minneapolis, a speech therapist who, like Adrienne, is married with two small sons. She's saying that she was just scolded by her youngest's day-care teacher for forgetting to pack his sippy cup this morning. Ever the poised professional, she had burst into tears. I reach for the phone. "I can't believe that my life revolves around sippy cups," she tells me. "I mean, I love my kids, but between working and taking care of them, I never get fifteen minutes for myself. I'm always in a hurry. I'm always exhausted."

As I hang up again, it hits me: These calls aren't interruptions, they're *illustrations* of the very state of flux that I'm trying to explore. My friends and I are caught in the Crunch: wrestling with how we define and redefine ourselves as "you can be anything" collides with "you can't have it all." In her book *Bird by Bird*, Anne Lamott discusses the mythical radio station KFKD—or K-fucked—which blares in the head of would-be writers. Through one speaker a voice assures the listener that she is brilliant and talented, while the other raps out a hit parade of self-doubt. The author's task is to find a way to turn down KFKD long enough to eke out a few coherent paragraphs. As a writer, I identify with Lamott's conceit (perhaps more strongly than I would wish), but it struck a deeper chord as well. Living as a woman at the beginning of the twenty-first century is in itself a creative act, an exercise in improvisation: The task is to assemble the newly fluid pieces of partnering, childbearing, and ambition to form a satisfying life. But since the options, while expanding, are still inadequate, an insidious ladies-only program has recently become a staple of KFKD, and, as my friends reminded me, it builds to a deafening crescendo during the Crunch. "Now is the time your career will take off," it booms, "but don't forget to find a husband. Hurry, have a child, the clock is ticking—but what do you mean, you're going to become a single mom or need more time at home? Don't lose yourself in your children or you'll never find your way back—but if you work too much, you'll ruin them. If you have a daughter, what will she say about your trade-offs? Remember how you felt about *your* mom? What's wrong with you anyway? Weren't you supposed to be able to do anything?"

The nascent conflicts younger women feel—struggles between autonomy and submersion, between pleasure and pleasing, between ambition and affiliation—do not, as they hope, easily resolve in this next phase. Instead, the pressures intensify as the bait-and-switch nature of women's choices grows more complex. Sometime in her early to mid-thirties, no matter what she does—whether she is single or married, avidly pursues a career or scales back, has children or does not—the contradiction between a woman's vision of equality and the tug of tradition will get her right in the gut, exploding like the space creature from *Alien* (which, fittingly, was the first horror/action film both produced by and starring a woman). As women in my interview groups discussed the gap between their expectations as younger women and their current realities—between what they believed was possible for women generally and what had proven true in their own lives—their tone was often embattled, even betrayed. Yet, they had gotten where they were through a series of steps: decisions about partnering, childbearing, work, and how to strike the best balance between their needs for connection and achievement. The way a woman in the Crunch thinks about those steps, and the way she (along with her partner) negotiates, capitulates, or resists them is crucial to shaping the course of her life.

Will I Still Be Me If I Marry?

"Wait, wait. My English major is about to come in handy." Laura Zagby, a reporter for a Bay Area newspaper, puts a hand to her forehead, racking her brain for a long-forgotten couplet. She's sitting in a café in San Francisco with her friend, Maria Sager, a high-tech consultant. At thirty-five, both Maria and Laura are, somewhat to their surprise, still single—although not for lack of opportunity to wed. Laura ended an eleven-year relationship when she was thirty-one. Since turning thirty, Maria has broken off one engagement and has flirted with another. "In my bad moments I think maybe it's too late for me to learn how to compromise enough to be in a relationship," she says, "and I grieve that, because I do want a life with a partner. But right now I'm the captain of my life: I decide what I'll do and when I want to do it. It's not so easy to let that go."

There are currently a record number of never-married women in their thirties.[1] It's unclear how many of them have actively chosen their status, but, once again, the concept of choice is a slippery one: Maria and Laura may have rejected marriage proposals, but both expected, and still expect, to marry. After all, Laura points out, "I should live another forty years, right? Well, that gives me an awfully long time to find that person to share my life with. And I'm happy to find him at any point."

Maria looks down with a pained expression. Unlike Laura, she feels pressure to partner, and to do it quickly, because she wants to have children. "To me, being part of the human community includes getting married and becoming a mother," she says. "The two are linked in my mind. But it's a quandary: When I've ended a relationship, I've found myself realizing that although being single is a lonelier life, it's a much easier one. I think that's a secret that the culture tries to keep: If you can pay the rent and afford to go out and have fun, single life is pretty easy."

Laura's and Maria's feelings about marriage had grown more complex the longer they remained single. On one hand, the pressure to find a mate—which comes from the culture, from parents, from a longing for intimacy, and a desire to be "normal"—grows more intense and is often enmeshed with a panic over the biological clock. At the same time, women like Laura and Maria expressed a surprised contentment, almost a guilty pleasure in a life that they neither expected nor wanted a few years before. "It's not that I don't suffer all the things a single person suffers," Laura says. "There's loneliness, lack of intimacy, lack of sex. Or just being hugged or touched by someone on a regular basis. I miss that very much. And I suffer on long weekends and on holidays and all those times when it's hard to be single."

"And dating is a nightmare," interrupts Maria.

Laura nods. "But there is also a particular joy in waking up in an empty bed with the whole weekend ahead of you. And certainly being single is a *lot* better than being in an unhappy marriage."

The two women sit in silence a moment, then Laura smiles. "I've got it," she says. "I remember the poem: 'She fit with his requirement/dropped the playthings of her life/ to take on the honorable work/of woman and of wife.' "

"That's exactly it," Maria says. "It's like, if you're not careful in relationships, you can let yourself go."

The Good Wife

In *Parallel Lives*, her book of "high gossip" about Victorian celebrity marriages, Phyllis Rose writes that marriage is a political experience, the primary one in which most of us engage as adults. "Humans invoke love at moments when we want to disguise transactions involving power," she writes. "Perhaps that's what love is—the momentary or prolonged refusal to think of another person in terms of power."[2] Rose focused on the nineteenth century, but for today's women the nature of that power struggle is not so different: They strive to transform marriage so that they can maintain a sense of independent identity, of mastery, of efficacy within it. Barb Wieneke, a thirty-six-year-old marketing director in New York, sums it up: She wanted to marry without turning into a "wife."

Barb is one among a group of women I meet who volunteer at a social service agency in New York (the group also includes a divorce lawyer, two secretaries, and a stay-at-home mom). She's fashionably slender with blue eyes and a highlighted bob, wearing a black dress and matching Hush Puppies. She has been happily married for six years. "I feel so connected to my husband," Barb says, "and we're great pals. But to this day something about the phrase, 'this is my *wife*' "— she wrinkles her nose—"it just doesn't sound like who I think I am."

"It's like it defines you," agrees Michelle, thirty-two, who has also been married six years, albeit less happily than Barb.

Barb nods. "Your whole identity as a person gets swallowed up in it."

Both women and men, according to pioneer family therapy theorist Murray Bowen, must balance a need for individuality in a marriage with the pull toward togetherness.[3] But for women, who are more likely to define themselves through relationships, that's a particularly challenging task. Writer Dalma Heyn found that just as at other key junctures in female development, such as going through puberty, becoming sexually active, or becoming a mother, a woman feels a tremendous internal push to conform to a vision of ideal femininity when she marries: to be compliant, selfless, to mute her desires—her anger, her needs, her erotic feelings—for the sake of others.[4] In Heyn's lexicon, a "wife" tries to gain pleasure by giving it up. A "marriage," on the other hand, ought to be a relationship in which pleasure and responsibility are both mutual and reciprocal. The hitch is that for many women, as we've seen, suppressing desire has become second nature long before they marry.

I ask Michelle why she thinks she married in the first place, and she pauses for a long time. "I thought I loved my husband," she says with the slight accent she brought home from her stint as a graduate student in England. "But in the end, I think I really just wanted to make sure that I was all tucked away. I never really thought about the conflicting messages I have in my head: 'Be married and safe and always be polite and never hurt anyone's feelings.' And on the other hand, 'You can do anything, push as hard as you can. You can achieve anything.' " She sighs. "The one I followed in my relationship was the more docile one, I guess."

By contrast, women who said their marriages were "great," who had avoided the trap of the Good Wife, often said they "feel like myself" with their partners; they described relationships that were a balance between independence and interdependence, that were rich with intimacy and a sense of play. Kat Ungar, thirty-five, a magazine editor in Virginia, was married once in her early twenties—she now half-jokingly calls it her "training marriage"—and has been wed to her current husband for five years. "I wake up every day and I'm grateful and thankful to be with him," she says. "He's supportive of my work. We're really compatible intellectually, and we have fun: We read the same books, have interesting discussions, we love to do the same things, go to movies, travel together. . . ." She stops, seeming flustered. "But that's only part of it," she says. "It's much deeper than that. I think we have the most acceptance that we can in a relationship and still be independent people. To me that's the challenge, to adapt to the other person but hang on to who you are."

Whether they were happily or unhappily wed, women often described the decision to marry as a pragmatic one. It was time, they said, or they felt internal and external pressure to marry, or they couldn't envision building a life alone. Those who had reached their mid-thirties felt an additional urgency: They wanted to have children. A few months after talking with Kat, I met Lindsay Cronk, a thirty-six-year-old marketing consultant in Portland who recently became engaged to her boyfriend of six years after telling him to either marry her or move on. "I started thinking, 'Jesus, I'm getting old,' " she explained, " 'and it's going to take time to find my soul mate if it's not him. I might never have children.' But it was disappointing, because I thought I'd leave a man before I'd give him an ultimatum like that. I mean, I love this man. I'd like to spend my life with him. But it's also *time* for me to pick a lifelong partner, and it's *time* to have a family. He isn't hitting that time crunch. If he wanted to, he could wait another ten years. If it was possible, maybe I would too."

Marriage to one's best friend remains the best predictor of psychological well-being for both sexes as well as one of the greatest sources of pleasure.[5] The hope of attaining that, and the lack of imagined alternatives, may be enough to keep women dreaming of the ideal even as they often convince themselves to accept less. "I want to be a wife in an equal and loving relationship where we treat each other with a lot of respect," says Lindsay. "I'm very attached to that image. I want it to be in an unusual and spectacular marriage. When we struggle I have resentment and disappointment because my expectations are so high. Right now that's the only thing that worries me."

Naturally Lindsay would like to be in a "spectacular" marriage. Who wouldn't? And why shouldn't her standards be high? Certainly it would be lovely if partners intuitively understood each other, if needs were magically met, but that is illusion, generally achieved only at great cost to a woman's psyche. Sociologist Arlie Hochschild has found that while "ideally" women would like an egalitarian marriage, they don't really "want" it: When they have to choose between pushing for equality in their relationships and keeping the peace—that is, acting as the Good Wife—they invariably choose the latter.[6]

Listening to women talk about marriage forced me to reflect back on my own choice. I was crazy about Steven when we got engaged after a year of dating and am grateful that I could separate the decision to partner from the one to parent. Yet, although I wasn't eyeing the biological clock, I was keenly aware of another ominous tick: that of the social clock, which monitors when one "should" marry or have children, and whose relentless advance is regularly announced on special broadcasts of KFKD. I was twenty-nine when we met (he was thirty-eight) and felt the pressure to move on to the legitimacy of marriage. Although it's difficult to admit, in retrospect I believe that would've made it easy for me to have made a bad choice in a mate. I feel lucky that I enjoy my marriage and believe that I'm a more loving person because of it. Yet, like many of the women I talked to, while I've fiercely resisted the idea of being a "wife," I've also noticed how easily I slip into the role, especially when it seems, at least in the short term, to benefit me: Too often, for instance, particularly in the early years of our marriage, I viewed my earnings as mine and Steven's as ours. I wanted to be equal partners, but, somewhat like Abbey Green, I also wanted him to take care of me. I wanted him to respect my work, but I didn't want us to depend on my income. It took a long time, and quite a few arguments, to realize I couldn't have it both ways, to decide, as Steven would put it, "what kind of relationship you want to have."

The fact that my misgivings centered on money is significant: If, as Phyllis Rose wrote, love is the refusal to think of another person in terms of power, it positively balks at recognizing the role of economics in a couple's relationship. Yet, money is not only one of the most common sources of friction in marriage, but, as base as it may sound, it's central to the balance of power. As family therapist Betty Carter puts it: "It's the golden rule: whoever has the gold makes the rules."[7] Like it or not, money is often an equalizer (lesbian couples are the exception to this: Women are less likely to measure their worth by their salaries, so they seem to more successfully maintain domestic equality despite significant earning disparities).[8] Since women, from the time they graduate college, both track themselves and are tracked into lower-paying work; since the fields dominated by women continue to pay less than those dominated by men; since women, in virtually every profession, earn less for the same jobs than their male peers; since, as we've seen, young women are less likely to envision their careers as providing primary support for their families; and since young women still, despite their financial independence, want to retain the option of being supported by their husbands, it's an equalizer that remains both out of reach and sometimes incendiary to broach. Few couples openly discuss the role of money in their relationship and the balance of household power. That's partly because, by the time they marry, those issues have already, tacitly, been decided, based on the woman's choices about education, work, and her mate.[9] Yet, those silent bargains often have unforeseen consequences down the road: They will determine the leverage she has in negotiating chores and childcare with her husband.

Children:
To Have or Have Not

"People ask me all the time, 'When are you going to have children?' " says Teri Van Sels, who directs a small women's counseling center in Virginia. We're talking on the phone one afternoon, after she's re-sponded to a Web query I'd posted looking for women who were con-templating motherhood. Teri reports her age as thirty-one-and-a-*half* years old, as if both staving off and acknowledging the urgency of her situation. She married at twenty-five, far younger than she'd expected to, but recently, she says, she's started to feel oddly behind her peers: "One of my college roommates just had a baby," she explains. "We went through late adolescence and early adulthood together, started graduate school at same time. Now she's sailed into this motherhood thing. So, suddenly I'm thinking, 'Wait, shouldn't I be doing this too?' And I don't know: A child would add a whole different dimension of experience to my life, but I don't know if I really want to have one, or if it's just that I think I'm supposed to. How do you separate what you want from what is expected of you?"

Teri was one of the few women I spoke with who openly considered what she called the "amazing possibility" of not having children—amazing because it still feels taboo. The rise in professional and personal options may have pushed the rate of childlessness among women to nearly twenty percent, the highest since the Great Depression,[10] but rejecting motherhood outright—even toying with the idea—is, for most, still, well, inconceivable. Usually, when I asked if they'd considered childlessness, women were taken aback. Most had never seriously questioned motherhood, although few could articulate why, precisely, it was so important to them: They felt a tangled mix of social expectation and something more elusive. "I guess if you asked me before I had kids, I would've said it was just an urge," says a thirty-five-year-old mother of two in Minneapolis. "It was like an instinct. I wanted to pick out cute little clothes, to put pictures on the fridge and plan birthday parties. I wanted someone to love me in that way. I mean, basically, my husband and I loved each other, so we had children. I don't know if that was just what society tells you or if it was natural. But we never discussed *not* having kids."

Children bring wonder into their lives, women say, a chance to reexperience childhood, a deeper sense of family connection. But there's something else too: Motherhood has become increasingly central to women's conception of femininity, far more so than marriage. According to psychologist Jeanne Safer, few can imagine children as an obstacle to fulfillment rather than its source.[11] Yet, according to a large-scale study of women's life patterns, remaining childless has no long-term impact on a woman's well-being,[12] and another study discovered that childless couples are as happy as parents who have good relationships with their children—and happier than those whose relationships are distant.[13] Despite that, the women I met who were contemplating childlessness described few happy models: They worried that if they weren't mothers, they would be cut out of the mainstream of life, lose touch with parenting friends, and be perennially forced into awkward justification of their choice. "You can feel so out of it," says a psychologist in Chicago who is still debating whether to have kids. "I imagine this is what it must feel like being a gay person. You're leading a lifestyle that's so unconventional, and people are always wondering about you."

Nearly all of the women I spoke with liked children; that wasn't the issue. Their ambivalence pivoted on a lack of conviction that even under the best of circumstances—Teri Van Sels, for instance, has a husband who is willing to be an equal partner and is in a family-friendly workplace—they could navigate motherhood with their essential selves intact. "I worry that I couldn't be selfless enough to be a mother," she says, "not that you have to be totally selfless. But my mother was."

"Not putting down people's choices, but I wouldn't want to have a child unless I was going to spend time with it," says a chemist in San Francisco who is also thinking of forgoing motherhood. Yet, at the same time, she thinks she'd "go bonkers" if she stayed home. Those perspectives troubled me: Were these women truly exercising new options by contemplating childlessness, or were they, as much as the woman who burns herself out trying to "do it all," acquiescing to a cramped definition of motherhood?

Women who wanted or had children described the same internal conflicts as those who did not, but they weighed the trade-offs differently. Often, they believed children would answer basic existential questions of meaning. Recall that during the Promise years women imagined motherhood would provide a kind of pure unconditional love that relationships with men might not. Although they recoiled from the silence of the Good Wife, they embraced the Perfect Mother—the woman for whom childrearing supersedes all other identities and satisfactions, whose needs are either relinquished to or become identical to her child's—but they'd given her a modern spin: In a melding of feminist and feminine ideologies, they believed the best way to assert and nurture the self was through submerging it in a child, ignoring the fact that mothers' and children's needs often conflict.[14] The cost of that contradiction could be enormous. In retrospect, women told me, they believed they'd overidealized motherhood, which set them up for what writer Susan Maushart calls "baby shock."[15] "Before you have a child, you only hear how great it is," says a thirty-four-year-old office manager and mother of two in St. Paul. "Now if a woman said to me, 'What's it like?' I would tell her everything, for sure. 'It's going to be stressful, and it's going to be hard. Sometimes you are going to want to say, "You know what? I don't even want to be here. I don't like my kid. I don't like my husband. I want to go." There will be a lot of changes you don't expect: financially, professionally, and emotionally. And lots of changes in your marriage.' "

Motherhood Versus Marriage: The "Near Peer" Slide

"When we were DINKS—you know, 'Double Income, No Kids'—we went out to dinner all the time," says Carrie Pollack. Carrie is sitting among a group of six women in a living room in Philadelphia. The four others who are mothers nod sympathetically. "We went to the movies, we had a lot of social contact. But once we had our daughter, everything began to focus on her. It brought us closer together, because we're both so invested in our kids, but at the same time, we've kind of lost a little bit of each other along the way." Tears well up in Carrie's eyes and she blinks hard. Earlier, she had said how deeply she loves her husband, how grateful she is to have married him. "It frightens me," she continues, "because I see myself as a good wife, but am I really a good wife? I mean, the kids are totally the top priority, but I don't want to lose what my husband and I have."

From Philadelphia to Minneapolis to San Francisco, the women I spoke with described the same tensions developing in their marriages after children were born: They loved one another as parents but had lost the connection as lovers and partners, particularly if the husband was in a demanding profession. "Kids have changed our relationship for the good and the bad," says Alicia, thirty-seven, in St. Paul. Alicia's husband is a physician while she stays home with their three children. "When we do things together as a family, that's the best. But our relationship seems to be getting lost in the crunch. I think it's his job that puts the strain on our marriage. There are not enough hours in the day, so that's what gives. We rarely go to bed at the same time anymore. Our connection is over laundry at ten o'clock."

"Well, I think it has a lot to do with sex," says Gena Scapelli, thirty-eight, in San Francisco. Gena, a part-time technical writer with two sons, sits on a couch in her living room, chatting with a group of women who initially met in a childbirth class. "Because you lose some sex drive when you have kids," she continues, "especially when they're young."

Faye Winfield, thirty-two, agrees. "I'm frightened that we don't have the desire," she says. "We have sex about once every two months. Does that mean we don't love each other anymore?" A stay-at-home mother with one son, Faye is a sensual-looking woman with long, hennaed hair, scarlet lips, and a flowing Gypsy skirt. "I don't want to be a divorce statistic," she continues. "I'm frightened that not having sex is a sign that there is something really wrong, and it's going to keep going wrong."

All these women are experiencing firsthand what studies bear out: When the first child is born, marital satisfaction plummets and continues to dip with the birth of each baby, rising back up as children grow older and leave home.[16] Lack of time, lack of sex, lack of intimacy, money worries, and conflicts over childrearing all contribute to a fraying connection between partners, a diminished sense of joy. In that litany, however, one underlying cause is often overlooked: the failure, as journalist Joan Peters puts it, to "modernize motherhood" in a radically changed world.[17] The moment a child is born, most couples still tumble into traditional roles despite their intention not to, and, when they do, their lives begin to diverge.[18] Whether or not a woman works, she makes concessions to parenthood in a way that men, for the most part, still do not: Words like "balance," "trade-off," and "work-family conflict," had, by the century's end, become as feminine as pink tulle. That makes sense when one recalls the conflicted expectations of the younger women. They were quick to testify that financial independence was the key to personal freedom and egalitarian relationships. Yet, despite a surface desire for equality, they were preparing for something else.

Lindsay Cronk, for instance, the newly engaged marketing consultant in Portland who said she dreams of a "spectacular marriage of equals," veers away from that ideal within seconds when I ask her about parenting. "I want it to be equal," she begins, "but I accept that

I'll do more than he will. I would want to be able to say 'I have to go on a business trip' and have him be comfortable taking care of the child. Or go running for a couple of hours and have him be comfortable with that. But if he were making enough money, I'd be willing to take on more of that domestic stuff."

What Lindsay envisions (and what most of the other mothers I spoke with *live*) is what sociologist Pepper Schwartz calls a "Near-Peer" relationship, and it describes the majority of couples in America once they have children.[19] Near Peers like the idea of equality, Schwartz says, but for a combination of economic and psychological reasons— the mother's pull toward the child, the presumption that she is the "better" parent, or that only women can "choose" to stay home—they have not been able to attain it. A Near-Peer mother may expect to contribute to the family income, but her career is secondary. Both members of the couple consider the husband the primary breadwinner and tacitly value his job more: They protect his time and income at the expense of her professional advancement, of his connection to their children, and, ultimately, of a collaborative, intimate relationship with one another. The resentment women eventually feel over taking on too much of the childcare and housework—even if they chose it, even if they're not gainfully employed—has been well documented.[20] Meanwhile, what Schwartz calls "the provider complex" has repercussions for men, too, by cutting them out of the family's daily workings and emotional heart.[21] Family therapist Betty Carter attributes the current high divorce rate to the traditional backslide, and psychologists Philip Cowan and Carolyn Pape Cowan found that the more conventional a couple's division of labor, the less satisfied they are with themselves, their relationship, and their roles as parents.[22] Since most couples fit the Near-Peer description, those are uncomfortable truths.

"I remember that my sister told me how threatened her marriage was by having kids," says Gena in the San Francisco mothers' group. "And I thought, 'Oh, that will never happen to us. But it did. It wasn't *just* having kids. It has to do with how hard Victor works now. And sometimes I resent that, because he comes home late and he's tired. But I work two days a week too, *and* I've been with the kids for hours and I need a break. . . ." She shakes her head, frustrated. "But then, I feel so lucky because I have this bond with the kids that is so powerful that he can't even imagine. He loves the children and is very close to them. But it's just a totally different thing. I think he has just shut off a lot of the feelings that to me are so powerful and profound." Gena pauses, considering what she's said. "But, on the other hand," she adds, "he is really involved compared to his own father."

The trajectory of Gena's comments was typical: from a growing sense of distance between her and her husband, to her irritation with his lack of participation in the nitty-gritty work of childcare, to taking refuge in the unique bond she shares with her children, and, ulti-mately, letting him off the hook because he's a better parent than his own father was. That final twist reminded me of something that soci-ologist Arlie Hochschild once said: that comparing men to their fathers sets the bar too low—we ought to be comparing them with women.[23] When I mention that to Gena and her friends, their reaction hovers somewhere between dismissive and defensive. "Well," says one, "you can't really expect *that*." Later in the evening I try putting it another way: It seems to me that women, whatever their arrangements, feel like lesser mothers than those of the previous generation. Mean-while men, even with minimal participation at home, feel like better fathers. "That's true," Gena acknowledges. "Because most of the men we know *are* better fathers. But I don't know any woman who doesn't struggle."

I'm the Mother, Dammit

Gena had mentioned the singular "powerful bond" she shares with her children. For many women, that intimacy is the essence of motherhood—it's not just a reflection of what they do as a parent but of who they are as a person. The old TV show got it wrong: Deep down, most women feel that it's *mother* who knows best. She is the one who holds the secret to everything from tending to a sick child to doing laundry without turning the white socks pink. The truth is, there is a power in that "powerful bond," and women can feel conflicted about giving it up, about ceding control to their husbands even when the weight of "doing it all" overwhelms them. Inevitably, as I peeled away the layers during interviews, women would admit that the battles they had with their husbands over household divisions of labor weren't entirely the men's fault. "It's like I'm caught in this whole dynamic," admits a thirty-one-year-old filmmaker who was part of the San Francisco mothers' group. "I want to put the baby to bed, and yet I want him to do it. I want to be in charge of the bills, but I want him to do it. It's like I want power over all these things. And I try to give them up, I do. But it's hard for me. I guess I feel like I want to have control over everything."

In *When Mothers Work*, journalist Joan Peters found that even when women work full-time, perhaps *especially* when they work full-time, they cling to maternal control. Micromanaging their children's lives—retaining a sense of authority over packing lunches, choosing clothes, and coordinating activity schedules—is what makes them feel that they are Good Mothers. For working mothers, who can feel like they have to prove their devotion to an invisible chorus of critics, that can seem particularly important.[24] Holding tight to the small stuff can also make a woman feel, more generally, in control. Psychologist Terri Apter found that women convince themselves that if they could only be more organized, if they only had more energy, life in the Crunch would be easier. Although they were aware of external constraints and resented them, they sought answers from within, believing they could triumph through force of will. Under the sway of that illusion, they avoid considering the cost of mother management to their own well-being.[25]

"Oh, that control thing," says Jill Roedel, thirty-five, rolling her eyes. "It's something I definitely have to work on." Jill is a vice president at an insurance company, who has gathered a group of four friends for me to interview in her suburban Minneapolis home. She has short brown hair and green eyes and is dressed in sweatpants and a T-shirt. Her husband has taken their three daughters to gymnastics lessons, but she had commandeered them all into a major house-cleaning before they left, in preparation for my visit.

There was a time, Jill says, when her oldest was about nine months old, that her husband took on more authority at home. It was a kind of accidental equality, driven by necessity. Jill had just taken a new job, one that required out-of-town trips. "Suddenly I was gone for two days at a time. He *had* to do the diapers, he *had* to make the formula, he *had* to give the bath. So it gave him the freedom to figure out how to do things on his own without my looking over his shoulder."

Her husband has stayed more involved than Jill expected, but once she stopped traveling, she slowly reasserted authority. "I'm not a very good delegator," she admits. "But the truth is, it would still be scary for me to give those things up. I'd be scared he wouldn't do things right because—" She breaks off, searching for an example. "Okay," she continues, "one day he dropped our oldest daughter off at a Brownie event where I thought lunch would be provided. It wasn't. Luckily, the troop leader worked something out for her, but I cried that night. I kept thinking, 'What a failure I am as a mother to not even think of what my daughter is going to eat for lunch.' " Jill looks at me, to make sure I understand what she's saying. "I didn't think 'He's a bad father,' " she emphasizes. "I didn't blame him. I feel like if my house is messy or my kids don't have clean clothes, people are going to judge *me*."

The phrase "Bad Mother" affects women like kryptonite. It's one of the most effective checks against women pushing for fuller lives. The Bad Mother risks damaging her children through independent needs and outside interests, such as a profession. She is the evil twin of the Perfect Mother who lives solely for her children, whose needs are completely in sync with theirs. For me, the most poignant illustration of the Perfect-Mother bind was among the mothers of girls: Not only did they feel vulnerable to self-recrimination, scrutiny by other mothers, and societal reproach, they fretted over how their daughters would someday judge their choices. In this Perfect-Mother permutation, women had to be nurturing, ever available, and all empathic, while at the same time being the opposite: credible models of autonomy and professional accomplishment. Understandably they projected their own anxieties onto their daughters. I wondered, since the mothers of sons seemed to worry less about modeling female independence, whether the more conventional expectations of boys were being perpetuated as well. "The fact that I'll have a daughter makes me want to concentrate on my career again," says Eleanor Hwang in Philadelphia, who is seven months pregnant. Eleanor has stayed home with her son, but she's unsure of whether that's the right course with a girl. "My husband is my son's role model," she explains, "but I'll be hers and I want to set a good example. I don't want her to consider me old-fashioned or dependent. I'm so scared she'll be the opposite of what I want her to be. But then, I'm really ambivalent about what she *should* be."

You're *What?*
Work and the Good Mother

If working mothers feel compelled by the culture to prove their devotion to their children, they feel equally pressured at the workplace to do just the opposite. When a woman becomes pregnant, the onus is on her to prove that motherhood changes nothing—that it won't compromise her productivity or split her loyalty, although, for both men and women, it both does and should. Women describe being found guilty of motherhood until proven innocent, and the scrutiny starts as soon as they "come out" as pregnant.

One afternoon I join Emily Sorenson, thirty-six, an associate partner at an international business consulting firm, and two of her friends in Emily's suburban Chicago home. "Most people assume you're going to have a child," Emily says, "but when you actually *do,* they move your classification from 'career-minded' to 'not career-minded' and your first year back they pay a lot of attention to your work habits. I was fortunate that my husband had real predictable hours and wasn't traveling much, so I could work as hard as I needed to, and that gave me credibility. So, they've given me the opportunity to prove it, but I did have to prove it. And you feel that consciously."

Emily is a petite woman with regulation corporate-length brown hair, sparkling brown eyes, and a devilish smile. The fact that she has *three* children, she says, made her even more suspect. "When I announced that I was pregnant the third time, everyone looked at me like, 'You've already had your quota,' " she recalls. "My boss actually said to me, 'How many kids do you have now?' I said, 'Three, how many do you have?' He has four. He shut up."

"Does his wife work?" asks one of her friends, a sales rep for a pharmaceutical company who has two children.

"Absolutely not," Emily shoots back, and all three women laugh.

The trouble is that the senior men who set the tone of most corporate cultures still, disproportionately, have stay-at-home wives. Even the best among them, women say, don't truly understand the demands of parenthood; at worst they harbor the belief that women ought to be at home. More disheartening, though, were the conflicts women reported having with female employers: with childless women who believed, sometimes more strongly than men, that women with children are uncommitted to their work—sometimes even with other mothers who'd made different choices. Over coffee in a colleague's kitchen in St. Paul, Kristen Dornfeld, thirty-four, tells me she quit a sales job she'd loved over the terms of her maternity leave. "My boss, who was female, asked me to come back after four weeks," she says bitterly. "And she had two children!"

"Oh, gosh," says Vicki, an office manager at the company where Kris now works. "Get real."

"And I did it," Kristen says, indignant. "A week later I asked her for a month's leave of absence, and she denied me three times. The last time was my resignation."

"And she was a mom?" Vicki says.

Kristen nods. "And she was a mom."

Given the pressure they feel to "prove themselves" or recede from the workforce, the pressures of the Near-Peer relationships at home, the double whammy of the Good and Bad Mother, and the prevailing sense (particularly in elite fields) that they still have to put on a false, masculinized self before going in to work each day, it's no surprise that women show a steep drop in job satisfaction beginning at age thirty.[26] After all, the conflicts were already brewing. In her 1998 study of female lawyers, legal scholar Nancer Ballard found that even so-called "family-friendly" firms assumed that successful lawyers either had no family obligations or had spouses who freed them to devote most of their time to work.[27] Perhaps during the Promise years, women can accept those terms, but as they enter the Crunch, the contradictions grow ever more painful. "The trouble is, women in law often have husbands with equally demanding jobs," says an environmental lawyer and mother of two in Oakland, California, who is struggling to put in the hours to make partner. "So, it's really hard. Some take the mommy-track route until they're ready to come back full-time and try for partner. But what does that mean? That two years after a child is born you go to work sixty hours a week again? Do you go back full-time after four years? When they're six and three? At what age is it okay for both parents to work sixty hours a week?"

I ask her why it's so important to her to make partner when the price is so high, but even as the question comes out of my mouth I realize it holds an implicit accusation. Would I ever ask a working father why he wants or needs to make partner? But she doesn't seem to notice. "I want to be in charge of my own destiny in my practice," she responds. "I want to be involved in decision-making in my firm. When you've been working in a field for nearly fifteen years, it's not appropriate to be labeled a senior assistant anymore."

If the workplace was questioning the depth of mothers' commitment to their jobs, Ballard found that motherhood often inspired women to question the way that commitment was measured. Unfortunately any choice they make is booby-trapped: Submitting to the firm's vision of success forces them either to give up family life or play superwoman. But by quitting, they reinforce what employers suspected all along: that women are high-risk hires, that the glass ceiling is about individual "choices" rather than gaping structural flaws.

Who Am I If I Stay Home?

"I just assumed that of *course* I would work after my first child was born," says Lonnie Holub, thirty-eight, who is sharing a pizza with a group of mothers in a South Dakota college town. Lonnie is a full-bodied woman with thick, dark hair and a throaty laugh. As we talk, she nurses her daughter, who is six months old. Three years ago, when her son was born, she was a social worker who traveled regularly through the state. "Then, one night, I got stranded in Sioux City, and my breasts were full and I didn't have a pump with me. So I drove home in this snowstorm and almost went into a ditch. My husband said, 'Can't you just quit?' And, you know, it hadn't even occurred to me. I just had this fear that I had to work."

What were you afraid of? I ask. "That if I didn't work I'd have no identity," she says, waving her free hand. "That I would be lost, that I wouldn't have any status anymore. And, you know, that whole thing that the little woman who stays home is just a bore. I had all of those fears. And that night, they all lifted. The next day I quit, and I've never looked back."

Fifty-five percent of women go back to work within a year after the birth of a child.[28] Still, in the 1990s, for the first time in decades, there was a slowdown in labor-force participation among women of childbearing age.[29] Among the mothers I met, a series of interconnected pressures and pleasures—part push, part pull—had influenced their decisions to leave the workforce. A number of them, like Lonnie, had fully expected to return to their jobs, but something—external circumstances, or a more visceral tug toward their baby than they had expected—intervened. Sometimes they found they liked the role of mother-manager, or they could not find adequate childcare, or they believed that their spouses were either unable or unwilling to be an equal parent. Almost universally they were married to men who worked long hours, earning far more money than they ever could. That allowed them the luxury of "choosing" to quit their jobs, but it also created a situation in which they felt they had to: The demands of their husbands' jobs, which they felt were inviolable, left them solely responsible for childcare and household management. Layering those tasks over full-time work quickly became overwhelming.

Some women also realized that work was not the primrose path to personal liberation they expected it to be. They discovered they were not as ambitious as they had once thought, or their careers had not rolled out as planned. Maybe the demands of their profession were too intense, or the atmosphere too dehumanizing. Often, their vision of success clashed with their employers'. Maybe they couldn't, or wouldn't, demand more power, more money, more respect, or more personal satisfaction from their jobs (men, incidentally, often reach similar plateaus, but they have little choice but to soldier on through). The socially acceptable option of staying home with children allowed both a legitimate out and also a time for reevaluation.

In San Francisco the women in the mothers' group I interviewed all consider themselves stay-at-home moms, although several work ten to fifteen hours a week. To them, staying home is, in part a rebellion against the ascent of the marketplace as the greatest good. "I became sort of outraged at society for promoting this idea of women going back to work when, at least for me, it seemed like a crime against nature," says Alanna, thirty-nine, shaking her head in disgust. Alanna was a full-time therapist before giving birth to her son three years ago. Now, although she has a bare-bones practice again, her priority is being at home. "There are parts of society that I try not to have much to do with, that are commercialized and crass and seem disrespectful of what we are trying to do for our kids. They're like, 'Why aren't you out there contributing more?' I am keeping my child healthy and continuing to do the work to make him feel secure, and wanted, and loved. That's a major contribution, I think."

"I remember reading in a women's studies class about this whole fifties paradigm of how couples became Mrs. Inside, Mr. Outside," says Faye, who was a teacher before her son was born. "It was supposed to be very uncool. Now I am Mrs. Inside, and my husband is Mr. Outside. But there is a way that we are valuing the Mrs. Inside even if it's just in my little inner circle of friends and in my relationship. Mrs. Inside is worth more than people think."

Philosophers from John Ruskin to social historian Christopher Lasch have made similar arguments. They see the family as a refuge, the last defense against encroaching consumerism. Lasch believed the American Dream has been cheapened, reduced to a standard of living, and that feminism is partly to blame: Women's liberation has been co-opted by narcissism, by the culture's blind worship of individualism and indifference to the needs of children.[30] The problem is, that view subjects women, and women only, to an all-too-familiar higher standard of morality, encouraging us to believe that "self-interest" is the same as "selfish." By making Good Mother martyrdom the noblest course, it also minimizes men's ability to foster fruitful connection in the home.

Regardless of why women stayed home—whether the choice was morally based or practical or simply felt inevitable—without outside work they worried about how to maintain a sense of individual identity and wrestled with feelings of cultural invisibility. "A lot of my peers say, 'Oh, isn't it nice that you're staying home and parenting,' " says Faye. "But it's like kind of a hollow 'isn't it nice,' because then they always say, 'Well, what are your plans after *that*?' And I have to say, 'Okay, well, then I am going to do this. And it's going to be great. And I'm going to make a lot of money. It's going to be really good.' Even though I'm not sure really what's going to happen. Or when."

Gena, who is sitting across the room from Faye, nods thoughtfully. "I had this epiphany the other day," she says. "Both kids were in bed with me, and I was looking at them. It had been one of those days where I was just beating myself up because I don't produce anything tangible, and I can't even keep a house clean. The kitchen was a mess. I had finished only one load of wash, and I didn't even put it away. So, I was lying in bed and looking at these two little boys, and my epiphany was 'This isn't such a bad product to produce. This is pretty great. I have these cute little babies, and they are healthy.' But sometimes it's hard to sustain that feeling."

Stay-at-home mothers do have a distinct advantage over those who work: They can grab the Perfect Mother high ground. Although there's no evidence that other care harms children, the prevailing belief is that mother care is best. Nearly half of Americans still believe that the ideal family consists of a homemaker mom and a breadwinner dad.[31] Yet, that begs the question: What happens if a stay-at-home mother's efforts *don't* result in "better" children? If their choice can be legitimized only by their children's happiness and success, stay-at-home mothers risk seeing their children as an extension of themselves, exerting too much control over them and allowing their own identities to become bound up in those of their sons and daughters. "That's one of my big fears," admits Gena. "My mother stayed home with the kids and she just never seemed to have found herself. She hasn't to this day. And she haunts me. I don't want to be overly dependent on my children."

Meanwhile, the stay-at-home mothers I met do raise disturbing questions about our culture's definitions of personal success, about the lure of materialism, and about the lost value of home and regeneration in contemporary life. Is accruing the most stuff really the ultimate measure of success? Can upward mobility confer meaning? Too often, rather than becoming the centerpiece of a larger, gender-neutral discussion, those questions fall into the cracks of women's "choices" and get lost in the defensiveness and anger of the Mommy Wars, or the skewed debate over so-called "family values." The truth is, caring for children, despite the lip service paid to it, continues to be one of the country's lowest priorities. Righting that balance may involve acknowledging the labor of stay-at-home moms, but it goes well beyond that. It includes a reevaluation of the pay scale of childcare providers and teachers, of the structure of corporations, of the faux family-friendly policies of government. It demands that men become primary in their children's lives. It challenges women to develop a new vision of satisfaction, one that goes beyond either career or family as the central source of identity. It requires a more expansive definition of motherhood that does not continually pit a woman's well-being against her child's needs. Those are points, perhaps, upon which both women who work and those who stay home can agree.

BALANCING THE NEEDS and demands of motherhood in a half-changed world is notoriously complicated, whether a woman works full-time, part-time, or stays home. Perhaps it's not surprising, then, that over time women talk less and less to those who've made choices different from their own—to their mutual loss. In the following four chapters I look more deeply at questions of motherhood and marriage as they typically unfold in women's thirties. Setting out to understand why women mother, as well as why they don't, I spoke with those who were ambivalent about childbearing and ended up taking a new look at myself. I also spent time with Dana Rosen, whose maternal impulse was so strong that she conceived her daughter via donor sperm, giving up the dream of bearing a child with a partner and becoming a mother on historically unprecedented terms. Carrie Pollack, a lawyer specializing in child abuse cases, assumed she would have an egalitarian marriage, but to her surprise found that once she had a child, she and her husband preferred traditional roles. Emily Sorenson imagined the opposite: She thought she might become a stay-at-home mother but came to believe her career benefited her self-esteem, her children, and her marriage.

Chapter 6

Pinning the Butterfly

THERE WERE TIMES WHILE reporting this book when I felt like a taxonomist searching for a perfect specimen. I was searching for someone with whom to explore the impulse to mother, the conflicts it gives rise to, the nature of the very new idea that women have a choice about bearing children. But after conducting dozens of interviews with women who were wrestling over whether or not to have children, my net was still empty. Ambivalence, particularly over motherhood, is a fluid thing, uncomfortable to live with both personally and culturally. It's a state that changes, that incites change, that often feels too raw to discuss.

Some of the women I met during my two-year search had never spoken of their doubts about mothering to anyone—it made them feel that aberrant, that guilt-stricken. Three times I thought I'd found the right woman. A therapist in Atlanta backed out as I was planning a trip to visit her, explaining that the issue was just too hot: She and her husband had hardly been able to discuss it between themselves. A video editor in Chicago canceled for a different reason: She came home one day to find her husband of twelve years had moved out, filed for divorce, and cleaned out their joint bank account. Just like that. "I guess I don't qualify for your study anymore," she said sadly. A third woman, in Omaha, became pregnant. As I discovered, one way to counter ambivalence is to make a nondecision: to play fast and loose with birth control and just see what happens (or, alternatively, to keep delaying until it's too late).

Then, through a posting I'd put on the Internet, I found Belinda Gee, thirty-one, a Ph.D. candidate in Comparative Literature at the University of California. Belinda lived just a few miles from my office, so we agreed to meet on a Wednesday morning for coffee, a time, as it turned out, when the café scene is all about moms and babies. A small boy in a stroller, chugging on a bottle, eyed us as we walked in. Belinda's gaze drifted over to an adorable golden-haired girl who played happily with an old Pac-Man machine against one wall. "You see a little girl like that and you think that you'd like to have a kid," she observed. "Not so much to pass along genes. It's the desire to have a role in creating a good, productive person."

Belinda, a Chinese American woman with a round face bisected by small rectangular glasses, was dressed entirely in black—black platform shoes, black bell bottoms, black shirt, black jacket—and wore a shade of lipstick I think I've seen at the Mac counter. Her long black hair was wrapped into a knot at the nape of her neck. The effect was a bit severe, but her smile was shy and friendly. She was about to begin her second year of applying for academic jobs. It's a competitive market, she explained as we sat down with our tea, even tighter if she wanted to get tenure; the degree is just the first hurdle. At the same time, she was beginning to feel pressure from her in-laws, her friends who already had children, even from her husband, to get pregnant. "I always assumed that I'd be a 'career first' kind of woman," Belinda said. "But, as time goes by, I have a new reaction to seeing children. Maybe it's the biological-clock thing. On most days I still think, 'Oh, my God, do I want *more* work? Do I want to be *more* frazzled and burdened? Is my husband going to put in his share? Am I just being domesticated? What about my career?' I mean, there are so many reasons *not* to have kids. But then, it's a lopsided debate." She extended one hand, palm up, weighing. "The emotional side, and social pressure are so strong"—she said, then extended her other hand—"even though there are so many intellectual reasons not to do it." She looked back and forth between them and shrugged. "It's kind of a tossup."

Belinda's confusion was typical of women who were contemplating motherhood: They'd reached pivotal junctures in their careers—they were completing long years of training, stepping onto partnership tracks, being offered more powerful, more lucrative positions—but so were their husbands. They didn't see how pursuing those options would jibe with the demands of parenthood. Or, more to the point, they did see: The responsibility for accommodating would probably fall largely on them, and when it did, they worried about who they would become. "I'm afraid that we would fall into the traditional mom and dad roles, which is what I never wanted to happen," Belinda said. "As it is, I have complaints about my husband not doing a lot of household work, so I wonder, is this going to be a partnership, or am I going to be basically a single mom with a husband?"

In subtle ways, Belinda admitted, she was already preparing for that inevitability. Over the past few years her husband, who works in Silicon Valley, had moved into jobs where he could make more money and command more respect even though it's meant more stress and longer hours. Belinda, meanwhile, had made a different set of decisions. Passionate about labor rights, she'd earned a law degree, then opted against practicing, in part because, if she ever did have children, she felt the hours required of lawyers would be untenable. She'd also dreamed of a life in politics, but that, too, seemed incompatible with having a family, too intrusive on privacy. Teaching, if she could get a job, would pay less than law, but, she reasoned, it would be more flexible and she could still make an impact; yet, even in academia she'd seen women's careers suffer after motherhood, especially if they went part-time. "I can understand why so many women decide not to have children," she said. "If you have to get looks from your colleagues, or snide remarks, or people just don't take you seriously, and the opposite of that is to be childless and be able to do as many or more things than your male colleagues, and career is important to you, why would women choose to have kids?"

It's been difficult to sort it all out, and lately, perhaps in response to that complexity, Belinda has noticed her professional goals are growing vague. "All the ways in which I was ambitious in my twenties—political projects, activism—all the ways I wanted to make a difference seem to have muted down," she said. "It's not because I believe any less in the principles, but it's a matter of priorities. At the spur of the moment I'm making decisions to take care of the home first, to take care of the husband. I'm sure that will intensify if I have a child. The great struggle for immigrants' rights will just have to wait until next weekend or something." She peered earnestly over the rims of her glasses. "I would like to believe I'm committed to those ideals, but I see myself making these choices. So . . ." She let the sentence hang, stared into her cup of Earl Grey.

I told Belinda I'd like to talk with her again and interview her husband as well. She agreed, but her schedule was hectic, and I was about to leave town, so it was over a month before we connected by phone. When we did, Belinda had news. "We sort of got pregnant by default," she said a little sheepishly. "We agreed to not be real careful, but the trouble is, now we haven't had all those discussions we should have had before we got pregnant, the kind of stuff you and I talked about: What are our lives going to look like with a child, how much time I'll devote to career. I sort of freaked out about it at first, but I'm happy."

I congratulated Belinda and hung up. I wondered whether she and her husband would ever have those talks, or whether they'd also "default" into the traditional roles she'd feared. I wondered about the impact of that on their relationship—and on their child. Still, my overriding emotion was frustration. Belinda was no longer balanced on the precise fulcrum I wanted to examine. I was back to square one—for the fifth time. Then, quite suddenly, I realized what the real problem was: I was looking for someone to substitute for myself in these pages, to represent my own conflicted feelings about children and motherhood. I was trying to hide behind the stories of Belinda Gee, the woman in Omaha, the therapist in Atlanta, the video editor in Chicago.

The butterfly I was really trying to pin down was me.

Into the Chasm

A couple of years before I met Belinda Gee, on a trip to visit my parents in Minneapolis, a woman sitting next to me on the plane struck up a conversation. We chatted for a few minutes, then, inevitably, she asked, "Do you have kids?"

As any childless woman in her mid-thirties knows, that's a deceptively simple question. I took stock. I could say No, but I have ten nieces and nephews, which would "prove" I loved children and thus was acceptably feminine. I could say No, not yet, indicating my every intention to join the fold of normalcy. Or I could do what I did, and just say no.

Just no. Simple as that. Of course, I knew what would happen. The woman drew back just a fraction, looking uncomfortable. I could read her thoughts as clearly as if she had a cartoon bubble over her head: "Is she infertile? Selfish? A child-hater? Is she a lesbian?"

I couldn't take it. I let her off the hook.

"I do have ten nieces and nephews though," I said sweetly, and she smiled in return. We reached into our purses to pull out photos.

What if I'd told that woman the truth? That I love children, but there is a chasm between the abstract idea of having kids and the three-dimensional reality of what it means to mother. I was in the summer of my thirty-fourth year by then, and the ambivalence that had in part inspired me to write this book had only grown sharper. I knew that if I didn't make a decision soon, biology would make one for me. It wasn't that I felt any internal alarms going off; my life actually felt pretty complete. I loved having time, time to make last-minute plans with a friend—to *see* a friend—to go away for the week-end, or just to dash out to the grocery store without worrying about childcare. I relished lazing about on weekends, reading the paper or puttering in the garden. I fretted over what parenthood would do to my marriage. Steven and I were best pals, and, more than that, we were partners: He read the first drafts of my articles, I watched the rough cuts of his documentary films. We'd even talked about collaborating on a project. If we became parents, who'd mind the baby? A few weeks earlier we'd gone off to Hawaii and snorkeled over a reef holding hands. I'd tried to imagine future vacations—if we could afford them once we had kids—where one of us would stay with the children on the beach while the other swam out to sea. Sometimes that seemed a sweet tableau: I felt my heart swell at the notion of Steven as a father, of watching him with *our child*. Other times it felt like a loss. Maybe I was too selfish to be a mother. Or maybe I just ap-preciated what I had.

Then there was the potential cost of motherhood to the work I loved: Across the board, parenting stunts women's earning power and advancement. In journalism, a 1996 survey of Washington correspon-dents found that nearly half had never married and two thirds didn't have children. What's more, even given those sacrifices, they *still* got paid over a third less for the same work. And those who did have chil-dren were twice as likely as men to feel that parenthood significantly hurt their careers.[1] Joyce Purnick, the Metro editor of *The New York Times*, provoked a furor among her colleagues when in a 1998 com-mencement address at Barnard College she said she couldn't have reached her position had she been a mother. Parenthood and power, she implied, were mutually exclusive for women.[2] Purnick was later forced to backpedal, but given the numbers, I'm not sure she was wrong.

Institutions throw up barriers to success, but, as we've seen, women themselves also hedge, preparing to accommodate motherhood long before they actually face its challenges. In my interviews I'd begun to notice the phrase "do it right" cropping up, as in "if I'm going to be a mother, I want to 'do it right.' " That meant, as Mandy Warner, thirty-three, a business consultant in San Jose, California, said, "getting over the whole overachiever thing so I'll be able to stay home and focus on my kid." Mandy saw her "achieving" impulse as bad, as "over," inappropriate, certainly incompatible with the sacrifice required of the Good Mother. But how could she reconcile that with ambition, with the mantra she'd heard all her life that she could be "anything she wanted to be." Was that true only until a woman became a mother? As with Belinda Gee, it was Mandy's husband who wanted a child most—she'd put him off for four years. Yet, although she was sure he would be a "great father, far more involved than his own father was," neither of them expected him to make the adjustments for parenthood that she would. Good Fathers don't have to give up their dreams in our half-changed landscape. "We brainstormed about him staying home," she said. "He was real honest. He said, 'I'm a modern guy, Mandy, but I don't know if I'm prepared to go that far. My ego couldn't take it.' " Like most women, however, her ego had been trained to submit to the needs of others.

Listening to Mandy, I realized that I was also mulling over a choice without questioning its terms. I'd developed my own image of the Good Mother, who "did it right," and she looked a lot like my own mom—someone who was satisfied as a mother and wife, who was happy supporting others, making her mark through the accomplishments of those she nurtured. It's a sacrifice that she's insisted was no sacrifice. I knew I couldn't be that kind of mother, yet, like the women I interviewed, I felt like hers was the "right" way to do it. I feared devolving into a conflicted, discontented version of her, becoming a person who lost her essential self in motherhood while trying in vain to "do it right." Perhaps because of that, I minimized the rewards of caretaking, nurturing, even cleaning and cooking, seeing them only as burdens that subtracted from my identity, siphoned off from the independent life I'd worked so hard to create. I realized that like some of the more ambitious young women I'd interviewed, I'd seen the feminine as weak, and thought it was feminist to do so. In that sense, though, I was capitulating to the Good Mother rather than trying to reinvent her in a new, more balanced way. Was it possible to be a mother without being a Mother? In an interview, Gloria Steinem, who is childless, once said, "I'm not sure I would have been strong enough to have children, to live that life, and come out the other end with an identity of my own. The way I came to think of it was that I could not give birth to both myself and someone else. It was a choice."[3] I understood her point.

And yet there were moments when I could almost feel the weight of a child in my arms, when I felt that if I looked over my shoulder while driving, I would see an infant seat with a curly-haired little girl (or sometimes a little boy) looking back at me. I would imagine the songs we'd sing together, the games we'd play, the books we'd read. It was as if there were this shadow self hovering over me—me as a mother—that I couldn't quite shake. I would ask Steven what he thought of various baby names, and he would shake his head. "Peg, we don't *have* a baby."

When he tried to engage me in a more serious discussion, though, I would put him off. "Let's talk about it next month," I'd say, or "Wait until we go on vacation and have time to really focus." I didn't want the pressure, and, although he leaned a little more toward wanting children than I did, he was willing to take the out my confusion offered. After all, he reasoned, we were happy, in love, engaged in our work. "I don't feel a deep need to create another me or another you," he told me on one occasion. "Or even to continue some legacy, although I was raised to feel that way, since I'm the only son of an only son."

So, I asked, what should we do? "Well, when you're married

and really love someone, having children is a way to take your relationship deeper, to learn things about yourself and your partner that you can't learn otherwise," he said. "But I don't want to do it unless we both want to. I don't want you ever to say 'You talked me into this.' It has to come fully from you. And if you don't want to do it, I'll be fine. I won't have that many regrets."

The truth was, I *did* want him to talk me into something, although I wasn't sure what; it would've been the path of least resistance, a way to evade responsibility. One evening I marched into the living room, where Steven was stretched out on the couch, watching TV. He's a tall, stocky Japanese American man with a shock of tousled black hair, high cheekbones, and warm, dark eyes. As usual, he was dressed in a dark button-down shirt and black jeans. "I have an announcement," I said. "I want to have children."

He looked at me dubiously. "Okay," he responded. "Are you sure that's what you want?"

The next day I came to him again. "I've changed my mind," I said. "Let's not."

He rolled his eyes. "So, is *that* what we're doing?" I looked at him helplessly. How could I actively choose not to be a mother when it was still a possibility?

In her book *Reconceiving Women*, psychologist Mardy Ireland notes that motherhood is so inextricably woven into our concept of feminine identity that there's no term for a childless woman that doesn't imply absence. Even the politically correct "childfree" defines women in relationship to mothering rather than as individuals making a choice. The task for women who don't have children—whom she breaks into three groups—is to de-link the two. For instance, "traditional women," who wanted children but were unable to have them, must discover alternative sources of creative expression in order to live a satisfying life, or redirect their maternal energy by becoming devoted aunts, foster parents, or volunteers.[4] At the other end of the spectrum, Ireland calls women who make an active decision to pursue a creative destiny without motherhood "transformative women": While some may see them as suspect, even masculine, Ireland argues they may merely be reclaiming an unrecognized, or denied, aspect of femininity.[5]

Then there is me, smack dab in the category she calls the "transitional women": the woman who wrestles with society's expectations and her own, who delays childbearing, believing it will be possible "someday," who drifts, "getting older and older, never at the helm of her own life."[6] If she remains childless, the "transitional woman" has to acknowledge the loss of the possible selves she might have developed in motherhood—the invisible infant seat in the back of my car would have to go, along with the accompanying fantasies—and recognize the potential for different selves to emerge. If she can do that, like the "traditional woman," she can move forward in the quest for meaning, seeking other creative outlets, other opportunities to nurture that aren't merely compensatory, but are viable alternative paths to female identity.

Apparently I haven't gotten that far.

Breaking the Chain: A Daughter Who May Never Be a Mother

My parents live in a putty-colored split-level house at the end of a cul-de-sac, the quintessential 1970s suburban home. They still have the original variegated pink shag carpeting in the basement. The day after I arrived for a visit, my brothers, their wives, and their children came over for brunch. As I played with the kids, I watched my parents. My mom is getting older, but she's still vital: She wore jeans, a polo shirt, and sneakers, her hearing aids covered by her gray-blond hair. My dad is slim and tan; he still plays tennis three times a week. Every time I see him, I'm surprised that his hair is now snow-white instead of black. When we sat down to eat, he presided over the head of the table looking fully content, a patriarch who'd completed his career, raised his family, still loved his wife. My mother, the *über*-grandma, brought out platters of food from the kitchen, pausing briefly to play tea party with my three-year-old twin niece and nephew. She'd dropped a lot of hints about my having children over the past few years, but she'd never come right out and asked me about it. I am her third child; she's learned a thing or two about discretion.

That afternoon, after everyone had left, we sat at the kitchen table, chatting and admiring my dad's garden out the picture window. I took a breath. "You know, Mom," I said, "I've been thinking, I might not have kids."

My mother has very pale skin. I had no idea it could grow even whiter. She'd always assumed that, like her, I wanted children. I laid out the reasons: my happiness with my relationship, my devotion to my work. Her eyes looked stunned. She said very little. "Well, honey, I can't say I wouldn't be disappointed not to have your children be part of my life. But this is obviously something for you and Steven to decide." She paused a moment, collecting herself. "I just want you to be happy," she added, but she didn't look happy at all.

The next day she brought it up again. "You know this not having kids thing?" she asked. "I hope I didn't say anything wrong."

"No, Mom, you were really great," I said, perhaps a little too hastily. I didn't want to give her another chance to say more, anything that might hurt. "You didn't try to judge me, you just listened, and I appreciate it." She looked uncertain. Later I found out that she'd talked to one of my sisters-in-law about it, asking whether she thought I was seriously considering childlessness. It was unimaginable to her that I would forgo motherhood. One of the reasons I *did* want children was to have that bond with my mom. I felt uncomfortable, a little guilty, not about denying her a grandchild—she already had five—but about denying her a daughter who was also a mother, for depriving her, maybe even depriving myself, of a part of our relationship as women. If that were true, though, then I was back to not being fulfilled *as a woman* without kids. Could I create not only an alternative feminine vision for myself, but in my relationship with her? Our lives had been so different, our sources of sustenance and identity so dissimilar, children would bridge those gaps, make me feel closer to her on her terms. But, I thought, if I didn't have children, maybe she'd have to grow closer to me on mine, not through our roles as mothers but through our common bonds as women, as adults, as people in this world.

ON OCTOBER 31, three weeks shy of my thirty-fifth birthday, there was a message on my machine from a friend. "Listen," she yelled. I could barely hear her over the shrieking of her sons, whom, I assumed, were practicing their goblin arpeggios for Halloween. I was wrong. They were actually throwing simultaneous tantrums. "I want you to hear this," she continued, "so you'll know what it's really like to have kids and not feel so bad."

Occasionally she has asked me why I was even contemplating motherhood. I always brushed her off. "You love being a mom," I'd say. "You wouldn't give it up for anything."

"I do," she said when I called her back, "but you hear these women say 'motherhood is the most fulfilling thing.' You know what I say? Bullshit. It's fulfilling. It's rewarding. There's absolutely nothing that makes my heart melt like when my children look up at me with their big brown eyes. But it's not the most fulfilling. There's no one thing that can be the most fulfilling." That was an important reminder in a culture that often tells women just the opposite.

But that night, as I was shuffling through the photos from our Hawaiian vacation, pasting the good ones into an album, my heart suddenly went cold. As a child I loved looking at old pictures of my mother, my father, my grandparents. Who would see these? Who would care? I'd wanted to make the choice to have children affirmatively, not out of fear of the alternative, yet those fears dogged me. I feared I would regret childlessness after it was too late. I also fretted about being old and alone, especially since Steven was nearly ten years my senior. I knew from my reporting that, like gays and lesbians, childless heterosexuals create "families" in old age, networks of friends whose emotional support is as effective as that of biological relatives (although they're less likely to provide basic physical care). In fact, elderly childless women report that they're *happier* with their social relationships than women with children.[7] But that didn't satisfy me. Then I remembered Lois and Kiko.

Seventy and Childless:
Words from the Wise

Kiko and Lois were, respectively, sixty-nine and seventy-two years old and neither one had children. Lois never married, and Kiko had divorced in her mid-forties. They were originally friends of Steven's, women he'd met during the making of one of his films. I'd known them for the better part of a decade, yet never once, in all that time, in all my agonizing over childbearing, had I asked them what it was like to be childless as senior citizens. I can't explain why. Perhaps it was deference toward one's elders, a polite reluctance to get too personal. Or maybe I thought the conversation would be painful for them.

"So, you want to know how this happened that we're all alone and getting old," Lois said when I met the two of them at Kiko's for tea, and they both burst out laughing. We settled into the art deco furniture in the living room, Kiko's dog lying at our feet, chewing an old tennis ball. Kiko sat across from me, sipping on a root beer float. She's a Japanese American woman whose short, curly hair is still mostly black. She was dressed in a T-shirt, shorts, and Reeboks, her legs golden brown from her daily tennis matches. Lois sat next to her, tall and elegant with silvery bobbed hair and blue eyes, wearing slacks and a turtleneck, her glasses hanging on a chain around her neck. On the table between us was a suitcase filled with socks, which Kiko was selling on behalf of her niece, who owns an organic clothing business. "I'm selling Amway for mine," Lois confided.

Both Kiko and Lois had grown up assuming they'd have children; in their era, it was just a given. Yet, for one reason or another, they'd found excuses to avoid or delay marriage. Lois turned down one proposal for the chance to live in Europe for a year, then, at twenty-six, moved to Japan to work for the State Department. Since then she's earned two master's degrees, founded an English language school for nonnative speakers, and published a novel. "There was always so much to do, and it was all so exciting," she remembered. "I never said to myself, 'My God, I'm not going to have kids.' It just never seemed to me to be a necessary component of life."

Kiko, a retired administrative assistant who grew up in a farming town in the San Joaquin Valley, did marry at thirty-seven. Two years later she had a pregnancy that ended in miscarriage. "By then we were kind of old, especially for our generation," she recalled. "We looked into adoption, but that was going to take several more years. So, my husband said, 'Do you think we could have a good marriage without children?' " At first the idea shocked and unsettled her. It certainly wasn't what she'd expected. But after reflecting on it, Kiko realized she could. "And you know," she said, "it didn't seem like a loss. That sounds funny, because I always liked children and was always around them a lot. But I really didn't miss it, maybe because I *was* always around my friends' and my family's kids. They all called me Auntie Kiko. I took them home with me for weekends, we spent a ton of time together." She contemplated the suitcase full of socks. "This sounds immodest," she continued, "but I think that I'm the most important auntie in my nieces' and nephews' lives. And now that they're adults, we're real good friends."

Lois and Kiko are part of a tight-knit community of women, some of whom go back thirty-five years. They celebrate holidays and birthdays together. When one died of cancer a few years back, they cared for her until the end. Lois is also in a reading group, a writing group, and a group of retired teachers. Kiko volunteers for Meals on Wheels, at a local theater troupe, and as an adult literary tutor. Whenever I call them, they're always off to the theater or a museum, or in the midst of planning a weekend jaunt. Their lives are very full—far busier than my own. Still, I wanted to know what they thought would happen as their vigor began to fade. "How does the importance of your community change as you get older?" I tried diplomatically.

"By 'change' you mean . . ." Kiko began, then her eyes registered recognition. "Oh," she said. "Well, we all tend to say to each other, 'Since we don't have kids, we have to take care of each other in our old age. We should get a big house and live together.' " She looked at me pointedly. "Well, you know that's not going to happen." She threw her head back and laughed. "We'd just be at each other's throats."

A few years ago, Lois explained, their community of friends had found a good long-term-care policy and checked out local nursing homes. She'd had a lawyer write up her wishes and discussed them with her nieces and nephews. "We don't want to be a burden on them just like parents don't want to be a burden on their children," she said. "It's really not any different.

"You know," she continued, "it's not the end of the world if you don't have kids."

Kiko nodded. "As long as you're open-minded. I know I've lived a lot more interesting life having moved from the San Joaquin Valley to here. I look out my window every morning and I think, 'How did this little girl from Tulare end up looking out at the Golden Gate Bridge every morning?' And how grateful I am that I live here, where there's so much to do and so many interesting people to see and be with. I'm very happy."

Lois leaned in toward my tape recorder as if she were about to impart the wisdom of the ages. "Me too" is all she said.

My conversation with Lois and Kiko left me relieved. More than that, it left me feeling liberated. Driving home, I found myself thinking, "Maybe I *could* have a child," not because they weren't happy, but because they were, because the anxiety over what life would bring if I didn't have children had lifted. Knowing that I could be childless and truly live a satisfying life freed me to think in terms of my own desire. That day I felt my consciousness begin to shift.

The Lesson of Noodle Soup

In late November, three days after my thirty-fifth birthday, I sat in my office, a renovated laundry room in one corner of our house, watching the sun move across the sky through the bay window. It was a winter sun, bright but cold, emblematic of fading days, but I felt stronger, healthier, in better physical and emotional shape than I had in my life. I didn't feel old. As I turned back to my computer screen, Steven came in, bearing a bowl of udon, a kind of Japanese noodle soup, for my lunch. He set it down beside me, then quietly left the room. It was a small gesture, but I realized that in our relationship, those gestures were usually his. He was the one who worked the garden, who cooked, who found special things to display on the walls. He had made our home a sanctuary. It occurred to me that he was the kind of person I wished I were: the kind who could be accomplished in the outside world yet create a cozy environment at home without either role threatening the other. He had found the balance that I lacked. The longer I was married to Steven, the more I appreciated what he brought to our relationship. Ironically some of his strengths are those most associated with women. Through him I was slowly learning that I could have connection without submission, domesticity without a betrayal of self. Those lessons did not come easily to a woman whose feminism was built on the primacy of autonomy and achievement, who saw any step toward traditional spheres of femininity as backsliding. I write about women, but it took a man to teach me this.

Over the next few months, as I was mulling all of this, we met with some of the inevitable tragedies of adulthood, the ones that make you realize, in the saddest ways, that you are a grown-up. One of Steven's closest friends, a woman in her early forties, died of ovarian cancer, and just before Thanksgiving his father, who'd been sick for several years, died as well. The losses left us depleted, and, I suppose, with an even stronger urge to affirm life. A few weeks later, on the plane home from spending Christmas with Steven's family—the first without his father—we discussed having children one more time.

"I think you have to make a decision, Peg," Steven said gently.

I looked into his eyes, considering all I'd learned. "Let's have a child," I said, taking his hand. "Let's start trying in the spring." All the way home we held hands and giggled like kids ourselves, sharing a secret. I finally felt I could tackle the professional challenges, that I could balance my identity as a woman and an individual whether or not we became parents. I could only believe our child would be better for that. I was ready. I was excited. We were going ahead.

Two weeks later I was diagnosed with breast cancer.

Time Stops

On January 16, 1997, at 4:45 P.M., my surgeon told me over the phone that the tissue she'd removed from my breast to biopsy was malignant, and all the colors in the room went flat. The abnormality had been detected two weeks earlier on my first mammogram, the one I'd had as a baseline, as part of clearing the decks before trying to get pregnant. No one, not the surgeon, not the radiologist, expected this. "Dammit," I thought as I listened to her, "this can't be true. I have no family history of cancer. I do aerobics three times a week. I eat broccoli." The tumor was small, she explained, still too small to feel, and slow-growing. The chances that I would survive it, with a lumpectomy and six weeks of daily radiation treatments, were ninety percent.

"But what about kids?" I asked. "Can I still have kids?"

We could talk about that later, she said. I'd certainly have to put pregnancy off for a year, maybe two. Right now, though, we had to focus on getting rid of the disease.

Over the next few months my life went into a fugue state; I remember very little of what happened. I stopped reporting, since I couldn't travel during treatment, and tried to write instead, but it was hard to care about anything beyond my own terror. Mostly I stared out my office window, watching the light play across the redwood trees, letting the days go by me. My friends and family marveled over how well I was coping, but the truth was, I was struggling. My prognosis may have been good from the start, but getting cancer at such a young age didn't bode well for the future. I might die, I thought over and over, I really might die. All I wanted in that heightened, crystalline state was to have a child. I tried to feel that I hadn't made a serious, possibly irretrievable mistake by not having done it earlier. Two years seemed an eternity to wait, particularly given my age. Sometimes my grief was so intense, I could barely breathe.

To my surprise, though, those feelings didn't last. As the months went by, I began to trust that I would survive and, as my fear of death abated, so did my regret about missing my chance at motherhood. Simply being alive began to feel like enough. The old ambivalence even began to seep back, but I understood it differently. Despite my joy in reclaiming my old life, I couldn't ignore the anguish I'd felt facing death; I tried to pay attention to both.

By the time I was given the go-ahead to get pregnant, roughly a year after I finished radiation, making a baby no longer felt like a romantic project. We'd lost so much time already, and the disease had left me feeling alienated from my body, suspicious that it would betray me again. A month went by. Then two. Sex quickly lost its tang, its joy. Steven complained that I had made it into a military maneuver with my temperature charts and my boxes of ovulation predictors. I longed to be younger, to simply be able to throw away the pills and make love.

My focus had shifted from the idea of having a child to the goal of conception to proving that I was normal, that it wasn't too late, that I could win one for the Gipper of older moms. Five months went by. Then six. We began infertility testing. Briefly it appeared that the problem lay with Steven's sperm count. I was surprised by my response— I was almost giddy. *It wasn't my fault.* It wouldn't have mattered if I was twenty-six or thirty-six or forty-six. If the trouble was with him, I felt let off the hook; if it had been with me, I would've felt like it was a result of my "choices" and punished myself forever. It turned out, though, that the doctors had been hasty and Steven's sperm was fine. We'd already discussed and rejected the possibility of fertility drugs, but as six months turned to seven, then to eight, I began to reconsider.

Then, in mid-August my period was late. I took a home pregnancy test that came with the ovulation predictors. That blue line jumped out. I ran to my car, drove the five minutes to Steven's office, and wordlessly showed him the test. We stared at each other for a good thirty seconds. "You're pregnant?" he asked. I nodded. I sat on his lap and we hugged and laughed. Then we looked at each other again. "You know," he said. "I suddenly realized how much courage it takes to choose not to have children." I nodded, I knew exactly what he meant. The future rolled out before me like a well-worn path; I had only to place my feet in the footsteps.

I thought that my doubts would magically disappear once I was pregnant. Most of the time I was excited, dreaming about little outfits and cute names. But I was also struck by flashes of the same old fear: that my ambition, my relationship, my *self*, would evaporate with my waistline. Would the baby come between Steven and me or enhance our bond? Make us better partners or send us careening into separate worlds? Were our lives about to change for the better or for the worse? All I knew was that they were going to change.

One night, when Steven came home, I was immersed in Rhona Mahony's book *Kidding Ourselves: Breadwinning, Babies, and Bargaining Power*. "It says here," I proclaimed, "that fathers need to spend as much time alone as possible with a child early on, even if it means breast-feeding less. It's the only way he won't get relegated to the assistant role, especially since we automatically assume women know more about babies than men."[8]

"That seems obvious," Steven said. "That's what I'd expect."

"You would?"

"Sure," he said. "Besides, I'm not worried about any of this. You know why?"

"Why," I said.

"Because I'm going to be a great mom."

I looked up, astonished. He had just summed up years of reading I'd done, studies by sociologists, psychologists, and other journalists which concluded that for women to achieve full equality, men needed to become more than "involved" fathers: They needed to truly think like mothers—and women needed to allow it.

At eleven weeks we went in for an ultrasound, full of confidence that all was well. I had been horribly sick for the previous few weeks, which was usually a good sign for fetal viability. The technician ushered us into an exam room and poured a cool, slippery liquid onto my stomach. She ran the ultrasound wand over my abdomen, then left the room for a moment, returning with a long phallic device. I slid it inside of me and she looked at the screen again. "Hmmm," she said again. "I think I'll get the doctor."

Steven and I looked at each other and we knew. The pregnancy was over. I felt myself slipping into the familiar numbness of medical emergency. The doctor came in, broke the inevitable news, and ushered us to plastic chairs in the hallway while he contacted my obstetrician. "Are you relieved?" I asked Steven.

"Maybe a little," he said. "Mostly, though, I'm sad."

We went through the rest mechanically. The D&C, the bleeding, telling our families and friends. They expected me to be devastated, but, strangely, I wasn't. I was sad, of course, but I didn't have a hard time sharing the excitement of my two friends who were expecting babies the same week I had been. I was happy for their happiness, ready to welcome the little lives they were creating. I was relieved that I'd gotten pregnant at all; if it happened once, surely it could happen again.

The Only Sane Response

Three days after my miscarriage, I was scheduled to give a talk about teenage girls and self-esteem at Washington University in St. Louis. I'd been brought to campus by a foundation that gave scholarships to exceptional female graduate students across the disciplines. The night before I spoke, I shared a table with some of the current fellows at the foundation's annual dinner: One of the young women was in law school, one was studying to be a psychologist, a third was earning a doctorate in physics, and another was earning hers in philosophy. They were an extraordinarily bright, inspiring group of young women, and chatting with them refueled me. I asked them about their hopes and fears for the future. Their biggest concern, unsurprisingly, was how to balance motherhood with a productive career: The very time they'd have to make the big push for professional success coincided with when they'd hoped to have children. "I don't want to have to wait until I'm thirty-five to have kids!" one of them exclaimed, and the others nodded, their faces grim.

I nodded too, sympathetically. It really wasn't fair. Then, suddenly, I thought, "Wait a minute! I'm nearly thirty-seven and I don't have children yet. These women don't want to be *me!*" It was a shock. On one hand, they looked at me starry-eyed, as a role model, a woman who wasn't that much older than they were and was successful in her career. At the same time, they feared becoming me. It was disconcerting. Which was I? Shining example or cautionary tale? Transitional woman or transformative? Or both?

THE MISCARRIAGE TURNED out to have further complications, and it was over six months before I was allowed to try to get pregnant again. That brings me to today, age thirty-seven and a half, still thinking about becoming a mother for the first time. It's not what I expected, or what I wanted, but it's where a combination of choice and circumstance has led me. I'm still not willing to relinquish the potential, mothering self inside me, but if it turns out I have to, I hope I can do it gracefully, with a little grief and a lot of faith that there are many ways to live a woman's life. I'm not sure I fully believed that before, nor did the women I interviewed: They still felt too little choice over one of the most important decisions a person can make, and the fusion of feminine identity with motherhood only made it harder. I can't say I've fully come to terms with the conflicts I feel, but perhaps that's to be expected: Ambivalence may be the only sane response to motherhood at this juncture in history, to the schism it creates in women's lives. Some days I'm still not sure whether getting pregnant is the right course, whether I'm succumbing to peer pressure or lack the courage to forge an identity, a sense of community, a sense of femininity, without a child. Even as I write that, though, I feel a twinge of guilt. Am I wrong to admit those feelings? Should I cover the tracks of my ambivalence in case I do have children, let it sink like a pebble into a dark, serene pool of mother love? What will people think of me as a mother if I admit that I wasn't so sure? What if it turns out that even if I love my child so much that as a friend has said, "I would kill for him," I'm still not ever, ever sure?

Chapter 7

And Baby Makes Two

DANA ROSEN WAVES AT me from her front porch as I drive slowly up the tree-lined Oakland, California, street where she lives. Her one-year-old daughter, Kayla, balanced on Dana's hip, waves too, breaking into a drooly grin. They are both rosy cheeked and a little breathless, having just come from an afternoon at a nearby park: The stroller is still in the front yard, and Dana holds the keys to her apartment, the lower unit of a stucco duplex. Framed by the pillars of the porch, they form a classic portrait, but one in which mother and child are a study in contrasts: Dana has short, dark hair, a pleasantly bird-like nose, and kind brown eyes. Kayla, on the other hand, has a strawberries-and-cream complexion, sapphire peepers, and pale, cottony wisps of hair. Dana smiles when I ask if there are any blondes in her family, acknowledging the subtext of my question. "Not as far as I know," she says, kissing Kayla's flaxen head. "I imagine this all comes from the donor's side."

Giving Up the Dream

It is fashionable these days to call unmarried women of a certain age, a certain class, and, usually, a certain race who intentionally bear children "single mothers by choice," but Dana, whom I first met among a group of five women at a Berkeley sperm bank, made it clear that was a bit of a misnomer. Certainly, it's a *choice*, but not one she wanted to have to make.[1] "My first choice," she explains, "was the Dream."

Dana is sitting at her dining room table while the baby naps, sipping tea from a mug decorated with pink footprints and the words "With Love from Kayla," a heart replacing the "o" in "love." She is wearing jeans, a long-sleeved black T-shirt, and green suede shoes. Since she's still nursing, she's heavier around the hips and belly than she was before her pregnancy. A silver ring circles the middle finger of her right hand; the fourth finger of her left hand is bare. Her two-bedroom flat is dominated by the detritus of infancy: Baby gates line one wall of the living room, blocking off Dana's computer, stereo, and CDs from tiny, inquisitive hands. The table where we sit has been shoved against one wall to make room for toys, books, and a walker that looks like a hovercraft. I comment on her salt shaker, a ceramic princess leaning over, lips puckered, to kiss a crowned pepper-shaker frog. "My brother and sister-in-law gave me that," Dana says with a half-smile. "Everyone has their wishes for me."

Dana had her wishes for herself as well: The Dream she mentioned (seconded by every unmarried heterosexual mother I interviewed) was that she would have a loving husband who would be a committed father, whose career, while not too demanding, paid well enough to allow Dana the option, once they had their two children, to quit her job as a lawyer for the Environmental Protection Agency.[2] There is nothing about Dana that would suggest she would find herself, by her mid-thirties, so far from attaining her fantasy. She is an engaging, attractive woman, easygoing and attentive, the kind who goes out of her way—Coffee? Cookies? Sandwich?—to make a guest feel comfortable.

Her relationships with men had been typical enough too, with the same joys and the same tacit tension over losing oneself in love that so many women I spoke to described. Twice she came close to marriage: In her mid-twenties she became involved with a man who was funny, athletic, loved kids—he even led a youth group. They dated for six years. "After we broke up, I remember telling someone, kind of glibly, that what I'd really wanted was someone who would see all my faults and love me anyway," Dana says. "It took me a long time to understand that he *did* see all my faults, but he *didn't* love me anyway." At thirty-three she fell in love again, with a gentler, less critical man. But shortly after they met, she was transferred out of state, and when she returned a year later, the romance fizzled. "I started to feel there was something seriously wrong with me," Dana recalls, "like my radar was off and I was doomed to always be attracted to the wrong guys. I really felt helpless and hopeless. . . . I'd lost any sense that I was on track with my own life."

Dana sighs. Perhaps, she says, she hasn't married because she's ultimately been less willing to make compromises than other women. Perhaps she is more sensitive to—or more guarded against—what she calls "that insidious eating away of yourself that I know can happen in relationships, even in not very dramatic ways." Perhaps it was simply luck of the draw. For whatever reason, Dana found herself single and childless at thirty-five—that magic if arbitrary age when women in our culture who are not mothers begin to feel an intense urgency about their biological limits. Over the next year or so Dana found herself moping around, and she feared she was becoming the kind of person she couldn't abide. "I was dating a lot," she remembers, "but I felt like I had a neon sign on my head that flashed 'desperate.' My joke to myself was that I'd go out on a date and say, 'Hi, my name is Dana, and I'm thirty-six, and I'm a lawyer, and who are you and what's your sperm count?' "

It was around that time that the idea of having a child without a partner began to percolate into her consciousness. "It wasn't any one thing that pushed me toward this," she says. "I just didn't want to drift into childlessness." Dana decided to take a year to learn everything she could about single motherhood. She took a friend who'd had a baby on her own out to lunch for a chat, then did the same with several friends of friends. She consulted psychologists about the impact on children of being raised by a single parent. She read Jane Mattes's book *Single Mothers by Choice* and, through it, found a local SMBC support group. The first meeting she attended was at a rambling old house in Berkeley. Twenty women, ranging from their twenties to their mid-forties, gathered in the backyard, all with children they'd borne on their own. "I'd met women individually," Dana says, "but this was a critical mass. I thought, 'this is real.' They had all found a way to do it regardless of circumstance, economic situation, family support. And they were all happy they'd done it."

While still statistically small in number, women aged thirty-five and older are actually the fastest growing group of unwed mothers: At a time when the teenage birth rate is dropping, their rates of childbirth have more than doubled: from 2.4 percent in 1980 to 5.8 percent in 1995.[3] And that doesn't include those who've adopted children. Surely, there is strength in numbers, comfort in community, and in the SMBC group Dana found that. She never set out to be a trailblazer. "I want a lot of the traditional things," Dana explains. "I'm not the type who's going to butt heads with people and make them think about doing things differently." And yet, she adds, she's "enough of a feminist" and "well-enough educated" to feel a certain sense of entitlement, a birthright to self-determination.

Bearing a child on one's own as an economically and socially independent woman can be a radical act, challenging the definition of

"family," separating sexuality, marriage—*men*—decisively from repro-
ductivity. From that perspective, it's not surprising that in 1992, Vice
President Dan Quayle would blast the sitcom character (and single
mom) Murphy Brown for "mocking the importance of fathers by bearing a child alone and calling it just another 'lifestyle choice.' "[4] On the
other hand, most single mothers feel that, as women, they are somehow incomplete without children—a notion that however subversively
it is expressed, is profoundly traditional. In *On Our Own: Unmarried
Motherhood in America*, journalist Melissa Ludtke found that older unwed mothers, who are often professionals, felt that they'd sacrificed
their feminine identity to succeed in the workplace; bearing a child
was their way to reconnect with it.[5] Yet, like their married sisters
who undergo long-shot fertility treatments, the quest can grow obsessive, making it difficult to see alternatives, to develop an expansive
feminine identity that does *not* include motherhood.[6] By the natalist
nineties, motherhood supplanted marriage as the source of romantic
daydreams: A baby became the new Prince (or Princess) Charming,
conferring true happiness and fulfilled femininity.[7] Perhaps it's not
surprising, then, that women would consider bypassing the middle
man—the husband—if necessary. The youngest among the women I
interviewed often joked that if they hadn't found a guy who was marriage material by the time they were thirty-five, they'd head for the
nearest sperm bank, and half the women surveyed by the Institute for
Social Research in Los Angeles said that if they were childless by their
forties they'd consider it too.[8]

Several months before I met Dana, I interviewed Cheryl Zinko,
a forty-year-old therapist in San Francisco who had been trying to conceive a child through a sperm bank for two years. Insemination on its
own wasn't doing the trick, and months of increasingly potent fertility
drugs hadn't worked either. Now she was considering in vitro fertiliza-
tion, using both donor egg and sperm, because adopting would feel
like a failure. "I feel this incredible longing to carry the baby," she explained. "It must be pretty fundamental." Cheryl had had an adventur-
ous life: She'd traveled the world, had two careers, many lovers, and
lots of close friends. She was grateful for those opportunities. And yet,

her sense of legitimacy, her very self-worth as a woman, had been narrowed largely to whether or not she could bear a child.

"Sometimes I wonder if I'd want to be a mother so much right now if there weren't this incredible pressure in our culture," she said. "It's relentless. There's no really positive image of women without children. When I was growing up, there was Mary Tyler Moore. She was successful and had a career and a value to her life and she was completely content. Now they're doing an update where Rhoda and Mary have children. That makes me so angry. It's bullshit. So I wonder: If there weren't all this pressure, would I feel so strongly that I have to do this? I'm not sure. I probably would want to, but I might embrace this effort differently."

SEVERAL TIMES DURING our interviews I ask Dana what her life might have been like had she decided against having a child. It is the one question, no matter how I phrase it, that she has difficulty answering. "I really couldn't imagine *never* having a child," she says. "I guess I was afraid of what that would be like. To some extent, this is the part of me that couldn't be the feminist I was reading about in college. I wasn't sure I could define my life as being meaningful without having a child. And I worry about that, because I don't want Kayla to be the meaning of my life."

Over the ten months that she attend the SMBC meetings, sorting out her deeper motivations became Dana's central preoccupation. Her research provided lots of facts, but she still felt stuck. The obstacle to making a decision was clearly psychological. Did she want a baby to fill a void that ought to have been filled by something else? After all, a child wasn't a consolation prize, something to stave off loneliness. What did motherhood mean to her? What if it meant she'd never have a husband? How did she define family? Womanhood? Selfhood? Satisfaction? She began seeing a therapist and realized, over the next few months, that some of her doubts had nothing to do with single parenthood but were the ones that afflict many women. "I wondered if my life would ever amount to anything," she says, "would I make a contribution to the world after I had a child if I hadn't done so by now? Because I was simultaneously going through this process of thinking about a career change. I wanted to do something that felt more spiritually satisfying. And I thought, if I have this baby, that means making a choice to put that pursuit second."

But the biggest barrier was that Dana continued to want what she couldn't have, or at least couldn't be sure of having: a marriage she'd have time to enjoy before parenthood, a husband who would be a father for her child. "One of the things my therapist said to me was 'You're trying to make a decision based on an option that is not in front of you.' " She says, " 'You can wait to have a partner and hope you can still have a baby. Or you can choose to let that go and have a baby on your own. But you can't choose to have a baby with a partner.' And I thought, 'Hey! Cut it out! You're going to keep on sitting here in exactly the kind of indecision for the rest of your life that you swore you wouldn't!' As a friend said to me, 'If you wait for the perfect thing, Dana, you'll never have anything.' " Reckoning with that was a turning point.

In December 1996 Dana made her decision. At a local sperm bank she chose five possible donors from a thick binder of candidates. "It was like looking at personals ads to the nth degree," she recalls. "I was very conscious of how weird it was." She scrutinized the men's health histories, read about their occupations, their hobbies. She also tried to get a feel for the intangibles: intelligence, creativity, sense of humor—"All the things I would've looked for in a partner," she says. "I don't know if I can articulate exactly what I liked about the one I chose though. It's like great art: You know it when you see it." During her lunch break on the day she ovulated in January, she took a vial of his frozen sperm, packed in a cooler of dry ice, to her doctor, who thawed it and injected it into her uterus. She'd been told it might take months, or years, to conceive, that frozen sperm wasn't as reliable as the fresh stuff, but luck was on her side: Two weeks later she was pregnant.

Why Single Is
Not Necessarily Alone

On Sunday night Dana and her mother, Phyllis, are in the kitchen, inundated with vegetables. Dana has signed up for a service, popular in the Bay Area, where she pays a flat weekly fee for a box of locally grown organic produce, which she picks up a few blocks from her house. What she gets is a crap shoot, but, as Dana says, it teaches you to "eat seasonally." In late fall, however, "seasonal" means a mountain of kale, chard, spinach, and other greens. The service provides recipes, but still, it's a lot of leaves. Phyllis is washing them all in the sink, not just the ones for tonight's dinner but for the whole week. "Otherwise she'll never use them," she says, "they'll just rot and get thrown out,"

Phyllis is a young-looking sixty-six-year-old who has retained the New York accent of her youth. She's physically fit with short brown hair, glasses, and skin that is only just starting to wrinkle. She's wearing gray waffle-textured pants and a matching vest with a white turtleneck underneath. As they work, she and Dana catch up on news about friends, chat about a trip they took to Yosemite. The galley kitchen is tiny, but the two women never bump into each other: They have developed the intuitive choreography, the awareness of one another's movements and habits, that comes with intimacy. Dana's mother drives in from Sacramento every Sunday night and stays until Tuesday morning, providing childcare on Monday while Dana is at work, but that doesn't begin to describe her role. She often makes several nights' worth of dinners before she leaves for the week; she buys groceries, runs errands, does a couple of loads of laundry. She also provides Dana's only regular adult company. It is, Dana tells me, like having a wife.

When she's not at Dana's, Phyllis is employed as a social worker. She went back to school for her master's after Dana's younger brother left for college. Her training, combined with meeting classmates who'd left bad marriages and survived, encouraged her to ask questions about her own life, questions that culminated, twelve years ago, in a divorce from Dana's father. Looking at Phyllis now, it's hard to imagine the emotionally timid person Dana describes from before the divorce. Upon meeting me, Phyllis says straight out that she has misgivings about allowing a reporter into her daughter's home. "I feel very protective about Dana," she explains, "This is not personal. I just don't know you."

"We've had family members say 'You know what Dana's doing is wrong, don't you?' " Phyllis tells me as Dana hoists up Kayla, who has been playing on the floor, and plants her in her high chair. "I said, 'I don't know any such thing.' What I know is that in my heart I wish it could have been otherwise. But once she made this decision, I decided to do whatever I could to support her." She grimaces. "And I told that person, if they couldn't do that too, to make themselves scarce."

No one has ever said anything derogatory to Dana herself about Kayla's conception, although, she says, given how hard the decision was for her to make, it wouldn't have surprised her. "I did have a very good friend who asked me, 'Isn't it sort of selfish what you're doing?' " she says. "And the answer was definitely yes. But some part of me thinks it's *always* a selfish act to have a child."

"It's narcissistic," Phyllis says from the kitchen. "You want to recreate yourself."

Dana nods. "The question is, is it somehow more selfish of *me* because I'm bringing a child into a situation that is not ideal?"

Kayla bangs her spoon on her tray like a starving inmate demanding food. Dana laughs and puts a bowl of Phyllis's homemade chicken soup in front of her. "And I think the answer is yes," she continues, "although it's a matter of degrees on the spectrum. It's true that there are a lot of children out there whom I could adopt, who might otherwise be in a series of foster homes or institutionalized or whatever. I struggled with that for a long time. But I really, really wanted to have a baby, and I felt as though I could provide a good enough life that I wouldn't have to spend the rest of my life feeling guilty about having had her."

Dana's pregnancy was not an easy one. The last trimester brought home what it meant to be a single mother—both that she didn't have a partner to rely on, and that for a woman who makes this choice there can be a vast difference between being single and being alone. In her sixth month, just before she was supposed to move out of the house she was then sharing with housemates, Dana began to have contractions. She was forced to put her belongings in storage and move in with friends, who waited on her while she remained supine. Briefly her condition stabilized, and she found an apartment (although she couldn't move in) and told her friends they should take a planned vacation. While they were away, though, her water broke—seven weeks early. Worried and frightened, Dana called a cab and went to the hospital by herself. She was there for another four weeks while her doctors staved off labor. "My life became a horrible disaster area really fast," Dana remembers. A person who had always prided herself on her self-sufficiency, she asked everyone she could think of for favors, including moving her boxes into her new flat and unpacking them so she'd have somewhere to go once the baby was born. "I had never experienced asking for help on that level," she says now. "And for a long time it was depressing. But, ultimately, it was liberating. I didn't know I'd feel so good about it—and so good about the world—and that I would feel so much love because of it."

Dana had fantasized about giving birth at home, or in a warm bath, where the baby would be welcomed gently into the world, but that wasn't going to happen either. In the end her labor was induced, and when it came, it came full-on: "Wham! Like a truck!" she says, pounding her right fist into her left palm. Instead of the natural childbirth she'd envisioned, she was hooked up to monitors and an IV. It was fast, it was hard, but it was uncomplicated. Phyllis was right by her side.

"It was such a powerful experience," Phyllis says, looking over at Dana and Kayla. "My own daughter"—her eyes well up—"I was sitting there, remembering when she was born. It was just . . . very beautiful."

"Mostly I wanted her to hold my hand," Dana says to me, then turns toward Phyllis. "And I didn't want you to leave me."

It was Phyllis who cut the cord that attached her granddaughter to her daughter. Dana's sister-in-law and closest girlfriend were there too, and her brother arrived from Seattle soon after Kayla was born. It was a Friday night, the beginning of the Jewish Sabbath. Dana's brother picked up dinner, wine, and candles and brought them to her hospital room. Dana, her mom, her best friend, her brother, her sister-in-law, and her new baby blessed the Sabbath candles together, said the prayer over the wine, and celebrated.

Confessions of a Perfect Mother

At Totland, a playground that is specially designed for infants, there are sandboxes and baby swings, low wooden climbing structures and dozens of donated (and often broken) Big Wheels, dump trucks and sand toys. Phyllis brings her granddaughter here most Monday afternoons to play. There is a slight chill in the air, but that doesn't stop Kayla, who promptly crawls into the shade and proceeds to dig around in the damp, cold sand. We sit on the edge of the sandbox and watch her. "Sometimes I think it will be hard for me if Dana gets into a relationship and tells me to back off," Phyllis muses. "I'm so bonded to Kayla." She worries a bit that Dana may have a similar problem. "If emotionally she puts all her eggs in Kayla's basket, she may have a hard time letting go. I think Dana's smarter than that, but smart isn't always where it's at. I hope she can do that."

When Dana was Kayla's age, Phyllis certainly couldn't imagine her daughter's life would turn out as it has. "I wanted her to have it all," Phyllis recalls. "To graduate college, and be a lawyer, and be a wife and mother, and be happy and have a sense of personal accomplishment, gratification, joy. And she does have that. I just didn't know it would look like this." She looks down at Kayla, who is jubilant, digging in the sand.

Phyllis swallowed hard when Dana first brought up the idea of have a child on her own. She knew how badly Dana wanted a baby—she was pretty desperate for a grandchild herself—but single motherhood? "I thought, 'she hasn't a clue about how difficult this will be,' " she recalls. "But I told her I would not judge her, and I don't. Of course, I have lots of thoughts on the subject. I wish she didn't *have* to do this. It's way too hard. On some level it's unfair both to her and the baby." She shrugs. "And I think it's the best thing she's done."

Sometimes, Phyllis says, the difference between her daughter's life and her own amazes her, the change over a generation has been so extreme. Phyllis was married with two children before she was thirty years old. She was the kind of mom who sewed Halloween costumes and drove car pools and had a plate of homemade cookies ready when her children came home from school. In fact, Dana often compares herself negatively to her own mother because she won't be able to do those things for Kayla.

"You're kidding!" Phyllis says when I tell her this. "I'll have to dissuade her from that notion." Dana, she insists, is a far better mother than she ever was. "Yes, I was home. Yes, I baked cookies, and I was the swim team mom, and I made the sandwiches for all the other kids after practices, and made costumes. But the kids paid for that. I expected them to be appreciative of what I was doing for them, and to be 'good' as a result, to reflect well on me. And that's a crock. You're supposed to do things because you want to do them, not because of what you expect in return."

Kayla lets out a wail: She's fallen backward trying to pull herself up on a Big Wheel and bumped her head. Phyllis rushes over to comfort her, carrying her over to the baby swings. She places Kayla in the seat, squats in front of her, and pushes gently back and forth until her granddaughter begins to clap and smile.

Phyllis may have looked like the perfect mother, she continues—from the outside, the Rosens looked like the perfect family too. Occasionally she wonders, had she not found the courage to shatter the mythology of the "perfect" family and the "perfect" wife by divorcing her husband, whether she could've so easily accepted her daughter's decision to have a child on her own. "I don't know how I would've reacted to Dana, to someone making her own rules, if I was still like that," she says. "I had a lot of fear about striking out on my own, about leaving what seemed to be a perfect situation. And I suspect that if

I thought I couldn't break the rules myself, I would've thought she couldn't do it either."

Phyllis catches the swing and stands up, pulling it toward her, holding it suspended in midair. Kayla grins and Phyllis kisses her before letting the swing go. "And look what I would've missed," she says to me before catching the swing again. She turns and speaks straight to Kayla. "Look what I would've missed!"

"I Didn't Go Through All This to Not Be with Her"

Dana's "office" at the Environmental Protection Agency is a minute cubicle amid a maze of minute cubicles in a federal building in San Francisco. It has a spectacular view of the Bay, of tour boats and sailboats skimming along water, of sea gulls sawing circles in the sky, but Dana rarely notices. Her chair faces a panorama of a different sort, what she calls her "Kayla shrine," an ever-evolving display of about two dozen pictures pinned at eye level to the fabric walls of the cubicle. She points to a picture that shows the Rosens as a seemingly "normal" nuclear family: mom, dad, Dana, her brother, his wife, their daughter, and Kayla. "Both my dad's wife and my mom's boyfriend were there, but they aren't in the picture," Dana says. "It just worked out that way." She contemplates the snapshot for a minute. "The first time we were all together after the divorce was when my niece was born. She's adopted, so it was my dad, his wife, my mom, my brother, his wife, me, and the birth mother, who was sixteen. I looked at us all together and thought, 'Well, this is the new American family.' "

Dana turns her attention to a stack of papers on her desk. She's a staff attorney for the EPA, working to enforce federal pollution laws. It's a job that suits her. Coming of age in the late 1970s, she was encouraged to enter a field that had the cachet of being dominated by men, but the area of law she chose, advocacy work, is closer to women's traditional occupations, with all the advantages and disadvantages that entails.[9] She's never felt a barrier to the promotion of women at the EPA, no real glass ceiling, in part because there's no partnership track. The atmosphere is loose, the dress code casual. This is the kind of place where, when she announced she was pregnant, bags of maternity clothes appeared on her desk, the kind of place where no one batted an eye when she explained how the baby was conceived. As a federal employee, it was relatively easy for Dana to shift to a four-day week, which she's doing until Kayla is one, although it's meant that she's burned through all of her savings.

Therein lies the rub. Dana currently nets about $40,000 annually, which is not only rock bottom for a lawyer, but in the economics of the Bay Area means that as a parent, she's barely scraping by. The rent on her flat is $1,500, and childcare eats up an additional $650 a month. Food, diapers, clothing, doctor's bills—they all add up to more than she expected. Dana mentions her money crunch frequently although breezily. Like many of the women I interviewed, she never expected to be the sole support of a family. "Part of me always wanted to be militantly uncaring about how much I made," she explains. "I never wanted to make a choice about my career based primarily on money." That's a luxury, she's discovered, that a single mother can't afford.

At 12:15 Dana picks up the phone and calls Kayla's day-care center to say she's on her way down. The biggest perk of her job may be that the agency has on-site day care, which Dana uses three days a week. The center, on the first floor of the building, tends to dozens of children, from babies through preschool-aged. The infant room is broken into several areas, each scrupulously clean: There is a carpeted section with books and rows of identical toys, an area padded with bright-colored, soft mats; nooks for changing and feeding the babies, cribs for their naps. Near the bottom of the wall, at a crawler's eye level, construction-paper goldfish swim through an azure sea, each carrying a snapshot of one of the children and his or her family. The room is not exactly cozy—it's a little too institutional for that, especially with the fluorescent lights—but it's pleasant. When we enter, three caregivers are playing on the floor with five babies, one of whom is

Kayla. She squeals with joy when she sees Dana, who scoops her up and kisses her, inhaling her sweet scent.

Dana carries Kayla into the staff room, which, since the door has a lock, doubles as a nursing area. One of Dana's colleagues is already in there with her shirt off, double pumping breast milk. "That's such a gruesome process," Dana says, settling into a rocker. "At first I tried pumping in my boss's office—she was out sick for a long time— but even though I locked the door and put a note on it saying I was in there and not to disturb me, one of the office workers, an older man, actually went and got a key and walked in on me."

The other woman rolls her eyes. "And there's just nothing you can do," she says, glancing at her exposed breasts. "It's just like, 'I am a cow, yes, please go away.' "

As they pump and nurse, the two women begin to discuss a case they are working on together. "We come down here, take off our shirts, and have meetings," the other lawyer says cheerfully as she buttons her blouse and gets ready to leave.

Dana has told me that in some ways she feels like she has to squeeze motherhood into the margins of life: rushing to get Kayla fed, dressed, and out the door by about seven each morning, shuttling her back and forth on the BART train, nursing her in a glorified coat closet. On the other hand, watching her now with her colleague, I realize that she's also on the vanguard (if unwittingly) of those who are forcing a more permeable boundary between work and home, who will not allow the concerns of one to be separate from the other, hidden behind an invisible curtain: a world in which the workplace makes provisions for two women who want to discuss a client while nursing side by side.

There wasn't a moment from the time she contemplated single motherhood that Dana didn't know that she would have to go back to work within a few months of her child's birth. But, for women who go to such lengths to have babies, for whom motherhood is so deeply defining, returning to work is particularly complicated. Just as she would've far preferred to conceive a baby in the context of a marriage, Dana really wanted to raise her child the old-fashioned way too. "I loved being on maternity leave," she says. "I loved being able to wake with her, to nap with her if I needed to, to take a walk with her in the afternoon, to have the day based on her rhythms and not on this artificial schedule that requires us to get up at this hour and get to work. It hurt me to think of having to wake her in the morning and having to leave her with someone all day long, even if they were taking good care of her. I didn't go through all of this to have a baby on my own to not be with her."

If she'd had a partner, Dana says, she might have done what she preferred to do: stayed home until she felt ready to go back to work, no matter how long that took. And she might have been happy doing that too, who can say? But what has been surprising to her, what she might never have had the opportunity to discover if her circumstances were different, is that she *likes* much about being a working mother. It forces a kind of balance in her life that she otherwise might have let slide. "Even though I didn't want to go back, and I would quit in an instant if I could, I enjoy working more than I thought," she admits later, when we return to her cubicle. "The truth is, I appreciate the relationships I have with people when I'm here. And I hope this doesn't sound contradictory, but having Kayla has also, in some ways, made me care more passionately about the kind of work I do. It's made me want to have a job that I really love. First, because it makes me a happier person and makes me feel I'm doing good in the world. And also, I know that as much as I wanted to have a child, she can't be my reason for being. I have to make another contribution. Both for my own self and for her."

We Don't Have a Daddy

A few days later I meet Dana at 5:45, just as she's leaving work, pushing Kayla in her stroller. It's been raining all day, a dreary, relentless drizzle, and Dana struggles to keep both herself and Kayla dry as they make their way along the traffic-clogged street. Dana has dark circles under her eyes and her skin looks drawn: She was up until three last night, trying to meet a work deadline while tending to Kayla, who had a nasty diaper rash. She couldn't face the sodden commute on BART this morning, so she drove in, even though parking costs eight dollars a day. Unfortunately, every other commuter in the area seems to have abandoned public transit as well: The approach to the Bay Bridge is jammed, a line of brake lights disappearing into the fog up ahead. Dana grips the steering wheel with one hand and with the other dances a stuffed puppy in front of Kayla, who is fussing in her rear-facing child seat. "She spends so much time strapped into things," Dana observes, shaking her head. "Strapped into her stroller, strapped into a cart at the day-care center, strapped into the car seat, strapped into her high chair. At least on BART I can take her out and play with her."

By the time we get home, it's after 6:30 and we're all starving. Dana hauls in the clean diapers the service left on the porch, quickly changes Kayla, makes her a dinner of leftover salmon, potatoes, and zucchini, and heats up the lentil soup Phyllis left behind for the two of us. Ideally, she tells me, she and Kayla are home by six. That way they have a solid two hours to play after dinner before it's time for bed. When things go smoothly—which, between traffic and Kayla's rash they haven't tonight—that's Dana's favorite time of the day.

The phone rings, but Dana ignores it, as she usually does at this hour. "I want to make the evening sacred," she says, "yet I find it really hard, for four nights in a row, to not return phone calls or look at my mail or pay the bills. Usually, I end up waiting until she goes to bed to do chores around the house, then suddenly it's eleven o'clock, and I'm thinking, 'How am I going to manage tomorrow?' " Dana shrugs. "I suspect that's exacerbated by being a single mom, but probably any parent would tell you the same thing."

Kayla finishes her meal—Dana has barely touched hers—and points to a group of photographs on the piano, saying *"Ba-ba-ba"* enthusiastically. Dana picks her up and they look at a photo of a friend's newborn twins. Kayla points to a picture of Dana's father. *"Ba-ba-ba!"* she says again. "That's your daddy," Dana tells her, then quickly corrects herself. "I mean *my* daddy. Your grandfather." Dana hands me the frame, a present from her stepmother, which contains two pictures:

The first shows Dana at seven, in profile, her neck stretched long, nose to nose with her dad. He is clean-cut with dark hair and wears a T-shirt under his doctor's lab coat. They're both smiling. The second picture, taken in the cockpit of a small plane, was snapped more recently. Dana is now an adult, and her dad, who sits in the pilot's seat, has a graying beard. But they're still in the same position: nose to nose, grinning.

Some of Dana's friends have told her she was lucky, as a single mother, to have a daughter rather than a son, as if girls need male guidance and support less than boys. Although she understands the logic, Dana doesn't really buy it. "I think daughters need a father *differently* than sons, but not less so," she says, putting the photographs back on the piano. "I was extremely influenced by my father, and the idea of his absence in my life is inconceivable. I mean, his complete nonexistence?" She shakes her head. "It's hard for me to imagine who I'd be, how I'd be formed, what my psyche would be, what my goals and ambitions and drives and fears would be if my father had simply never existed in my life." She shakes her head again. "Unimaginable."

Dana doesn't know exactly how she'll compensate for that lack in Kayla's life. It's one of the questions she hasn't answered to her satisfaction. Dana's father, while not as integral to their lives as Phyllis, is still an active presence. She tries to establish close ties between her male friends and Kayla too. Sometimes Dana even considers moving to Seattle to be near her brother, whom she thinks is a wonderful male role model. Then there is the donor himself. Dana chose an identity release donor, which means that once she's eighteen, Kayla can gain full access to his records, including his name, address, phone number, and social security number. In Sweden ID release is mandatory, viewed as the most ethical way to conduct donor insemination. Here is it far less popular and quickly reduced the donor pool to just a handful of viable candidates. Most of the women I interviewed had opted against ID-release donors, either because there were so few of them or because they didn't want the potential for emotional entanglement or disappointment down the road. Dana, however, disagrees. "Those of us who have children in this way refer to 'the donor,' " she says. "But to Kayla he's her biological father. And biology is not insignificant. I want her to at least have the chance to know who her biological father is.

"I do wonder, though, what this will be like for her growing up," she continues. "Will she think that if she only knew him, all her problems would be solved? Will he take on this aura of a perfect man?" She looks down at Kayla, playing on the floor. Kayla has wound a Slinky around her neck like an Elizabethan ruff and waves regally at her mother. "Hi!" she says, and Dana smiles. "And what would it be like for me, if she decides to meet him, for our relationship?" she adds, and then sighs. "It seems so far away right now, I can't wrap my mind around it. And to some extent we'll only really know all that after we do meet him."

Dating and the Single Mom

Until January first, when Dana goes back to work full-time, Friday is errand day. This afternoon she pushes Kayla in a grocery cart up and down the cavernous aisles of Costco. Her mission: to find a disposable helium tank for one of her SMBC friends, whose child is having a birthday party this weekend. Since she's here, Dana is also picking up a ten-pack of tuna and some other odds and ends. As she cruises past a display of improbably giant jars of maraschino cherries, she bumps into a friend from her synagogue, whose cart is piled high. The woman asks Dana if she's coming to Saturday morning services. "We're having a special Kiddush," she says, referring to the reception after the service.

Later, in the checkout line, Dana tells me she would like to go to the service, it would be fun, a nice outlet for her, but she doubts she will. She can't go without Kayla, and it's impossible to predict whether she would make it through. Since Kayla was born, Dana has had virtually no separate social life or even time by herself to get a haircut, read a book, exercise. That's typical: Aside from economic concerns, the biggest challenge for single mothers—whether they bear their child out of wedlock, adopt, are widowed or divorced—is to create that much-needed rejuvenation time.[10] So far Dana hasn't minded. But after a year she's beginning to consider the occasional break. Last week she hired her first baby-sitter so she could have dinner with friends, but at twenty dollars for the sitter and fifty for the evening out, it was too expensive to do often. Sometimes I wondered how Dana's isolation from other adults affected our interviews. My sessions with her tended to last longer than with other women. In part, that was because she had a great deal to say—and I had a lot of questions—but I suspected she was also enjoying the novelty of companionship.

As for romance, Dana says, that's a distant memory. Her last date was during the first trimester of her pregnancy. I'm a little shocked to hear her say she dated at all while she was pregnant. She didn't set out to, Dana explains, but twice during those early weeks friends offered to fix her up, so she went. She'd heard stories about women who met and married Mr. Right while they were pregnant, although it hadn't happened to anyone she knew personally. Among the single mothers I met, none had been involved with a man since giving birth. They didn't go so far as to say that single motherhood precluded marriage, but they had accepted that it reduced the possibility. At any rate, Dana came clean within the first hour of the dates. The men were curious, she recalls, even supportive, but they weren't interested. Neither one called again.

We pull into Dana's driveway, and she comes around to the passenger door to unstrap Kayla from the car seat. Kayla reaches her arms up toward her. "You are the sweetest child," Dana croons as Kayla embraces her. "The sweetest, sweetest, most affectionate. I love you *soooo* much." Kayla flings her arms wide at the elongated "soooo," and Dana and I laugh.

"Sometimes the hardest thing about not having a partner is not having someone to share all those moments of joy," Dana says. "I'm very, very lucky because I have my mom. So I have more of that than I had a right to expect I would. But I still miss it. I miss having someone to come home to at the end of the day besides Kayla. I miss all of the things I like about a good relationship. The affection. Someone to curl up with on the couch and rent a movie with. And I miss not seeing someone I love in her when I see her. I see her and love her, but she's not the reflection of a partner that I love and created her with. It's an ephemeral thing, but I miss it."

At the same time, Dana doesn't romanticize having a mate. "This is not just to justify my position," she says, "but the reality is, sometimes my friends have a helping partner but not always. And sometimes they have struggles with their partner, and there is resentment. There is no one in my life who is not fulfilling my expectations, or not doing for me what I think they should. And every help I get, particularly from my mother, but also from friends who helped me move, or bring over videos, or one who came over when I was sick once to watch Kayla so I could take a nap—to me these are all unexpected gifts. Now, if I were *expecting* all that and someone was letting me down, my attitude would be very different."

I open my mouth to challenge her on this, but she stops me before I can say anything. "Yes, taken to the extreme, this attitude would indicate that having a lobotomy was the best way to go through life, or to just not have any expectations, which I don't believe," she says. "And I don't want to build myself this lovely little castle where I shut out the possibility of a partner because I've rationalized my own choice. I really would rather have a partner. There's no question in my mind. But not just any partner."

Dana carries Kayla into the kitchen and rummages around for a banana. I ask her if she feels like she and Kayla are a family. She stops where she is, smiles, and blushes deeply. "Oh, well . . ." she says, and laughs nervously. No? I ask. Dana shrugs shyly and looks down at Kayla. "What do *you* think?" she asks her daughter. "Of course, you don't know how to say yes." Dana looks back at me. I'm still waiting. "It's a good question," she says. "Mostly, yes, in that Kayla is my daughter and I am her mother. There isn't anything lesser about our relationship at all. And, after all, statistically a lot of families don't look like the image that you think of when you think of a family. On the other hand, I do find myself noting it when someone says to me,

'And how's your family,' when someone *refers* to us as a family. I find myself being pleased that that person perceives us that way."

LATER THAT NIGHT I watch Dana nurse her daughter, rocking Kayla to sleep with the bedroom lights turned low, a Hebrew lullaby on the tape recorder. Kayla rests in the crook of Dana's arm while Dana hums quietly. She may have wanted the Dream—she may still at times mourn not having it—but, it seems to me that she *has* created a family. Kayla is well loved: better loved than many children with two parents, better loved than many children whose fathers eventually leave them. Dana has a child she adores, work that she enjoys, family and friends who support her, and a sense of gratitude for all of it. "I feel so lucky," Dana told me. "I feel like I live in this state of grace, of being grateful pretty much all the time. Truly grateful, not resentful-grateful, but *truly* grateful for all the help and support that the two of us have in our lives." Perhaps it's not ideal—and Dana might be the first to admit that—but then, every choice has its own sets of rewards and costs, even for those who have achieved the Dream.

Chapter 8

The Tug of Tradition

THE CORRIDORS OF THE Springvale mall in suburban New Jersey, like those across America, are encircled by the shiny links of national chain stores: The Limited, The Gap, Ann Taylor, Banana Republic. But it's not their dazzle that lure Carrie Pollack and Robin Keillor on this wet summer day. The two women ignore the siren song of Calvin Klein lingerie; they are unimpressed by a display of Prescriptives lipsticks. They march straight from the minivans and Volvos in the mall's parking lot to its indoor courtyard which, it turns out, is jammed with similarly high-priced vehicles: the Seville LXI, the Century Regent, the All Terrain—names more evocative of luxury sedans than strollers.

We have arrived at the red-hot center of what Carrie calls "the parallel universe" of stay-at-home moms. In front of us, dozens of children leap in gleeful chaos around a mock lily pond, plunging from plastic toadstools, squirming through hollow logs, and rolling around the blue-mat water while the adults supervise from carpeted steps. "Well, ladies and jellybeans," Carrie says, beaming at four-year-old Julia, eighteen-month-old Sam, and Robin's son, Michael, "What do you think?" At thirty-eight Carrie is just shy of five feet tall, dressed in blue jeans, a T-shirt, and sandals. Her dark hair is pulled back into a ponytail; her large brown eyes, under straight-cut bangs, are slightly asymmetric, giving her a friendly, quizzical look. It's easy to see why, back when she was a district attorney prosecuting child abuse cases— before her own children were born—she could win the trust of even her most traumatized clients.

She and Robin take a seat as the children skitter, stocking-footed, into the fray. The women chat briefly about Julia's and Michael's nursery school, where they met, then fall into a distracted silence. Robin runs a hand through her highlighted hair and fiddles with her necklace. Carrie hops up to make sure Sam isn't trampled by oblivious older children. Robin fusses over her four-month-old baby. Carrie checks on Julia. For the next two hours the only time they talk about anything other than the day's events is when I ask a question. Then it becomes clear that they know very little about each other.

"You were a physical therapist?" Carrie says to Robin. "I didn't know that."

"Absolutely," Robin says, nodding. "I have a master's. I didn't know you were a lawyer!"

Around us the stairs are filled with women. It may be 1997 in the real world, but here in the parallel universe, it looks more like the 1950s. There is a smattering of grandmothers and nannies, but mostly these are full-time moms. I see exactly two fathers during our visit here, and only one is without his wife. As that man walks by, Sam stops what he's doing and stares, eyes wide, until he's out of sight.

"Sam always stares at men," Carrie explains. "He's not used to seeing fathers during the day."

"I'll Never Be Dependent on a Man"

Like the other women I interviewed who primarily tended children— many of whom had left prestigious jobs—Carrie seemed a little surprised by where she'd landed, describing a kind of whiplash turn-around from her younger, more ambitious self. But the truth is, neither a woman's early childhood experience nor her expectations during the Promise years nor even a feminist orientation can predict how she'll navigate the choices and constraints of motherhood. Instead, it's an evolving interplay between the opportunities she encounters at work and the circumstances of her marriage.[1]

Typically the new generation of stay-at-home moms I met were highly educated women, the ones who had been expected to waltz through the doors of opportunity that feminist pioneers had jimmied open for them. Often, though, around the time they became pregnant, they'd become disenchanted with their professions, disillusioned by the bottom-line values of the workplace, frustrated by a lack of advancement. Frequently they found their ambitions flagging. Meanwhile, their husbands tended to be in demanding careers with high earning potential but rigid schedules. Even if they had planned to be egalitarian parents, that prospect suddenly seemed economically and logistically impractical. Often these women also described an especially strong pull toward their infants. Childcare became—partly by default, partly be design, partly by desire—their responsibility, and combining full-time motherhood with a career quickly became untenable. With very little discussion—and certainly without questioning the husband's role as primary provider—these women found themselves slipping into traditional roles.[2]

Carrie and Brian Pollack, however, were a little different. Brian was one of the rare men in America to take a six months unpaid paternity leave when his daughter was born. Meanwhile, Carrie loved her job and was adamant about her economic independence. We discuss this one morning while sitting at the dining room table of the Pollacks' modest, happily chaotic home. Next to us, in the living room, a playhouse dominates one corner. Along the walls, about two feet up from the floor, Carrie has taped up crayon drawings of dinosaurs. Toys are strewn along the couch, across the hearth, overflowing from boxes onto the floor. In the Pollacks' world, stay-at-home mom does not mean live-in maid.

"This will explain everything about me," Carrie begins as Sam toddles in and out, showing off toy trains and picture books. Carrie has mastered the maternal art of split conversation and talks simultaneously to Sam and me without missing a beat. "When I was six, my mother entered me into this Little Miss Springtime contest. *That's Mommy's tea, Sam. Tea. It's hot.* The judges asked me, 'Do you want to get married and have children when you grow up? *Dah, dah. Good Sam. You like those noises.* And I paused and said, 'Yes, but I want to become something first.' *Oh, you are very tidy. Much more than Mommy.* My mother had already drilled that into me."

By the time Carrie was a teenager, she understood that her mother had her own incentive for instilling Carrie with the popular idea that she could "be anything she wanted to be." She had sacrificed her own opportunities when she'd dropped out of college to marry. Her husband, the suave, martini-drinking father Carrie adored, turned out to be chronically unfaithful. Carrie came to see her mother as trapped, humiliated by her husband, underappreciated by her two sons (and sometimes even by Carrie herself); the couple divorced when Carrie was in her early twenties. "Seeing my mom in that situation and watching her struggle with it"—Carrie shakes her head—"I knew there was no way I was ever going to let myself be completely dependent on a man. I wanted to be my own person, to earn my own money."

Carrie's father may have made a poor husband, but he loved his little girl, and he took it upon himself to nurture her budding ambition. "He thought I had a very analytical mind," she says. "He was a very important intellectual force for me." She flirted with a career in social work but, under his influence, decided that law was "where the power was." Still, as for many of the women I met, power, as it's traditionally been defined, was less appealing than Carrie had imagined. Like Dana Rosen, she gravitated toward work that was lower paying and full of idealistic purpose—more admirable and also more in keeping with conventional, feminine values. Of course that's not an innate preference: As author Rhona Mahony points out, there is a disproportionate number of women in legal services (as well as the helping professions): They're freer to be more "moral" on the job than their male classmates, since their marriageability is less dependent on their earning potential.[3] After a disastrous summer internship at a corporate firm, Carrie became an assistant district attorney in Baltimore specializing in felony child abuse cases. "They threw me into that division without any training just like they throw in everyone to see who would sink and who would float," Carrie says proudly. "And I floated."

Carrie was exceptionally good at her job. She won sixty out of sixty-four cases she tried before juries, most involving intrafamilial abuse: There were the two small boys who'd been raped by their mother's boyfriend, for instance, or the man who'd been raping his granddaughter since she was five. "When those jurors came in guilty, it was the greatest feeling in the world," she says. "Because I had protected this kid. I was keeping this guy off the street for at least five years—that was the minimum prison sentence for the rapists. It was incredibly satisfying. I loved it."

By her late twenties Little Miss Springtime had fulfilled her childhood dreams as well as those her parents had for her. Carrie was independent: supporting herself, rising in the ranks at the DA's office, and relishing her freedom. She was starting to think about marriage, but children? They were the last thing on her mind. "I remember being at a party," she says, "and this guy said, 'I'm real interested in you, Carrie, but I would only date a woman who, if she married me, would stay home and raise our kids.' And I said, 'Well, you are barking up the wrong tree.' "

She glances up with a half-smile at the Q-tip-and-glue mobile hanging from the dining room light fixture. "I guess that's sort of ironic."

Who'll Mind the Baby?

A few hours after we return from the mall, Brian Pollack strides in the door and yells a greeting. He's a bearish man with an unruly mop of reddish hair, pale, freckled skin, and a warm, patient expression. Carrie had told me that Brian was not, as she put it, "drop dead," and that was just fine by her. She had long ago decided that there were two ways she could protect herself from her mother's fate. One was by having a career. The other was by not dating handsome men. "I associated good looks with philandering," she'd explained. "You know: debonair, tennis playing, handsome. That was all my dad. I ran the other way from men like him."

Carrie had other criteria too, which were surprisingly well thought out and, essentially, egalitarian. She avoided men who were too ambitious, who would want to put in long hours at the office at the expense of relationships. On the other hand, she wanted a mate with a sense of professional pride, who was as stable and directed as she was. When they met, during Carrie's first year of law school, Brian didn't seem like that man. A year younger than she was, he had dropped out of college and was working in a bike shop. They dated for a while, but Carrie broke it off. Then, five years later, Brian called her again. He had graduated from law school in the Midwest and was coming back east for a job. Would she like to get together when he came through town? When she saw him again, she says, she just *knew*. Six years ago they were married.

"It has surprised me that our love has grown," Carrie confides now. "I never thought that I could love him more than the day we married. But I'm just crazy about him. And I think part of that is the joy of seeing him with our kids."

Brian goes upstairs to change into a T-shirt and jeans—completing the transformation from employee to daddy—then jumps in with the children while Carrie finishes dinner. He's at a bit of a deficit, having missed the day's small dramas. He doesn't know, for instance, that Julia is not supposed to be picking the best pieces of lettuce out of the communal salad bowl, or why Sam has developed an obsession with the drawer where they keep their audiotapes. Still, where pure joy is concerned, Brian is right on target. "Daddy!" Julia shouts when she sees him; then she calls out the letter "Y."

Brian stops short and feigns surprise. "Oh," he says. "Are you cold? Do you need a sweater?" Julia giggles, delighted, and calls out the letter "I." This is their "chilly, chili, Chile" game, something Brian invented to help Julia understand homophones. Julia calls out the final letter of one of those three like-sounding words, and Brian responds with a sentence that conveys the appropriate meaning. "I?" he says, pretending concern. "No, we're having something else for dinner tonight." Julia dissolves in giggles again as Brian sweeps her off her feet for a hug.

The Pollacks have strong views about childrearing, views that they call "countermainstream," and they've made significant personal sacrifices to do what they believe is right for their family. Brian works for the government in a job that is both less interesting and lower paying than one in the private sector or academia, but the hours are regular and twice a month he works a four-day week. With just one income they've given up vacations, evenings out on the town, new clothing and furniture, and the kind of luxury items most Americans take for granted, such as a CD player or a VCR. Brian's parents chip in by helping them with their mortgage, and Carrie's mom provides childcare when they need it. To the Pollacks, putting children first means putting in time at the expense of both personal ambition and material comforts. They are both firmly against day care. Carrie says that because of the nature of her work, she is fearful of abuse, and each of them brought up what they called "benign neglect" by nannies and day-care workers. It's a position that Brian, in particular, who thinks of himself both as a liberal and a feminist, is surprised to have adopted. "I have some fairly violent feelings that I never used to have regarding the 'great experiment' we are engaged in that results largely in the neglect of almost all children," he told me. "So many kids up and down the economic spectrum are placed with, to my mind, inappropriate care-givers, whether in an institutional setting or at home. The bottom line was, one of us was going to stay home."

Which of them would be that "one," however, was an open question. Brian, in fact, seems almost sheepish about how their child-care arrangement turned out. After dinner he motions me down the basement stairs, where he can speak more freely. "In keeping with the fifties retro family that we are," he jokes, "we keep secrets from the kids." The basement is damp, with no natural light. It is where the Pollacks keep their NordicTrack as well as Carrie's desk and computer. Brian sits in Carrie's office chair and turns to me expectantly, eager to answer my questions. If gender hadn't been a factor, he would have seemed the more likely candidate for full-time parenthood. Before Julia was born, Carrie liked her job far more than he did his, and was more dedicated to it. Whereas she speaks passionately about vindicating abused children, here is how Brian describes his job as a lawyer in the federal government: "It's pretty easy. It's well suited to somebody with as terrible work habits as I've got because I can goof off for days at a time and still get very good opinions. And because of conditions I don't understand, they keep throwing money at me, which has been a big help too."

Carrie's job was also more lucrative, although, interestingly, the Pollacks have different recollections of the disparity. Brian claims it was twenty or thirty thousand dollars. Carrie declares the amount neg-ligible, "probably five thousand." When Julia was born, they figured they'd each take a leave, then work out the next step from there. Car-rie would go first, taking the four and a half paid months that her job allowed, then Brian would put in for the six months unpaid parental leave his office provided. He was the first man to avail himself of the policy. "We weren't quite sure how they were going to respond to the request," Brian says. "But they were fine. I mean, it's unpaid. I got mostly stroked. Other guys said, 'That's really cool.' "

" 'Really cool,' " I counter, "but none of them did it themselves?"

"Yeah," Brian says. "And there *was* some of that 'There is no way I would have done it,' although I don't think because of career considerations. Because in our particular office, there wouldn't be any. I think it's more social roles."[4] Brian says he was fully prepared to make fatherhood his vocation, yet even before he left work, subtle cues from friends and family let him know he was expected to return to his job. Carrie's girlfriends said how lucky she was that Brian was "trying to understand *your* experience." Brian's parents proclaimed the leave "wonderful for the baby" as long as it didn't hurt his long-term earning potential. All around, Brian was hailed as forward thinking, or, as he put it, as "progressive and New Agey"—providing he went back to work when it was over.

Looking back on it, Brian believes he could have withstood such social pressure if he had enjoyed his early caretaking time with Julia. As it turned out, though, it proved devastatingly difficult. When he discusses those six months, a tone of defeat creeps into his voice. "Staying home with her was really tedious," he says. "I was surprised by the constantness of it, the lack of breaks that we so much take for granted in life. By midafternoon my entire mental focus would be on how long until Carrie would get home.

"A day doesn't seem that long when you are working," he continues. "But, boy, it's a long time when it's just you and this kid that doesn't speak, and she is always wanting your attention. And when she's asleep, then there are all these things that have to be done before she wakes up. There's absolutely nothing I have ever experienced that was always bearing down like that. Nothing even close."

I ask Brian if there was anything he loved about staying home with Julia. He leans back in his chair, hands clasped behind his head, and grins. "Oh, absolutely," he says. "Little things, like when she'd fall asleep with her tiny arms going around my neck. And also there was"—he pauses, groping for words—"there was the sort of general psychic feeling of being a father. It was very bonding. The feeling of parental love was absolutely tangible during that period, and that was nice. On the other hand, both then and now it was tinged with a lot of guilt at not being a better one. Not spending more time, not having more energy. And that was even more true when I was home. I knew I should be doing more with her. And a lot of times we would just hang out."

What struck me, listening to Brian, was that the experience he described mirrored that of so many new mothers. Professional women in their thirties are especially likely to feel isolated, numbed by monotony, and worried that their response makes them bad parents. They, too, are racked with guilt.[5] But the women had two things Brian didn't: a support network—other mothers, family members—to help them cope with the boredom, and a cultural expectation that they would simply endure it. After all, there is no shame in a father admitting he finds infants exasperating and then retreating to the workplace. But when a mother does the same, her devotion is called into question by others and by herself.

In Peer Marriage, sociologist Pepper Schwartz has noted that the culture conspires against egalitarian co-parenting.[6] That's even more true in the case of a male primary caretaker. Play groups, library programs, and school committees are all part of what Carrie called the "parallel universe" of stay-at-home mothers. Brian enjoyed the attention of being the token dad at Gymboree, but most men would not feel so comfortable. For their part, mothers treat primary caretaking fathers as alien and often not quite competent. Some confessed to me that they think of full-time fathers as "losers." That may partially explain why the percentage of stay-at-home dads in 1993 was virtually the same as it was in 1977.[7] Women may have been integrated into the male enclaves of the workforce, but men have neither entered nor been accepted into the parallel universe of mothers. The assumption, as Schwartz points out, persists in both sectors that a child's primary parent is her mother, and the father is a temporary substitute.[8]

That Kind of Mother

While Brian was crashing into the limits of the New Age Dad, Carrie was wrestling with her vision of the Perfect Mom. At first she reveled in being the working parent. "It was great," she says one afternoon as we drive along rainy tree-lined streets in her Volvo station wagon on our way to pick up Julia from nursery school. "I had my cake and could eat it too. Work was definitely more relaxing than being home. I took care of Julia in the mornings, then I disappeared to work. Then I came home and took care of her some more. And I knew that during the day she was with Brian. But on the other hand, I started to feel like he was home and I was missing all of this stuff." Work gradually began to lose its appeal. Carrie felt cut off from Julia. Besides, she'd reached a dead end in the job—her next promotion would be to a position that didn't interest her, and she wasn't sure what else she might pursue.

As Brian's paternity leave wore on, Carrie and Brian each began to articulate reasons why she would be a better full-time parent: Brian watched C-Span all day and Carrie didn't want the kids exposed to that much TV. Carrie was "more disciplined, more able to get the job done through the tedium," although with time, Brian admitted, he too might've learned to cope. Carrie was "ambivalent, but *less* ambivalent" about leaving work. "Carrie missed Julia," Brian said. "Either she missed her genuinely emotionally, or felt that she *should* be here for her." He shrugged. "It probably was a combination. I think the truth is, Carrie didn't want to be seen as 'that kind of mom'—the mom who was working and not staying home with her kids."

As we pull into the nursery school parking lot, Carrie tells me she's been surprised by the feeling of freedom she finds in motherhood. "I always come back to something that my mother-in-law said to me," she said, "that it is okay to mix it up in life. I was a real straight and narrow person, and stepping off has showed me that a job is not necessarily the be-all and end-all of who you are: It is good to take time, to exit from that place and do something different. I mean, it hasn't been all hearts and flowers. I've had doubts about what I've done. But all in all, if I could go back and talk to my younger self, I would say, 'Get ready for some really rich mixing it up.' "

It's an interesting twist on a woman's liberation: motherhood as a mid-career sabbatical, a time to recharge. Staying home allows Carrie not only the opportunity to enjoy her children but to do a little consulting, a little volunteering, and to think creatively about what she might want to do if she returns to the workforce someday. Sociologist Kathleen Gerson calls it the "domestic option," and it's something that in a postfeminist period women have unconsciously tried to preserve should work cease to satisfy.[9] Without this socially sanctioned escape hatch, they risk becoming little more than the Woman in the Gray Flannel Suit, a distaff Willy Loman.

In an ideal world, perhaps both men and women could take a break when their children were small to parent and to regroup, but as it stands, only women are allowed such a luxury (and not too many women at that). Yet, a "motherhood era" comes with considerable personal risk: It is predicated on both the assumption that someone else will always pay the bills and without regard to its impact on a woman's future earning potential. Stopping out of the workforce even for a year per child is, in fact, the biggest impediment to a woman's career advancement. It also severely limits her ability to save for retirement: A woman who takes seven years away from a forty-year career may end up with half the benefits of someone who stays in the workforce.[10]

I tell Carrie I'm surprised that a woman as insistent as she is about financial independence was willing to give it up. She sighs and nods. "It was really hard for me to become dependent on Brian," she says. "It's so awful to have all those eggs in one basket. I mean, God forbid something should happen to him. Not only would my world fall apart because he's my husband and I love him, but the very underpinnings of our family . . ." Carrie shakes her head, letting the sentence go unfinished. But that, she tells me, is where her consulting comes in. About once a month, or whenever work comes in, Carrie lectures at conferences of various professionals who investigate cases of child abuse. She doesn't know if it will keep her marketable over the long run, but at least for now it allows her to hold on to the notion of herself as a provider: She brings in between eight and ten thousand dollars a year.

"Maybe it's partly self-deception," she admits. "But I'm convinced that my financial input to the family is important. Several times Brian has said, 'Oh, we could get by, it would be okay. Don't worry about it.' But I've said to him, 'I *want* it to be perceived as important.' Then he is like, 'Oh, it *is* important. It is.' Sort of flipping. But it is *very* important to me that the money I make means something to our family."

Other Women's Choices

Sam has stayed behind with Carrie's mom while we take Julia to another play date, with a boy from her class. It's no accident that both of the children Julia has been paired with on my visit are boys. Carrie noticed that given the choice, Julia would play exclusively with girls, and it worried her. Julia's calendar—more complicated than that of most adults—is full of such deliberate plans. "The kids are now my work. They are my job," Carrie explains as we drive along. "And in the same way that I was a perfectionist at work and cared a great deal about the product and about winning and all of those things, that has been translated over to my kids. Basically every day there is an activity for one or both of them. Because I see my role not just as basic caregiving but as going that little extra step and enriching, enriching, enriching them. My mom did a lot of enriching for me, and I really believe that I'm partially the way I am because of all of her care and insight and investment. And it was my mom. It wasn't my dad. And that's what's happening here."

Carrie hadn't expected to be judgmental about other women's choices, but she regularly brings up examples of how careers come at children's expense, always beginning with a disclaimer, expressing empathy with working mothers. "I'm very surprised I respond this way," she tells me. "Because I think of myself as very open, and 'whatever is good for you.' But I see mothers who believe their nanny is good, and the person is really in outer space. Maybe they don't know. Or maybe they have lower expectations. But I sort of think, you have the kid, you are going to have to make some sacrifices, either the husband or wife or both, in your work life."

Meanwhile, Carrie says, the hard feelings are clearly reciprocal: Scratch the surface of respect for stay-at-home mothers and you will quickly find contempt. "People have actually said to me, 'You went to law school, you had this career, you threw it all away.' " She looks at me, indignant. "Just like that: 'Threw it away.' And I think, 'I didn't *die*.' I mean, not that I can tell anyway."

Women certainly have had both ample reason and ample opportunity to denounce one another's choices. Whatever a mother does seems to result in public censure and private doubt; that makes it difficult to accept someone else's accommodations without questioning your own. I suggest to Carrie that the only way to break out of this deadlock is to do what she and Brian rejected: to have fathers do more of the mothering. And yet, if people like them, who have a willing male, don't do it, how will it ever happen? "It's true," she says. "And I am the one who said no. I don't know who ever would. Do I know any fathers who are primary caretakers?" She thinks for a moment. "I guess not. I've certainly read about them."

THE HOUSE WHERE Julia's having her play date is the antithesis of the Pollacks': There is a new leather couch in the living room, Lalique crystal figurines, and an entertainment center that runs the length of one wall. While the kids play, Carrie and the boy's mother, Annette, drink coffee and eat Oreos, chatting politely about preschool: There is some controversy over the quality of next year's teacher, as well as resentment over the amount of time parents are expected to clock there. "There's an assumption that most of the women are home and we have nothing else to do but spend time at the preschool," Carrie says. "A lot of us take that opportunity to have one-on-one time with younger siblings or to take classes. And if they say it's not mandatory but it turns out that you're the only mother who doesn't show up, your kid feels awful."

"I didn't realize it was such a problem until something was scheduled on the day I had my amnio appointment," says Annette, a tall blond woman with a creamy complexion who is seven months pregnant with her second child. "The teacher told me, 'If you can't come, maybe he shouldn't come to school at all that day.'"

Carrie looks shocked. "Oh, Annette!" she says.

"I'm home to be with him," Annette says, "and I've been there for everything. So the one time I'm not, I'm made to feel like a bad mother. I can't imagine if I were working."

Journalist Joan Peters has pointed out that even as women have flooded the workplace, the "edifice of motherhood" has expanded: In addition to basic nurturing, the Perfect Mother is now expected to be a creative playmate, developmental psychologist, and educational expert, not to mention a ready volunteer.[11] Stay-at-home moms are as vulnerable as working moms to the pressure to do ever more. Carrie strives to imbue every activity that her kids engage in with "a purpose." Annette, whose baby has yet to be born, is reading a book called *The Second Child*, and is worried that subsequent children tend to have lower IQs than firstborns. She mentions that with her first, she felt she'd "failed as a mother" when she couldn't breast-feed ("I tried for six and a half weeks," she quips. "I really bonded with that pump"). Carrie has told me that she feels guilty because, although she spends a lot of time with her children, she sometimes drifts off when Julia chatters at her, or feels exhausted by Sam's perpetual motion. The impossible standards they set for themselves, shared by so many women, reminded me of the teenage girls I used to interview, who, no matter what their weight, saw themselves as fat. I don't know whether there's a Perfect-Mother equivalent to an eating disorder, but I wondered: How good does a mother have to be before she feels good enough?

As the afternoon wears on, it becomes clear that Carrie and Annette have little in common. When I ask Annette what she expected from her life ten years ago, for instance, she says, "I never had a career, just a job. And I just always wanted a baby. I always wanted to be a stay-at-home mom."

"You can see I don't connect with Annette," Carrie says when we're back in her car. "But that's another thing that gets sacrificed. You don't make friends based on who you want to be friends with; it's based on who the kids are friends with, what's good for them. So you lose that connection with women you'd have more in common with. I miss having those friendships."

When we'd picked Julia up from nursery school, Carrie had pointed out one of the other mothers to me, a woman who looked, at least superficially, like Carrie: While most of the other moms wore jewelry, makeup, and nail polish, this woman had wild, curly hair, glasses, and was dressed in jeans and sandals. Carrie looked at her longingly. "I think we'd like each other," she says now, perking up. "It's very exciting to see her. I've said to Brian that sometimes I feel acutely lonely. I really do. I'm trying to think, when have I been alone with other adults aside from him?" She squints in concentration, then gives up. "It's strictly phone contact."

I ask Carrie—since she's given up her job, her financial independence, and time with friends for her children's well-being—if there is anything that would make her feel she's gone too far, that she has become too subsumed in her role as a mother. "If I suddenly felt totally satisfied with motherhood alone," she says slowly. "That would be a warning sign that I was overly involved. Because I can't imagine ever being totally satisfied with this role. There's got to be ambivalence, and there's got to be other needs for self-expression."

"To tell you the truth, Peggy," she continues, "I don't understand someone like Annette. There is part of me that says, is she really as happy as she appears? And if she is, all the more power to her, but I just cannot imagine it. Is she too obsessed with her kid? She doesn't seem to be. But I know that I have other needs, and if they suddenly disappeared, I would think, 'What has happened? Why have I lost this need to do something other than mothering?' "

A Good, Happy Wife;
a Good, Happy Mom

When I first met Carrie at a group interview in Philadelphia, something startling happened. One of the other women had just talked about her recent separation from her husband, saying that it came as a terrible shock since they'd always been best friends. When I turned to ask Carrie a question, she was quietly crying. "This frightens me," she said, "because I see myself as a good wife. But am I really a good wife? Not only is my career somewhat submerged, but with two children there's not a hell of a lot of time for each other. My husband is so second tier. I don't want to lose what we have. I think we're both very much aware that's a possibility, but I know that's no guarantee. It's always possible, even when you thought you had a great thing."

A year later, as we drive back to her house, I ask Carrie if she remembers the incident, and she shudders. "I will never forget that as long as I live," she says. "When that woman was describing her husband, I'm like, 'Oh, my God, oh, my God.' Because, let's face it, she married a guy that she thought was a Brian. And it didn't turn out that way. And all of the safeguards that I put up for myself, that I didn't marry my dad—who's to say that one day something like that couldn't happen to me?"

Carrie says that despite their shared joy at having Julia, having a child changed their marriage far more than she would've expected, and two children have made it even harder. "The kids did bring us closer because both of us are so invested in them," she says. "But we've lost a little bit of each other along the way. We've said jokingly that maybe for the next eighteen years we're going to be on the back burner as a couple. But at the same time, I recognize that that's not possible. So there's a lot of tension. I want to be a good, happy wife, a good, happy mom, a good, happy career person, but all of those things sort of are colliding worlds. There's always this split-dom of never feeling able to really do one thing completely well."

Most of the couples I spoke with felt that children had both enhanced and strained their marriages, but traditional couples have a special vulnerability: As their roles diverge, they can grow apart, losing their connection as equals.[12] Brian and Carrie take that threat seriously. When during our basement conversation I had asked Brian how having children changed their marriage, his first response, too, was to tell me how it had strengthened their bond. "The joint-project nature of Julia gave us a focus," he said, "and also just the incredible joy of them. I think it was probably good for our marriage. On the other hand, it's hard to say. Since Sam, it's harder to be connected. We are very committed, very till-death-do-us part, but because of the stresses, pressures, energy drain, and projects, we don't have time for one another. So, in the short term, it has made our marriage less fun.

"And in the long term"—he paused for a moment, staring at the ceiling—"it might take a toll on our connectedness. It's entirely possible that our fifties scenario will continue and it will be the midlife crisis: having grown apart, without knowing each other because of our different roles as a couple. I think we're in danger of that." Brian nodded. "It's very real," he said quietly. "It's very real."

The Braver the Better

When she gets home from Annette's, Carrie sits down on the living room floor with Sam on her lap, watching Julia play dress-up in a silver lamé scarf and tattered party dress. She's playing princess, and Carrie keeps trying to inject pro-girl messages into her play. "You're so brave in your silver jacket, Princess Julia!" she says.

"I'm Snow White," Julia huffs, "not Princess Julia."

"And Snow White was brave when she went to that house alone, wasn't she?" Carrie says, then turns to me. "Frankly I think Snow White got a raw deal, having to do the dwarves' laundry and cooking." She turns back to Julia. "They should have paid her," she adds. We concoct a new motto for Princess Julia: The Braver the Better. Julia seems indifferent to it, but Carrie is pleased. She wants Julia to have a strong sense of self, a feeling of entitlement to be, well, whatever she wants to be. It's important to Carrie that the children see her working, that they see her mowing the lawn and Brian making dinner. Yet, when I ask her what she dreams for them, her response is nonetheless stratified by gender.

"I'd like Julia to have a job that she loved. I would like her to find that man that she loves. I'd hope she can be more thoughtful about some of these decisions than I was, thinking about them ahead of time. I would want her to be happy like I have been. And to be fulfilled in her love life and her work life."

Does she ever consider that Sam might want to be a homemaker? "I definitely think about it with Julia. But I want her to have a career first. Whatever she decides to do, I want her to have options. With Sam it wouldn't occur to me that he would stay home. It just wouldn't."

Mothering begets mothering. In the end, neither the stay-at-home mother nor the working mom who exhausts herself doing the "second shift" changes the social fabric for the next generation. So much of what Carrie, and particularly Brian, have done has been pioneering: his paternity leave, his compressed work schedule, their commitment to family time over increased wealth. Yet, how do those sacrifices add up if they do not ultimately expand their children's opportunities? If Carrie can't envision her own son as growing up to become the kind of man that her husband was prepared to be, who can?

Later I mention this to Brian and ask if he could imagine a more egalitarian split. "If we were both working part-time and I were in the same position, that might be the best," he says. "It would be harder for me to be here instead of in my office, no question about it. And my work would be also harder if I were part-time. But it would have some satisfactions too. If Carrie could envision what she wanted to do during her part-time, I think that would be ideal for her. But I'm not sure how much more she would want to do than she does now—maybe working a third time. Maybe that would be ideal. But neither of us can envision it—or we aren't aware how to make it work."

A WEEK AFTER I visit the Pollacks, Carrie calls me. "Talking to you was really thought-provoking for both of us," she says. "We've already made changes. This morning we woke up at five A.M. and had some 'alone time,' " she laughs, "which was *really* good.

"I've thought a lot about what you said, though," she continues. "If we couldn't have a full-time father, or something more equal, then whoever would?" She pauses for a moment, contemplating her own question. "Well, let me know if you find that couple!"

Chapter 9

Almost Everything

O N A SATURDAY IN mid-November—the year's first truly
cold winter afternoon—Halloween ornaments still hang from
the knocker of Emily and Dan Sorenson's suburban Chicago door. A
planter full of dead purple mums droops on the front stoop. The
unseasonable display stands out in this neighborhood of seniors and
full-time homemakers who have already decked their houses with
enough Pilgrim paraphernalia to fill the *Mayflower*. But with three children and a full-time job as an associate partner at an international

business consulting firm, Emily doesn't have time to be Martha Stewart.

The door opens when I knock, and a small blond head pops out. Lucy, who is two, grabs my hand and drags me inside like she's known me all her life, then resumes what she was doing—shrieking and tearing around the living room with her older brothers. Christopher, four, slips, and crashes to the floor in front of me.

"Chris, those socks aren't good to run in," Emily warns as she comes downstairs. Emily is thirty-seven, a petite athletic woman with reddish-brown hair that falls between her jaw and shoulder—well within the range of what Mira Brodie would call "corporate hair"— dark, twinkling eyes, and a perpetually amused expression. She's dressed in her weekend uniform: sweatpants, a Polartec pullover, and fleece slippers. Lucy careens by. "Those tights aren't good either, Lucy," Emily calls out. "You're going to wipe out too." Emily notices me and waves hello. "I see the kids are letting in strangers again," she says, laughing.

Dan comes in from the kitchen to put Lucy down for her nap while Emily gives Chris and Tim, who is eight, Oreos and a Casper video to keep them occupied while we talk. "See you next weekend!" Chris says, waving. The children start to head upstairs, only to be turned back by Dan.

"They're not supposed to eat up there," Emily explains, "but I figured they'd be done with the cookies before they got to the landing."

Dan saunters into the kitchen behind the boys. He's a tall, stocky guy with ruddy skin and blond hair in retreat on his scalp. He has a jock's stature—he always seems to be rocking back slightly on his heels—and a hoarse voice that makes him sound gentle and a little sexy. He watches his sons eat their snack, then washes their hands.

"Can you get him to bed?" Emily says, indicating Chris with her chin.

"Well, I'll get him into his bedroom anyway," Dan replies.

The boys scamper upstairs, but before they disappear, Chris pokes his head back around the corner. "See you next weekend!" He says again to his mother, "Next Friday night, Saturday, and Sunday!"

Choices and Chances

As much as anyone I met in three years of cross-country interviewing, Emily Sorenson has achieved the Dream: a satisfying, well-paying career; a husband who does his share of the childrearing; excellent day care for their three children; parents who are ready and willing to help out in a pinch; a comfortable home and solid investments in retirement and college funds. She is also the first to admit that her circumstances are a function of good luck as much as social change or strategic planning. After Lucy and Chris are asleep and Dan takes Tim out to run errands, Emily curls up in an easy chair by the fire in her den and ticks off the various obstacles working mothers face. "If you weren't in a day-care situation that you felt comfortable with," she begins, "or your job wasn't willing to be flexible, or your husband didn't do his share, or if you made a lot less money than he did—it's easier to make it work with similar jobs and similar incomes. Or, if you don't have any parents to call upon. All those things, if they worked against you at the same time, or even if a couple of them didn't work out, you'd just say"—she shrugs—" 'forget it.' And it just gets that much harder to keep it going with each child you have."

In addition to serendipity though, Emily has also made a shift in her thinking about motherhood: She's been willing not only to delegate physical acts of caretaking but to let go of the Perfect Mother ideal with its sweet rewards and undercurrent of control. Her attitude evolved, in part, out of professional opportunities—an ever-increasing salary and genuine pleasure in her work—but her own childhood played a part too. Emily was the fourth of seven kids. She remembers her family as happy and blessed, as close as nine people sharing a house can be; one of her few regrets is that Lucy won't have a sister, won't experience the intimacy Emily still feels, to this day, with hers. Like many mothers of the era, Emily's mom stayed home, but, loving as she was, she simply didn't have time to lavish individual attention on each child, nor could she and Emily's father attend every activity or school performance—in that sense they were similar to today's overcommitted parents, although for different reasons and with less guilt.

Her upbringing left Emily with two distinct beliefs: She wanted to be more involved with each child than her own mother had been able to be, but she also knew that they wouldn't need her constant presence to thrive. "My mother didn't sit around and nurture me all day," she says. "She didn't do stuff with just me by ourselves. She couldn't. She was taking care of all these kids. And it really turned out fine."

Emily could stay home with her children if she wanted to: She freely acknowledges that she "chooses" to work, but then, she says, so does Dan—either one of their salaries could carry the family. Aside from the economic benefits, she's convinced her career enhances both her mental health and her marriage. "I think you can have an equal relationship without both people working, but it's harder," she says. "If one is staying home, you start living in separate worlds on a daily basis. This way, we're both experiencing the same things, and trying to balance the same things and we don't tend to take each other for granted as much."

For many women the layers of support, coincidences of timing, and ideological shift that gird Emily's life seem so remote as to feel like a reproach, as unattainable an ideal as *The Donna Reed Show* in the fifties, or *The Brady Bunch* in the seventies. Yet, the balance—that most feminine of nouns!—Emily has achieved reveals much about the potential for change both in the home and the workplace. And the constraints that she still faces, even in the best of circumstances, also show its limits.

A Matter of Grace

Emily sits behind the desk in her new office, dwarfed by a punch bowl containing candy from her children's Halloween plunder. The sweets, as much as anything, signal her managerial style: "I am approachable," they say, "the kind of boss who listens and cares." For the moment, the bowl is one of the few personal touches in the office, along with photos of the kids and a pair of Mickey Mouse ears. Emily hasn't had much time to unpack in the last two weeks since she began managing one hundred consultants hired by a client that designs software for retailers. The consultants will bill about twenty million dollars this year, tailoring the software to specific customers' needs. Emily's job is to make sure the project remains profitable, that it's adequately staffed, that the employees feel rewarded, and the client is happy. "It's a job that will play to my organizational skills, my financial skills, my management skills, my negotiation skills—all my strengths," Emily says. "With this kind of work, the status quo is never enough. It's always, 'What can you do better? How can you generate more revenue?' I like being pushed. If I worked in an environment where the current situation was okay for the next ten years, I wouldn't be happy."

Even so, the job was a lateral move for Emily. Usually an associate partner would be on the road four or five days a week, trying to drum up enough new business to be promoted to full partner. Among other things, being partner would triple Emily's salary. "You can be successful here as a woman," Emily says. "They *want* you to be." But, despite the fact that her firm was recently named one of the hundred best companies for working mothers by *Working Mother* magazine, that success is still achieved on conventional terms. "You have to decide if it's worth it for you to travel that much, to work that hard, to make those sacrifices," Emily says. "A lot of the men I work with can't see past the money. They say, 'Em, if you can make that much, why aren't you doing it? Why would you want to sell yourself short?' But I think, 'How much money do you need?' And for what? So I can drive around in a new Mercedes and never see my family?" She shakes her head at the absurdity of it. "I can learn new things in this job, gain skills, and still have a normal family life. If I need to, I can be home in ten minutes.

"The only thing I'm not sure of," she continues, "is whether it's going to bother me to see my peers getting promoted, seeing them bypass me. Partnership is something you grow up with: like the way your mother tells you you'll go to college, so you assume you will. When you start at a firm like this, they use partnership as the carrot. And you want to be seen as achieving what your peers have achieved." She looks around the empty office with its dust-covered filing cabinets. "Well," she says briskly, "I have some time here to figure all that out."

Emily is still in the getting-to-know-you phase of her job. She spends the morning introducing herself to her new employees and shadowing her predecessor at meetings. One of the best parts of her job, she says, is that every few years she gets to learn about a new industry. She's particularly excited about entering retail because it's dominated by women. Before this Emily worked in manufacturing, where all of her clients, colleagues, and superiors were men. "Looking back, I was never considered to be one of them," she says. "No one was ever rude to me, but you're surrounded by these big men, and it's hard to come into your own: It's hard to feel like you can really be yourself and be given the respect you deserve without having to be too forceful or being perceived as too tough. A lot of it is just about style. I liked to approach things a little more diplomatically than most of them did. There wasn't much appreciation for—" Emily searches for the right word, finds it, and smiles wryly. "Grace."

For all the women I interviewed, from Mira Brodie to Abbey Green to Emily, gender differences in communication styles were a key issue on the job, especially in male-defined fields. According to linguist Deborah Tannen, women's typical way of expressing themselves is less effective in gaining recognition for their ideas, negotiating for a raise, gaining promotions and power.[1] Yet, altering their style to fit in with the boys, as Mira Brodie's mentor warned, isn't effective either. Women who are perceived as "masculine" may earn a grudging respect but tend to be disliked, even provoking hostility.[2] I notice that the notes I'm taking on Emily reflect that tension: They focus on such things as the soft cut of her suit, the intimacy of her management style, the impishness of her smile. It's as if I feel the need to signal her femininity to readers before I can explore her power. If I feel that pressure as an observer, imagine what it's like to live with.

The assumption persists that women are, by nature, kinder and gentler than men, even though few behavioral differences have been consistently observed among corporate leaders.[3] By the late nineties that expectation had taken a new twist: In a Korn/Ferry International study, senior executives (almost exclusively men) said they perceived women as more "empathetic, supportive, nurturing, relationship-building, and willing to share power and information."

But, instead of being detrimental, they claimed, those "feminine" qualities were the "leadership traits of tomorrow"—much as Abbey Green did. Meanwhile, the same executives saw men as more "risk-taking, self-confident, competitive, decisive, and direct."[4] In other words, nothing had changed or broadened in the way women were viewed by their bosses; the stereotypes had just been repackaged in their favor, at least on the surface. Women are still expected to tend to the emotional needs of their staffs and employers, to soothe hurt feelings and assuage ruffled egos. They're still, according to Tannen, expected to be the ones who work behind the scenes to keep things running smoothly, who take pride in their work but eschew credit.[5] "I know I feel better contributing in more than just the ways that give me good press," Emily says. "I'm not much of a self-promoter. It's personal satisfaction of doing things that need to be done versus just the things that will get me ahead."

But there's a price to "invisible" labor. By any measure of comparison—including title, age, company ranking—top female earners in Fortune 500 companies still earn as much as $60,000 less than men in lesser positions.[6] Meanwhile, the tensions that highly successful women describe between the satisfactions of caretaking on one hand and its burdens on the other sound remarkably like the pressures of motherhood. "It's almost like women who have both aging parents and young children," one senior manager told me. "You feel like, 'I'm not getting anything from above, because that generation can't give it. And from the people I manage, the expectations are much greater than they used to be, in terms of mentorship and guidance.' And then you're also cut off from other women, because there's so few at this level."

Eight years ago, when Emily gave birth to Tim, none of her peers in the company were mothers. Her male colleagues (not to mention her clients and supervisors) all had stay-at-home wives: They couldn't appreciate how difficult, how physically grueling, it could be to manage a job and a baby. "You're trying to be productive, but you're fighting fatigue constantly," she says. "I didn't feel like I had the support system, people who understood why I had to leave on time, why I was late some days, why I had to go take the child to the doctor, why I was so upset that I couldn't fit into my suits." She laughs and rolls her eyes. "It wouldn't necessarily have changed anything I did, but it would've felt less stressful if there had been more than just me."

She doesn't know what, exactly, kept her going. Pride in her work, perhaps, positive feedback, the financial rewards, the challenge of exceeding expectations. Certainly there have been times when the stress level has felt overwhelming, and she has considered walking away. Usually it's when she feels she's falling behind her peers, or she's disappointed a client, or hasn't done her best work. "I do sometimes think, 'Gee, work isn't going so well right now, so maybe I should stay home,'" she says, "which is *not* the right reason. A lot of women do that though, because the time you have children often coincides with change at work: It's the same time you'd move into management or the equivalent, and if you're getting some resistance, or they aren't supportive of mothers, or you aren't performing well at new levels, it would be easy to give up. But it's never been because I thought, 'Gee, this child would be better if I were home every day.'" Even during the most difficult times at work, Emily says, she's confident that her children are safe, happy, and as well cared for as they could possibly be with Jeannie, the Sorensons' nanny. "Without Jeannie," she says, "this would all be so much harder if not impossible."

A Stay-at-Home Mom Who Gets Paid

An hour after Emily and Dan leave for work, Jeannie, Chris, Lucy, and Jeannie's dog, Leo (which she brings along to the Sorensons' each day), pile into Jeannie's Ford Explorer and head out to their ritual weekly visit to Starbucks. Jeannie is thirty years old, slim, and blond, dressed in leggings and a brown turtleneck with a gray sweatshirt tied around her waist. Before becoming a nanny, she was a professional animal trainer. At the café she orders a decaf latte for herself; Chris and Lucy get chocolate milk and split a Snickerdoodle. Leo stays in the car.

"I love you," Lucy says as Jeannie disentangles her from her winter coat, scarf, and mittens.

"I love you a lot," Jeannie replies, giving the girl a kiss. "She's like my own baby," Jeannie continues, turning to me. "I've raised her since she was a newborn."

Before Lucy came along, the Sorensons resisted hiring a nanny, placing the boys in a home-based day care with several employees. Dan, in particular, was hesitant to leave a stranger alone in the house, un-supervised, with the children. But with three kids, Jeannie's salary costs about the same as day care, not to mention that she makes life a lot less hectic. Emily and Dan no longer have to rush the children out the door each morning by seven or race through traffic to pick them up on time each night. They hired Jeannie when Emily was still pregnant, so she could monitor the quality of the nanny's care during her mater-nity leave. Now, two years later, the Sorensons trust Jeannie implicitly, as if she were a member of the family, which she is, almost. This morn-ing, like every day, she arrived at 7:30, parked in the Sorensons' garage, tied up Leo in the yard, and promptly began preparing a peanut butter sandwich for Tim's lunchbox, making small talk with Dan. While he ate his cereal, she dressed the children, combed their hair, and gath-ered up their laundry. She is even trying to toilet-train Lucy. "Emily and Dan think you should wait until the child wants to do it," Jeannie admits, "but they don't tell me *not* to. So they do what they do on the weekends, and I do what I do on the weekdays. It may be confusing to Lucy, but I don't want to leave her in a diaper until she's four. So, sometimes we have differing opinions, but as long as it's not interfer-ing with the welfare of the kids, they don't mind."

When, over lunch the previous day, I asked Emily if there was anything Jeannie doesn't do, anything she held out as a mother's pre-rogative, she considered the question for quite some time. "I like to take them to the doctor," she said. "And, of course, school conferences, that type of thing. But that's about it." There was an incident recently, Emily recalled, where she felt just the tiniest bit threatened. Jeannie told them she thought one of the boys was getting too selfish, that he should take on more chores. "Initially, I thought, 'This is *my* kid, *I* know what's best,' " Emily said, "but the fact is, she observes him at times when I don't, and when I thought about it, I realized that she was right. He was ready to take on more responsibility, and it would be good for him. I appreciated her bringing it up."

Some people, I told Emily, would say that Jeannie was raising her kids. She nodded her head. "Yeah," she said simply. "I know they would." Some people might even say that Jeannie spends more time with the children than their parents do, and that's not what motherhood is about. "I wouldn't totally disagree with that," Emily said. "And it's not to say I wouldn't be happy staying home with my children, but I'm definitely happier not doing that. It sounds terrible, but I think they're better off if I'm happier. And right now when I'm with them I really want to spend all my time with them. And I guess I always want to be in the situation where I want to spend more time with my children."

Jeannie actually does think of herself as a stay-at-home mom but one that commands the respect of a salary, an annual review, and paid vacations. There are other perks too, reminiscent of the kind a grateful husband might have offered a full-time wife in the 1950s: Emily slips Jeannie an extra fifty now and again; Dan brings her flowers for no reason. Every year the Sorensons give her a plane ticket to wherever she'd like to go. The result is that Jeannie feels like her work with the children is fully appreciated in a way that it might not be if she were, in truth, a housewife.

"Dan and Em are so nice," Jeannie says. "But I look at it as, if I were staying home, this is what I'd do." She gestures around Starbucks. "I'd have my dog with me, I'd go to the gym every day. Dan and Emily are flexible with all that because they know I work long hours, from eight until six. And they back me up on discipline too. The last people I nannied for couldn't believe that their children would do something wrong."

Lucy and Chris finish their cookie, and Jeannie leans over to wipe their hands. With her blond hair and brown eyes, she could easily pass as their mother, and it surprises me to hear how rarely that mistake is made, particularly by actual moms. The uneasy détente between working and stay-at-home moms becomes more strained where nannies are concerned. During Chris's first year in preschool, Jeannie says, the other children's mothers pointedly ignored her when she dropped him off. "It's like they can sniff out that you're a nanny," she says. "It stopped bothering me after a while, but nothing has changed: Every day, all those women stand around, talking to each other before or after school, and I'm by myself. It's like they think you're evil for helping out." Or, perhaps Jeannie is a proxy for a disapproval that would never be expressed so overtly toward the working mothers themselves.

Jeannie takes a sip of her coffee. The truth is, in some ways she's more sympathetic to those preschool moms than she is to Emily. "Having raised this one from infancy, I have very strong opinions about staying home through the preschool years," she explains, glancing over at Lucy, who has wriggled to the floor. "I couldn't sever that bond every day to go to work and then reattach at night. But, people make different decisions. I guess you don't realize the consequences until they're older, and you hope that they're not too devastating."

We contemplate Lucy and Chris, who are now greeting everyone who walks in the door. "Em has told me so many times that she couldn't stay home," Jeannie continues. "And I think it would drive her nuts. So, if she knows that about herself and she can admit it, maybe the kids are better off with someone who can be patient with them through the day. But if she told me tomorrow that she'd decided to stay home, I wouldn't think about losing my job. I'd be so excited. Because no matter how much attention I can give these kids, it's not the same. I'll never be their mom." Jeannie laughs. "You can tell I have a lot of opinions about this. But that's all they are—opinions."

Jeannie's opinions, though, are the ones that persist in the culture, even among working moms themselves. Fewer than one third of women in a 1997 survey believed that two full-time working parents could raise children as well as if the mother stayed home or worked part-time.[7] As psychologist Rosalind Barnett has pointed out, the idea that mothers provide the best care for their children just *feels* right; the fact that a raft of studies have proven that high-quality day care is just as good seems as counterintuitive as looking at the horizon and concluding that the earth is round.[8] Yet, over the last twenty years, researchers have found no difference in social, emotional, or intellectual development among children in day care and those raised at home, even when they were placed in other-care as young as six months; the key to a healthy bond appears to be a mother's sensitivity to her child, the quality of their relationship, not whether or not she works.[9] What's more, children of working mothers don't differ on whether they feel they have too little time with mom from children whose mothers stay home; in fact, children in both camps are more likely to feel they have too little time with their *dads*.[10] Meanwhile, working mothers—regardless of whether they are pink-collar or professionals—are consistently found to be in better physical and emotional health than those who are not employed.[11] Even so, the allure of the Good Mother in the popular imagination, the belief that, as Anne Roiphe has written, Mommy should be the one to do it (whatever "it" is)[12] makes it difficult to believe that a child could be happy on someone else's watch, or that children might gain rather than lose with every loving adult who enters their lives.

Halving It All

At 5:45 Dan Sorenson comes in the door, fifteen minutes late: Emily is caught somewhere in rush hour traffic and Jeannie is in a hurry to get home. Lucy and Chris are playing with puzzles in front of a Disney video in the den; Tim is upstairs reading. "Yay!" Lucy and Chris yell when they see their father. Jeannie flips off the TV and hustles into her coat. "Daddy, let's wrestle!" Lucy says, flinging herself at Dan. He laughs and hoists her in the air. When he does, his shirtsleeve slips down to reveal an odd-looking bead-and-leather thong he fashioned to keep a trio of yarn friendship bracelets the kids made him from disintegrating.

"What did you do in school today, Chris?" he asks. Chris dashes out to get his Thanksgiving art project: a coloring-book turkey glued to a Popsicle stick. Meanwhile, Lucy darts in circles around and through Dan's legs. "Are you guys hungry?" Dan says. "What should we have for dinner?"

Dan turns the video back on despite a house prohibition against TV at night and goes into the kitchen. He pulls a Tombstone pizza out of the freezer and rummages around in the fridge for milk, baby carrots, and a couple of apples.

A few minutes later Emily walks in, yawning, looking beat. "I have a conference call at six," she says. She hugs Lucy with one arm—the boys yell, "Hi, Mom," from the other room—grabs the cordless with her other hand, and says over her shoulder to Dan, "Two things for you to think about: Christmas pictures, and that we can't get into the two restaurants we talked about for Saturday night, so we need to think of another one."

"How about Morton's?" Dan says.

"I'll try it," she says.

"I put in a pizza," Dan says as Emily leaves the room, phone in tow. She nods without looking back.

This isn't exactly the scene Dan imagined would greet him when Emily first told him she was pregnant with Tim. If Brian Pollack envisioned a postfeminist, egalitarian split of family responsibilities—or even believed he might stay home himself—Dan, initially, would have preferred the opposite. "I remember him saying, 'Are you sure you want to work?' Because he really didn't want me to," Emily told me. "He felt strongly that the kids would be better off not being in day care."

Every couple reaches certain moments of truth in their attempts to structure their work and family lives, moments that force them to reevaluate their most deeply held assumptions. Emily and Dan's first one came just four weeks before Tim was born, when Dan was laid off from his hospital administration job. Although his severance package could keep them afloat for several months, Emily's was the only certain income they had; even if they had wanted to, which she did not, it didn't seem like the right time to take on traditional roles.

For Dan, losing his job was a shock, particularly when he was about to become a father—a provider—and the experience has permanently affected his sense of professional security. Yet, whenever he or Emily brings up that time, they speak of it, perversely, as a stroke of luck. As it turned out, the layoff gave Dan something he'd never expected or even knew he wanted—a de facto paternity leave, one that, unlike Brian Pollack's, was by chance rather than design. He and Emily spent the first three months of Tim's life at home together, and Dan was alone with the baby for an additional month after Emily returned to work. He's quick to say that he would have loved Tim just as much regardless, but being home during his son's infancy gave him an expertise that he might not have otherwise gained. It was like an inoculation against the "tipping" toward the mother that generally occurs when she is home alone with a newborn: Her knowledge of the baby's schedule and responses give her more authority, which, along with the assumed superior knowledge of a Mother, relegates most men permanently to an assistant's role.[13]

"Having had that time, I obviously have a different relationship," Dan says as he slices the apples. He pauses, knife in midair, and starts again. "Well, I shouldn't say . . . Well, you do have a different relationship with each of your kids, but that time created some other possibilities. It was really—" He pauses again, then chooses the precise word that Brian Pollack had used to describe his experience with his daughter. "It was really *bonding*."

Even so, once Dan returned to work, Emily suspects she might have reflexively reclaimed most of the devil-in-the-details aspects of parenting, except that by the time Tim was a year old, she was on the road roughly half the month. Like other mothers I interviewed who traveled frequently, that forced her to let go of a great deal of mother management. It was simply physically impossible for her to be the one who cooked dinner, or gave Tim his bath, or left work early to take Chris to the doctor for his chronic ear infections. Maybe Dan didn't always perform those tasks quite the way Emily would have—the kids may, for instance, be more likely to eat pizza or McDonald's under his care than a meal prepared with the four basic food groups in mind—but he has done so much of what is still, really, considered mothering that both he and Emily insist they are interchangeable in their children's minds and hearts.

Several times during our interviews Emily described Dan as "more maternal" than she, which was unusual. Most women took great pains to tell me they were "mothers first," regardless of other roles. I wondered how those women would perceive Emily: Would they consider her less loving, unfeminine, selfish? Yet, if women want the equal partnerships they say they do, what choice is there but to allow—to *insist*—that men, too, become mothers, in the process loosening our own grip on that defining role? Perhaps, in order to balance the scales, it's sometimes necessary to tip them in the other direction.

EARLIER THAT AFTERNOON I had visited Dan at work, in a newly constructed office park about ten minutes from the Sorensons' home. He oversees a team of former nurses and paraprofessionals, nearly all women, at a company that provides managed health care for self-insured corporations; company-wide, three quarters of the one thousand employees are women. The CEO is a woman too, a working mother who once, when she mentioned during a party that she'd need to talk with Dan over the weekend, turned to *Emily* and asked, "Would nine o'clock Sunday be okay?"

Dan's is a more casual, communal workplace than Emily's, more conducive to the kind of flexibility parents of young children require. Just yesterday, for instance, he popped out in the middle of the afternoon to take Tim to a birthday party. The relaxed corporate culture evolved, in a large part, to suit the needs of its mostly female employees, but the truth is that couples who share household responsibility most equally are those in which the salaries are similar and the *husband* has a flexible job. Once again, that serves as a corrective to the tendency of moms to automatically do it all.[14]

Operating in a world of women, Dan says, a man becomes sensitized to certain things. He notices that more of his employees' husbands pull their weight at home than once did (and he's right—the time fathers spend on chores has increased by an hour a day over the last two decades).[15] But, he adds, most still don't (he's right about that too).[16] More troubling is how some of the women—people he describes as smart, capable, and assertive—transform when they're around their mates. "These are women who do incredible things at work," Dan says, sitting beneath a sailboat mobile in his office, "and they change completely in a social setting with their husbands. They become more passive. It's interesting to see but irritates me that they're not given the respect or credit that's due to them in their own households."

Emily has told me that some of her girlfriends say their spouses should take husband lessons from Dan; one's husband told her, presumably in jest, that she should stop talking to Emily entirely. But that just embarrasses Dan. He doesn't see himself as an avatar of social change; he's not even sure how he came to value equality so highly. "Maybe I'm hard-wired this way," he says, laughing. Or maybe it is, at least in part, because of two moments of truth he observed growing up. When Dan was six, his mother lost her right arm to cancer; for some time, until she learned to cope with her left arm, his dad did basic household chores and cared for Dan and his sister. A few years later, when Dan was in junior high, his father had his own health problems which kept him out of work for a year, so his mother went to work to support them. "I guess I saw that meeting the needs of a family wasn't about gender roles," he says. "They managed it all between the two of them and they got along fine. We all got along fine."

Dan laughs again when I ask him what initially attracted him to Emily. "I don't know," he says, leaning back in his chair, lacing his fingers behind his head. "Just the essence of who she is, I suppose. We had a good rapport from the beginning. I guess it was also probably her dedication, being driven and working hard yet being balanced. It felt very compatible to me. It felt very . . . equal." Equal is a word Dan returns to again and again when discussing his marriage, along with phrases like "balanced partnership" and "joint venture." He recognizes the advantage of sharing responsibilities on the home front but has been surprised by the benefits of sharing the provider role. He may have been willing to do it—even expected to do it—but it's been reassuring to know that he isn't his family's sole support. "I would feel more pressure in that situation," he says. "Now, if one of us were to be laid off, there isn't anything that changes tomorrow, next week, or probably in the course of a year. By establishing a financial base, the whole family feels more secure. And since we contribute equally to the expenses, should that stop—if one of us decides to try something new, or to stop working for a while—I think it would be an easier transition because we know that balance has been there."

Then I Get Up
and Do It All Again

By seven o'clock dinner is over. Emily takes Lucy to the sink and washes her hands.

"What did you do today?" she asks.

"Played puzzles," Lucy says, "saw a video, drawed, read books."

"Did you take a nap?"

"Yes."

The children go into the den to play balloon volleyball and Dan heads upstairs to work. Emily clears the table, puts the dishes in the dishwasher, and wipes down the counters. "This was an okay night," she says. "Sometimes I come home and they're starving and they're jumping all over you. I don't even change my clothes, I just try to get dinner started and get something in front of them so they're not nuts. On those days it feels like your only downtime is in the car. You find yourself wishing your commute were longer, which is frightening."

Dan comes back in with Lucy. "Hon," Emily says to him, "do you want to do baths?"

"Why?" Dan asks.

"I think they could all use one." She takes Lucy and gives her a hug. "We're going to take a bath," she tells her. "What does that mean?"

"No fussin' and no cryin'!" Lucy says gleefully. "And no pooping in the bathtub!"

Emily laughs. "That's right! *Especially* no pooping in the bathtub."

At 7:50 Emily and Dan have shampooed three heads and rubbed them dry, cleaned three sets of ears, wrapped three bodies in towels. By 8:45 they've each made the rounds of the bedrooms, reading books, singing songs, and turning out the lights. Emily yawns and ambles into the kitchen, bleary-eyed, for some Oreos and milk. "What do I do with the rest of my evening?" she says, making a sweeping gesture with her hand. "With all this time I have left? I call my mom or my sisters. I get into my pjs. I gather my reading material and I get into bed. At ten o'clock I go to sleep and get up and do it all again." Her eyelids droop, and she wills them back open. My questions are making her day even longer; tomorrow she'll pay with exhaustion. "It's *endless*. And, you know, my life isn't unusual. Maybe some people don't work quite as much as I do, and maybe they don't have the money for a nanny, but seventy percent of mothers work, and for us, this is the way life is."

Time, Emily says, has been the biggest trade-off in the balance she's struck between family life and work. Time alone, time with Dan, time with friends, and, particularly, time with the children. "I need another hour or two with them every day," she admits. "I would like to be home when they come home from school, to find out how their day went. We do that in the evening, we go through what they did that day and what friends they played with. Tim's teacher provides us with the schedule of what they're doing, so we can ask specific questions. But he comes home pretty enthusiastic and I would like to catch him right then." Emily sighs, munching on her cookie. "It makes six o'clock to eight o'clock more stressful because you're trying to cram everything into those couple of hours: eating dinner, cleaning up, doing their schoolwork, finding the time to have *fun* with them. It's hard to do. You can't do it. That's what causes most of the stress, not having enough time to do everything. It makes the weekend very intense, every second."

That time crunch, Emily says, is the only thing that sometimes makes her feel like the dreaded Bad Mother. It doesn't help that the world of children continues to be run as if women don't work, or can drop whatever they're doing at a moment's notice. In Emily's suburb, for instance, PTA meetings are held at three o'clock; class performances at Tim's school tend to be in the middle of the day rather than at the beginning; even tomorrow, Chris's preschool is having a Thanksgiving party at eleven A.M., which the parents are invited to attend. "There's no way you can be there at eleven if you work," Emily says, disgusted. "Who can do that?"

Lucy and Tim seem content with the way things are, Emily says, but Chris, who, like her, is the middle child, gets a little lost in the shuffle. He's the one who sings out "see you on the weekend" when he leaves the room, or wants to know on Monday how long until the next "stay-at-home day," or wants one more kiss and hug before Emily and Dan leave in the morning. "Chris wants Mom and Dad home every day all day," Emily explains. "Part of it is timing: He's only twenty months older than Lucy. He's not old enough to do the things that Tim does, and he's not the baby. So, he gets a little bit gypped. He doesn't get as much one-on-one time as the other kids. Dan will compensate by consciously making time to be alone with him. He'll take him out to breakfast, or he'll come home from work and eat lunch with him. And for some reason Chris likes to go to the grocery store, so I take him with me when I go shopping on the weekend."

If time is so precious, I ask Emily, has she ever considered buying more of it by cutting back at work? She shakes her head. Working part-time, she fears, would be the worst of all possible worlds, marginalizing her at the office and skewing the balance at home. She may be right: Women who've reduced their work hours report lower job satisfaction and little letup of strain at home.[17] "If you work part-time, I think you'd end up doing *everything*," Emily says, "because, hey, you're home. And granted you have more of the time to do some of it, but then you end up with less time overall."

For the moment, Emily says, the life she and Dan have created works for them, but she's not sure how long that will continue. "This has always been an experiment," she says. "In the long term, I'll always work, but that's not to say that I wouldn't consider stopping for a year or two as part of figuring out something different to do." She shrugs. "It's not like you make this decision one time and you've made it for the rest of your life."

Great Job, Great Marriage,
Great Kids—Now What?

On a Saturday morning Emily sits in her kitchen, scowling at a Williams-Sonoma Thanksgiving menu planner that came free with a turkey roasting rack. It claims she should've ordered her turkey two weeks ago. "I'm already behind," she says dryly. "According to this, I'll be okay if I can order my turkey, plan the menu, make my shopping list, and shop for staples all by tomorrow." She rolls her eyes. "Oh," she says, brightening, "and buy essential kitchen tools." She waves her new purchase in the air triumphantly. "I've got my rack!"

As Emily flips through cookbooks, writing down the groceries she needs for the holiday dinner, I decide to try out a list of my own. The previous night I'd spoken to a friend, a working mother of two young boys, who told me that she didn't believe the Sorensons were for real. "You ask her who stays home when a child is sick," she said. "And who plans the kids' birthday parties? And who does the homework with them? You ask her that. Those are the things that really get you as a working mom."

With those words in mind I ask Emily who buys the children's clothes.

"We both do," Emily says, looking up from her list. "Dan will go to the Gap and buy all three of them sweat suits." She thinks a minute. "He probably wouldn't go out and buy Lucy a dress," she adds.

I press on. What about doctors' appointments? She shrugs and writes down "sweet potatoes." "Again, because I've traveled, we've had to split that."

Birthday parties? Emily nods. "Dan does that. He just organized a hockey party for Tim."

Buying presents for other kids' parties? "Fifty-fifty," she says.

Remembering school assignments and library books? "I do it more, but not much more."

Hiring sitters? "If he has a social event he's planning for us, it's his responsibility. He used to say, 'I don't want to call the twelve-year-old,' but he's gotten over that. I sometimes have to push him on that a little though.

"There *are* certain things Dan likes to 'let' me take care of," Emily admits, "like cooking dinner. If he knows I'm coming home before 6:30, he will wait even if he's home first. And the more you let that happen . . . It's just very easy to fall into. It's too easy with all those 'little' things to say 'I'll just do it myself' and then complain about it later on. I see a lot of mothers who work full-time whose husbands don't do anything except maybe yard work, and I think, 'Oh, gosh, how difficult.' But some of it is really their own fault. You have to establish those responsibilities." Emily closes her cookbook and caps her pen. "Like, for a while I felt like I was the one who had to make sure Tim read his book of the day and did his spelling words and whatnot. But I didn't want Dan to be the one who takes him out to play hockey and then I'm the one who does the homework. So, we had to have a discussion about that."

Their biggest ongoing vulnerability, Emily says, is that Dan tends to be the "fun" parent while she's the enforcer, a dynamic that was common among women I interviewed, whether or not they were employed outside the home. She's countered by setting limits on his volunteer activities: recently, for instance, he wanted to coach soccer for both Tim and Chris, as well as to help out on Tim's hockey team. Emily refused, saying it would send the family in different directions on the weekends and leave her to run all the errands and take care of Lucy. "You want to contribute to your community in some capacity, but your whole family ends up paying for it," she says. "We haven't really resolved it. But one thing we've done is, if he has to coach and I have to be somewhere, he has to figure out the childcare. I've dumped that back on him. And he does it. He doesn't assume that if he has something scheduled, I'm automatically there to take care of the other children."

Even with a vigilant mother, a willing father, a cleaning person, and a lawn service, though, the Sorensons haven't eliminated the drudgery gap. In addition to cooking dinner (which, as an avid chef, is a burden she enjoys more often than she resents) and shopping for groceries, Emily is also the one who picks up the house each night to keep them from being buried alive by an encroaching mound of action figures. "But that's partly my fault too," she says. "I just wish the clutter didn't bother me so much." Dan, meanwhile, does the typical guy things, like home repair and car maintenance. He also does the laundry for the two of them (Jeannie does the kids'), "but that's not exactly the same kind of chore," Emily concedes. "It's a weekend-long project: He puts in a load, runs an errand, comes back. You don't have to be here to do it."

The observation that men's household tasks can be done at their convenience while women's tend to be more repetitive and schedule bound was a common one among women I interviewed,[18] but it's Emily's tone that catches my attention. There is no frustration in her voice when she speaks about the imbalance, no resignation, no edge at all. Perhaps that's because, although she and Dan may not have achieved precise equality, the elusive fifty-fifty split, they have negotiated something that's awfully close: Call it equity.[19]

Emily glances up at the clock: Dan is out with Chris and Lucy, and she's late taking Tim to his cousin's birthday party, which is across town at something called a cyberbowling alley. She calls upstairs for Tim to hurry and get ready and makes him a quick sandwich for the road. The lanes turn out to be lower tech than one would suppose: The attraction seems to be Day-Glo pins illuminated with black lights. There are also enough other flashing lights, fuzzily amplified announcements, and general cacophony to give anyone over the age of ten an instant migraine. Emily settles Tim in, waves at her sister, and skedaddles.

Back in the car I bring up something she'd mentioned on the phone before I'd arrived in Chicago: a sense, not exactly that there's something missing in her life, but that there might be if she doesn't figure out another dimension to it soon. Emily nods, remembering. "We live in the house we probably will live in for a long time," she says, "and I've been in the same position at work for a while, and even though I don't have anything to complain about, I think, 'Well, is this it? Is this my life?' There's nothing wrong, but I don't know if it's enough for me. I feel the need to . . . I don't want to say make my mark, but accomplish something unique. And I think if I continue on the path I'm on, that won't happen."

I ask her what, exactly, she feels that she wants to achieve. "I think that I'd like to have more of a presence in my own community somehow, rather than just within this huge, global company," she responds. "Right now, I feel like I lead this somewhat invisible life, and while I've never been someone who wants to be in the limelight, I feel like I'm too anonymous. I'm so focused on me: *my* family, *my* career. That's what working full time and having children is like—it's all you can do to maintain. There's not time to worry about everybody around you except to throw money at them, and you want to do more than that. You go through that whole thing of 'What do you want it to say in your obituary,' and mine would be very boring right now: long-term employee in a consulting firm, mother of three."

It's not that she isn't happy, Emily insists; in fact, it may be her very satisfaction that allows her to start asking a series of new questions, questions that go beyond simply surviving as a modern working mother. It may be that Emily is starting to feel the tug of the next phase of a woman's life—involving deeper questions about community involvement and personal satisfaction. We drive along in silence for a moment, then Emily says, "Dan asks these kinds of questions too. If he had his druthers, I think he would be a high school hockey coach. I haven't told him he can't be one, but I guess he feels like he has his MBA and a great position in a nice company, so how can he walk away? In some ways he's working through it the way women do: He's got all these parts of his life—his coaching, his spiritual needs, his family, and his work—and he's trying to get a balance among them." Emily falls silent again, then adds, "We're both trying to get a balance together."

Part III

Reconsiderations

Chapter 10

The Face in the Mirror

A FEW WEEKS AFTER my final conversation with Emily, at a sushi bar in Berkeley, California, I ask Nancy Roland, forty-five, to do a little reflecting on her own reflection. Nancy, a journalist and mother of two teenagers, is slim and muscular, in enviable shape: She runs regularly, skis, plays soccer. She has shaggy brown hair and blue eyes fringed with dark lashes. Like many of the women I've interviewed, she looks younger than her age, or at least younger than women in their forties used to look. Still, she says, lately she finds herself wincing when she looks in the mirror. "You think it's going to be great to be liberated from the tyranny of the 'beauty myth' and all of that, but it sucks," she confides. "You wish it could feel liberating, you want to want that desperately, but the fact is, it's overridden, and you don't want that. You want to still have 'it.' And instead you feel"—she searches for the right word, settling on the one I'll hear repeatedly—"you just feel *invisible*."

Most of the women I spoke with expressed dismay over the excessive value placed on women's appearance, especially about its damaging impact on young girls. But that didn't mean that some of them hadn't profited by their beauty, hadn't from time to time reveled in it. Now they felt a kind of cultural power slipping away. More than that: From puberty onward, they'd unconsciously learned to see themselves as others see them, to filter their own vision through the male gaze. If men no longer looked, would the women still be seen?

"The writer Annie Proulx talks about how, as a woman in her fifties, she loves going into a restaurant and not even being noticed," says a forty-one-year-old English professor in Seattle. "But that scares me. I've put a lot of things in place over the last few years, but not that piece: not what it will be like to be invisible."

Although they felt newly "invisible" on the outside, in individual and group interviews women also described something just the opposite: an internal drive to become *more* visible, if not to others, then to themselves. Even as they mourned a lost source of conventional feminine power, they seemed compelled, as they reached their forties, toward something deeper: an authentic personal voice. In some ways, the two issues—voice and appearance—were entwined. The changing terrain of their faces reminded them that life was finite. Although most of the women I spoke with, surely, would be around for another forty years, they felt newly conscious of time's passage, a sudden nagging sense, however illusory, of last chances. That was often reinforced by the recognition that their children were growing up, or that their fertility was on the wane, or by their first brushes with mortality: the death of a parent or the diagnosis of illness. It was all part of the transition, noted by psychologist Bernice Neugarten, from viewing life as the time since birth to measuring it by how much is left to live.[1]

"I feel this sense of urgency to figure things out," explains a stay-at-home mother of two teenagers in Portland. "You see that your parents are aging, and your siblings are aging, and your body is aging, and you realize there are limitations. You can't postpone things anymore."

Like Emily Sorenson, women told me that they wanted an intangible "something more" out of their lives. After being whipsawed by the contradictory imperatives of the Crunch years, they felt a push to recalculate priorities, to reckon with the consequences of their choices, to examine potential left unfulfilled, and reconsider what would bring a fuller sense of satisfaction. Working mothers spoke of wanting something beyond their jobs and family lives; women who'd stayed home saw that role coming to an end and wondered what would come next; women who didn't have children considered the option one last time; marriages were thrown into question; a new sense of responsibility to community emerged.

Women's central question during this "middlescence" becomes "What do I want now for *myself*?"[2] For some, who have been grappling most intensely with the silence of the Perfect Wife and the Good Mother, it is the first time in decades they have even ventured to ask. Depending on earlier choices they'd made or defaulted into, on paths pursued or abandoned, on how they'd addressed their needs for connection and autonomy, on how they'd construed feminine identity, the answers—their very ability to seek an answer—vary tremendously.

Having It All: Now What?

One winter evening in Minneapolis I share dinner with a group of friends who (tongue planted firmly in cheek) call themselves the Sob Sisters. They are all in their forties: "Anyone younger," says Kim

Beaulieu, a senior management consultant whose den we're in, "just wouldn't understand." Kim, forty-five, is tall and slender with short, spiky blond hair. She has two children: a teenager from her first marriage and a five-year-old from her second. Linda, who sits on the couch across from her, is an accountant, married, and the mother of a two-year-old boy. There's also Joni, who came straight from her job as marketing director of a medical supplies company and is still wearing her maroon suit and pumps; she's married with a five-year-old. And Eva and Renee, both self-employed as graphic designers. Eva, who is single and childless, is a lanky woman with a casual, sporty style. Renee wears a black shirt and black jeans, her blond hair cropped short. She wed her business partner at forty, and, three years ago, they had a son.

I've been trying to engage them in a discussion about work, but, for the third time in an hour, the conversation has strayed. I'm a bit exasperated as I steer them back on track; for their part, Kim and her friends seem disappointed with me, a little impatient. This is one of their precious evenings together: They want to talk about marriage, about motherhood, about *shoes*, for goodness' sake, about nearly anything but what they do from eight to five each day. "It's what we do, it's where we spend our time, and it's how we make money," Linda says. "But there are more interesting things."

Kim nods. "By your mid-forties you're supposed to have attained a certain level professionally, and most of us actually have," she says. "But it's just . . ." She shrugs. "So what? What are you going to do? Buy more things? Make more money?"

"I know for me it's a question of 'Am I really doing what I should be doing?' " adds Linda. " 'Is this really it? This profession? This career?' And I'm just not sure of the answer."

I'd asked to meet with these women specifically because, by the standard measures of title and salary, they were all professionally successful; I was looking for insight into the ongoing role of work in women's lives, the evolving nature of power and ambition. When I'd brought up the subject in other groups, the discussion grew stilted, the participants less animated. I'd tried different approaches, asked different questions, conducted further interviews, but I felt like I was

trying to start a fire with damp wood. Questions of career and achievement just didn't drive women the way they once had. The voice of
ambition I'd heard in women like Mira Brodie and Abbey Green had
modulated from eager to conflicted to disinterested. What had happened? Some, like Linda, had reached a crossroads. That's not unusual: Women often go through a period of career reappraisal around
forty. While both sexes find work less satisfying by that point than
they presumed they would, women, as a group, find themselves more
dissatisfied than men—they often report feeling frustrated, empty, or
exhausted by the personal cost of success.[3] Women are, of course,
more likely to have faced obstacles in their careers than men, whether
overt discrimination or an accrual of "microinequities."[4] At the same
time, they are also more likely to have turned down opportunity, to
have based career choices on flexibility rather than their potential to
challenge. Neither is a recipe for career engagement.

Many of the women I interviewed, like Kim Beaulieu and her
friends, had excelled in their professions, although few had reached
the highest levels—few women still do. According to economist Claudia Goldin, just one in six of today's middle-aged, college-educated
women with children can claim career success when "success" is defined merely as earning more than the lowest twenty-five percent of
college-educated men.[5] By definition, three quarters of male college
graduates hit that mark.

Certainly the choices and pressures made around motherhood
explain part of that gap, as do its penalties: Female executives, for instance, who had taken as little as a combined 8.8 months off for their
maternity leaves were found to have permanently sacrificed career advancement and earning potential.[6] Meanwhile, Good Mother guilt has
expanded to accommodate the increasing numbers of school-aged children. Working mothers of kids that age make an average of five trips by
car a day—twice as many as working dads—increasing the strain both
at the office and at home, and giving rise to the moniker "chauffeur
mom."[7] And whereas women were once warned that the preschool
years were the critical time to be home, suddenly "anyone can comfort
a baby"; it's the teen years when motherly presence is most essential,

when women who have already taken on the role of family psychologist as part of mother management feel renewed pressure to be home, waiting patiently for the moment a child decides to communicate with them.[8]

Still, motherhood accounted for only half the differential Goldin found in women's success rates. The focus on family responsibilities can actually obscure other, deeply embedded forms of discrimination. After twenty years in the workforce, whether or not they have children, most women have taken their share of lumps from bonking against multiple glass ceilings, not to mention slamming into the brick walls of bias. Female executives cite male stereotyping, old-boy networks, dead-end jobs, and pay inequity as greater obstacles to their success than motherhood—and they don't believe that it's just "a matter of time" before things change.[9]

In Silicon Valley, for instance, a place with young, less traditional companies, organizational behaviorist Joanne Martin found that high-ranking women's departure from their jobs often had relatively little to do with the pull to be with or have children, although that's what the companies tended to believe. "When you really talk to them, though, that's not why they quit," Martin told me. "They quit because the environment was punishing."[10] Confirming the suspicions of the younger women I interviewed, Martin's subjects felt isolated, both from men—who built pivotal, informal ties over drinks, golf, even chatting in the men's room—and from other women, who were scarce at their elite levels. They had often become uncomfortable with the excess of competition in their companies, with an excess of what Martin calls "anger expression." Many had been sexually harassed. Few had been adequately mentored. "Being a successful woman means going to work every day in an atmosphere that often excludes you," Martin told me. "The costs are simply higher than for men." Leaving, she added, became a matter of reclaiming personal authenticity for her subjects, as individuals and as women. "They say, 'I can't be a collaborative, open person in this environment,'" Martin said. "And 'I can't express doubt because that's seen as weak.'"

Perhaps it's not surprising, then, that for many women at midlife, the measures of success become more internally determined. One study of female physicians found that they became less concerned with outside validation as they entered their forties.[11] The authors hypothesized that the shift was a coping mechanism, a response to marginalization—sort of like deciding you don't want to be a member of a club that doesn't want you. And, doubtless, that's partially true. But it could also signal strengthened self-esteem, a liberation from the feminine compulsion to please: Rather than withdrawal, it could be read as a move toward true self-acceptance, toward establishing goals based on a woman's own desires instead of on others' expectations.[12] As anthropologist Mary Catherine Bateson has written, "A pattern chosen by default can become a path of preference."[13] In a world of mixed messages and double binds, where the promise that "you can do anything" comes with some nasty fine print, part of grappling with "what I want now for myself" may finally be deciding what constitutes an advance and what is a retreat.

One winter afternoon in Portland I sit in a café with educational consultant Debbie Frieze. Debbie, forty-one, is a tall, rangy woman with shoulder-length blond hair and expressive blue eyes. She has two daughters and, for much of her nineteen-year marriage, was her family's primary wage earner. In her twenties Debbie pursued her career goals single-mindedly (she aspired to become a college president). Today, she says, while she loves her work and feels privileged to have a role in shaping the country's educational system, but "my sense of ambition is very different than it was," she says. "Now I feel like the quality of my life is more important than my achievements. And 'quality of life' is that ambiguous thing that includes your relationships with people. It's also an ability to find outlets for creativity, whether it's music or writing: It's having wider margins in your life than you're able to have when you're really on a professional track. So career goals have become much a smaller piece of the pie of my life than they once were."

The questions women were asking about status, power, and ambition may have their roots in constraint, but they're still a valid critique of the way the work world operates. The limitations they faced in the workplace led them to consider a more expansive model of success, one that ultimately may be healthier for men too. Although women's desires to "balance" their lives gets more attention, men express similar needs, which grow more intense as they age.[14]

That's not to say that the women don't seek or enjoy power—they do. But by midlife most of the women I spoke with defined it differently than men, in a way that was more conventionally feminine: They were less comfortable with establishing dominance, more focused on influence and personal autonomy. As Kim Beaulieu says, "Oh, I want power. I like power. I want to be the one telling people what to do rather than being told. I want to be a decision maker. Not that I have to be at the *top* top, but I like to be in control of my work." The equation of power with self-determination, along with the barriers to advancement women still face, helps explain the much-touted recent boom in female entrepreneurs.[15] "I didn't want to work under someone," says Renee in Minneapolis, who owns her own graphic design company. "I have the personality that as soon as someone tells me what to do, I just start boiling. I need to be the decision maker."

Interestingly a decade's worth of research on women in leadership shows that women are actually more likely than men to express strong needs for power.[16] Despite that, I often found myself arguing with women, pushing them to acknowledge their own status. They would squirm, sometimes even admitting they felt that acquiring power was vaguely unfeminine—unless it was being used for "the greater good" of a company or society.[17] Women were equally conflicted about power in others, often subtly keeping one another in check. When Joni in Minneapolis begins to introduce herself, for instance, one of her friends interrupts her. "She has a big-deal job," she jokes.

"A *real* job," adds another.

Joni blushes and waves a hand dismissively. "Oh, come on," she says. It was all in good fun, but I wondered: Why the teasing and the denial? I was reminded of something that Peggy McIntosh, associate director of the Center for Research on Women at Wellesley

College, once told me. She'd been on a panel with several other accomplished academics and noticed that to a woman, each had begun her remarks with an apology or a self-deprecating comment—something that distanced her from her own expertise, that assured the audience she was not, essentially, too big for her britches. I realized I did that myself when I spoke publicly. As a woman, I'd been uneasy with my own authority, more afraid of being perceived as arrogant than unknowledgeable.

If ambition no longer motivated women, though, what did? Having found work that was both challenging and well compensated, Kim and her friends in Minneapolis felt freed to ask a deeper level of questions about satisfaction and meaning. As it turned out, that was leading them back to traditionally feminine avenues of sustenance: community involvement, personal growth, and spirituality. When they spoke of role models, rather than pointing to women who had "made it" by standard measures, they chose women who were personally fulfilled, who had succeeded in becoming truly self-defined, even if they'd done it on the most conventional of terms. "My mom was an at-home mom, and she really immersed herself in the community," says Eva. "She started a handicapped swim club, and she'd bring these kids over to the house for dinner. She was amazing. I feel like her obituary will be really great. And mine won't be." The other women in the room start to protest, but I'm intrigued. Eva, like Emily Sorenson, seems troubled by her own legacy: Each mentioned that her obituary wouldn't make good copy. "I'm not saying it won't be," Eva continues, backpedaling, "but I'm starting to think I would like to do more of that kind of stuff. That means more to me than 'She had this career.' I mean, I love my life, but I think I would like to define it more in a giving way, giving back to the community."

"Well, we've been defining ambition only in the workplace," says Kim, "and I think it's equally ambitious to give up work at this point to take on something you personally care about."

Suddenly the discussion springs to life. "I've always wanted to be a teacher," Renee says enthusiastically. "The ultimate would be to have my company up and running, teach a couple of days a week, and also set up an art studio at home. Then I'd have time for myself, time for my child, and time to give back to the community.

"I recently met a woman who is sixty-seven," she continues. "She just got a computer and she taught herself how to design Web pages. And she got a job doing that. She redesigned her life at sixty-seven. That's something, to keep growing and learning your whole life. And she goes to Mexico and does these yoga retreats. That's something that we might want to do now as opposed to just working harder."

In her study of women in business, anthropologist Patricia McBroom found that the most satisfied women had gone through a cycle: They had rejected traditional femininity in the workplace and tried to play by the rules as defined by men; that was followed by a period of uncertainty about who they were and what they wanted; finally they integrated a new, stronger definition of femininity into both the workplace and the home.[18] Kim and her friends had gone through a similar evolution: They had started on conventional career tracks and found them alienating; then they became self-employed or joined companies where the work environment was compatible with their values. Now their vision of success was expanding to include elements that were both traditional and restorative. For Eva, that has meant joining the board of a battered women's shelter. For Kim, it has meant becoming a leader in her church. For some women I met, it meant leaving their jobs entirely to spend time with their families, pursue personal passions, or find a career that felt more meaningful to them. For Renee, whose identity had been grounded in individuality and professional accomplishment, it meant taking her last opportunity to have a child.

Sometimes I found myself wishing that the women I interviewed had pushed just a little harder in male-defined domains. Their efforts would have made the path much easier for those coming after. Considering the trade-offs and obstacles they face though, why should women turn themselves into sacrificial lambs, with less balance and less joy in their own lives so their successors can have more? So few women actually break through the glass ceiling that every move made by those who do becomes freighted with significance. How else to explain the exaggerated response in 1997 when Brenda Barnes, one of the country's highest-ranking female executives, quit her job at PepsiCo to "spend more time with her family."[19] She was accused of betraying working women, held up as gleeful proof that women "can't have it all." Perhaps that's true—especially if "all" means having a demanding job while living up to the ideal of the Perfect Mother. Or perhaps, like the disaffected Silicon Valley executives, she was ground down by a male-defined workplace and used motherhood as a politic exit line (recall that when former Secretary of Labor Robert Reich quit the Clinton Cabinet, he, too, diplomatically claimed it was to spend more time with his family, and no one crowed that men "can't have it all"). Or maybe, having climbed the peaks of power and surveyed the view, she felt she'd earned the right to make a purely personal decision—one that wasn't meant to be a commentary on other women—about how she wanted to live.

Hitting "the Void" and Getting the "Er" Back

"Last week I was walking in the park, and I saw a couple of groups of young women with kids, just hanging out," writes Janet, forty-one. "And I remembered how deliriously wonderful that time was." My acquaintance with Janet has been made possible through modern technology. She is a friend of a friend whom I met only twice, briefly, but we'd struck up a sporadic e-mail correspondence about the paths our lives have taken. Janet lives in upstate New York, where she tends to her two children and is what she calls a "shadow partner" in her husband's business. All through her twenties she was the assistant director of a nonprofit arts organization, "very career-driven," but by thirty she found that she didn't like the work. She had her first child, "not really wanting kids, but more like a change." To her surprise, stay-at-home motherhood agreed with her. "You had permission to spend the day lolling at the beach or hanging in the park," she writes. "A big deal was walking around, looking at dogs."

As the kids grew older, Janet found they needed more attention, not less: She became a soccer mom and a chauffeur mom, and before she knew it, a decade had passed. "I thought I'd gotten over that sense of need to have a legitimate 'er,' " she writes. "You know, 'I'm a danc*er*, writ*er*, doct*or*, lawy*er*'—and learned to enjoy the multidimensions of my life. But lately I find that old 'er' envy rearing its head." Yes, she says, her husband considers her an integral part of the business's success, but in the outside world the credit has largely gone to him. Once she mentioned how "we" wrote "his" book, then caught herself. "That's an oxymoron, isn't it?" she wrote. " 'We' writing 'his' book."

For women whose identity is grounded in their significance to others, asking "What do I want now for *myself*?" can be particularly complex. If, when their children were small, they felt a kind of moral advantage over working mothers, a belief, deep down, that they were the ones who were "doing it right," now they were facing the consequences of tucking personal ambitions away. The difference between women I interviewed who'd stayed in the workforce and those who'd left was marked: The working mothers sometimes felt regret or guilt over missing small, irretrievable moments of their children's lives; often they pondered the meaning of success and power; but self-worth was not at issue. In fact, they often felt like excellent role models, especially for their daughters. Among women who'd devoted themselves to family, poor self-image was chronic. In part, that's because the culture still devalues those who care for children, who can't quantify their contribution with a paycheck. But it's also an inherent risk in following the Good-Mother mandate. Their task now, according to psychologist Ravenna Helson, who is conducting a long-term study of women college graduates, is to "accord [their] own interests as much respect as those of others."[20] Determining one's self-interest, though, particularly when you've fallen out of practice, can be quite a challenge. By midlife it can feel like separate ambitions never existed.

One morning in Portland I meet two stay-at-home moms for

coffee. Amy, forty-two, has two girls, ten and eight. She wears a fleece pullover and leggings, and her brown hair is pulled into a ponytail; she gazes intently through gold-rimmed glasses perched low on her nose. Elaine, forty-five, who has two teenagers, is a little wry and fiercely intellectual with straight dark hair that hangs past her jaw. A former teacher herself, she's been deeply involved in her children's schools. Both women are now facing what Elaine calls "the big void."

"When my kids were very young, I gave up on the whole thing of a career being a huge issue," Amy begins. "I was completely, one hundred percent, satisfied being a great mom."

Elaine raises an eyebrow. "There was a time when motherhood was enough for you?" she asks.

"Absolutely," Amy says. "I felt privileged to be able to stay home with them. But now my kids are growing up. I still could do it: I could be home and be an incredible cook and drive them everywhere and meet everyone's expectations. I think it's almost a higher level of person who can say, 'This is totally fulfilling to me.' " She shakes her head. "I wish I could."

"Well, I never felt motherhood was enough," Elaine declares. "Being the support system for a family is just not terribly rewarding in the long term."

I ask Elaine why she did it, then. "You feel like it's what you need to do," she answers, "and it makes you feel good. I didn't want to put myself in a position where I'd place the family second. Family is first to me. But then, when you put yourself second so long, or third, or fourth, or fifth . . ." She sighs.

Amy nods. "That's well put," she says. "Family is first. But family grows up, and now I want to do something else. And that's okay as long as it doesn't cause a huge stress on the family. That's something that I'm always bouncing between."

"Your needs and your family's needs?" I ask.

"My family's needs *are* my needs," Amy says.

Women who "mommy-tracked" their careers express similar conflict: a confusion, as psychologist Terri Apter put it, over the high cost of something they believed was good and valuable.[21] "I really feel like I've missed the boat now that my daughter is older," says Lydia Chang, forty-six, whom I meet among a group of women in Los Angeles whose children attend the same school. "I look at other women my age and how they've grown in their careers. I don't really have a career and I feel crummy about that. I know I'm a good mother and it was no sacrifice to give up a very time-consuming job in order to stay home and bake cookies with my children. And I really worked hard to foster freelance work so I *could* be home. But now I don't have that satisfaction level with my work, and I certainly don't have the financial security. And I feel like, 'Wait a minute, what am I doing?' "

The traditional mothers' anguish may have been more acute than that of most of the working women I interviewed, but they raised similar protests about the conventional definition of success. They, too, questioned whether income ought to be the sole measure of a person's worth, whether professional achievement brings personal satisfaction. Some looked to athletics or artistic expression for a renewed sense of identity. Others turned to volunteer work. Jackie, forty-four, a stay-at-home mother of three in Portland, told me that by the time her youngest was in school she had "lost the ability to relate to adults." After going through treatment for breast cancer four years ago though, she found her niche in the broader world: developing a volunteer program at a local hospital that matches newly diagnosed women with "navigators" who guide them through the thicket of medical options. "I feel like I've found what I was meant to do," she says, "and it helps me as well as helping them. It's a wonderful, empowering thing." Recently Jackie was asked to offer the patient's perspective at a statewide medical conference. "Public speaking is one of my greatest fears," she says. "But every time I do it, I grow a little, and that makes me feel better about myself."

Jackie's success underscores the potential of community involvement, but it also has its complexities: While women's volunteering is important and has been both training ground and springboard for leadership, it is, like stay-at-home motherhood, unpaid and, consequently, largely undervalued. That may be why, although volunteering raises women's self-esteem at midlife, paid employment tends to lift it higher, even if it's just a "job job" rather than a career.[22] More im-

portant, without retirement funds of her own, a woman becomes economically vulnerable in the second half of life. Nearly half of women
sixty-five and over are widowed, and when a husband dies, most of his
pension goes with him. Should he need nursing care, Medicaid won't
kick in until the couple has virtually exhausted their savings.[23] That's
why a full eighty percent of widows now living in poverty were not
poor before their husbands died.[24] "It's a well-kept secret," says psychologist Laura Carstensen, who studies aging. "Women who did
everything right—women who married affluent men, who raised their
kids, who saved and invested, can lose it all."[25] The women I spoke
with had differed over the need for continued financial independence
once they had children, with those who stayed home or reduced their
commitment to the workforce, minimizing its importance. As part of
asking "what do I want now for myself," Carstensen's scenario may
provide compelling reasons to revisit that issue.

Women who plan to stay home, even for a short time, ought to
consider how to remain professionally viable, what they need to do
to keep up their skills or develop new ones. Before having her girls,
Rhonda, forty-three, one of the mothers gathered in Los Angeles,
hated her job as a nurse. By the time her oldest was in first grade, however, she realized she'd better settle on another career. "There was this
mother who was up at the school all the time," she says. "I remember
looking at her and thinking, 'What is she going to do when her child
doesn't need her anymore?' And then I thought, 'My God, that's going
to be me!'" Rhonda decided to go back to school for a degree in accounting. "I just took baby steps," she explains. She worked around
her children's schedule, taking one or two classes at a time until she
got her CPA credential. Now she's a financial consultant specializing in
health care. "I didn't see myself as someone who could get out there
and succeed," she says, "But I've proved to myself that I could."

Rhonda's use of the phrase "baby steps" struck me: I'd heard it
several times before from women who were reentering the workforce.
It seemed an interesting choice, particularly for those who were in the
process of watching their own children become less needy, first tod-
dling, now racing toward independence. They, too, were trying to catch
their balance, taking tenuous steps away from the demands and the

comfort of being needed. Rhonda says her new self-sufficiency has even enriched her marriage, bridging some of the gap that can develop during the Near-Peer slide. "I understand the pressures he's under better than I did," she says of her lawyer husband, "and it's helped him to understand me more when I've been on a deadline and he's had to be the one to run to the kids' activities. Or to not be able to get there and to have to explain to them why."

Rhonda got her "er" back. Some of the other women I met doubtless will as well. Renee's role model—the sixty-seven-year-old in Minneapolis who had reinvented herself as a Web page designer and yoga devotee—may have even more resonance for this group. Of course, not all of them had prepared as diligently as Rhonda. Some weren't even sure how to begin. One woman told me, ruefully, that she was waiting "for an idea to drop out of the sky." And another explains, "I'm seeing that these years are ticking by, and the choices I might make could take education. That takes time. I don't want to reenter the workforce at fifty-five. As it is, I may reenter at forty-eight." She shakes her head. "There's real limitations."

The Good Wife at Midlife

"The urge to merge, the desire to be joined, is so powerful when you're young," says Debbie Frieze, the education consultant in Oregon. "It's stronger than the urge to be fully yourself. But once you are joined, the urge to be fully yourself obsesses you." Debbie and I are driving along a two-lane highway in her Jeep Cherokee, on our way to her house for dinner with her book club, the heat blasting to keep us warm on a rainy winter evening. She is explaining how she'd followed the lure of the Perfect Wife, and how, recently, that's begun to change. "The metaphor I always use is that the day I got married was the day I stopped playing the cello," she says. "I didn't play again until I turned *forty*." She turns from the road for a moment and looks at me, her blue eyes wide, incredulous that she so easily discarded something she'd loved so much. "So," she continues, "that's my metaphor for voice: I got the music back."

At the transition to midlife, psychologist Terri Apter found that women typically reevaluated their marriages, wanting more equality, more mutuality, both in practical matters and issues of intimacy.[26] They wondered why they had been willing to dismiss their feelings in small (and sometimes not so small) ways; they reckoned with the degree to which they'd compromised in marriage, ways that were inauthentic to themselves. As they awoke from the slumber of the Perfect Wife, they felt compelled to shift the power dynamics, sometimes subtly, sometimes quite radically. For several of the women I spoke with, that meant pushing marriages, even reasonably good ones, to the brink.

"I think most people would've thought we had a very good marriage, but there were certain things missing for me," says Judy Winkler, forty-six. Judy is among a group of running buddies I meet in a Virginia college town; two of the others are married for the second time; a third is divorced. A former schoolteacher turned journalist, Judy is a diminutive woman dressed in overalls and a turtleneck, with reddish-brown hair that she's in the midst of growing out. Earlier, she mentioned that since turning forty her goal has been "to uncover who I really am, to rediscover it." Part of that process involved taking another look at her twenty-year marriage. About three years ago she made the decision to leave.

"I was no longer willing to repress the essence of who I was to try to preserve what I thought was the marriage," she explains. "I felt voiceless to a degree. It was nothing he consciously made happen; it was the synergy between us. So I thought, 'I'm going to take this leap and see what happens.' " The separation lasted for a year. "I fully expected that he would say, 'Okay, let me help you pack your things,' " Judy recalls. "But he decided he really wanted to work on it with me. I think it jolted us into being more aware, and that awareness is still there.

"But I never wanted not to be in it," she adds. "I loved him."

Back in Portland, driving down the highway with Debbie Frieze, she, too, remembers how, after sixteen years of marriage she separated from her husband for eighteen months. Several years earlier they had moved to North Carolina, which Debbie had resented but accommodated, so he could pursue a Ph.D. She supported the family and also began graduate work herself in the evenings, earning an MFA in creative nonfiction writing. "In many ways, going to graduate school gave me back myself," she says. "I got to figure out who I was on paper."

As part of her new consciousness, Debbie realized that her marriage had gone off kilter. "It's always a struggle to maintain those lines of communication," she explains. "I certainly choked down a lot. I didn't say what I was really feeling about following him and then I'd blurt things out. . . . I always had to follow him and figure it out. That really irked me. I was not silent on that." She considers that a moment. "Well, I was silent in the sense that I didn't really *act*, I told him how I felt but I kept following lockstep." At the time, their separation was hard on their daughters, who were seven and ten, but, as with Judy, it brought Debbie and her husband closer as a couple. Since they've reunited, their marriage has been more open, more emotionally honest. "I look back on that time as a kind of midcourse correction," she says. "I feel a little battle scarred from it, but it was totally worth it. I couldn't have said three years ago that he was my best pal. Now he is, and that's what needed to change."

No one forced Judy to "repress the essence of who I was" just as no one forced Debbie not to "really act." Yet over the years, the role of wife had subtly made them "voiceless." They were lucky: Both emerged from lengthy separations feeling their marriages were stronger, more intimate, more what they dreamed they'd be. Both say their husbands are now their best friends, which, according to experts, is the key to marital satisfaction.[27] Interestingly a wife's confidence in her own strong voice is also critical. In his studies of long-term marriages, psychologist John Gottman found that an imbalance of power threatens a relationship, and the key to mutuality is the husband's ability to accept his wife's influence (men are singled out because, even in an unstable marriage, women accept their husbands' influence). That plays into another of Gottman's discoveries: Two thirds of marital conflicts are irresolvable, but again, the problems themselves have less impact on the marriage than the couple's ability to discuss them as friends, and that involves a husband signaling that he puts "us" ahead of "me."[28] It may also, sometimes, require a wife to put "me" ahead of "us." To truly talk as friends, a woman has to take a risk: She has to fight against the tendency to be agreeable in relationships, to "choke things down." She has to overcome the Perfect Wife's expectation that her husband ought to intuit her needs. After all, that's neither the obligation nor the entitlement of friendship.

Few of the women I interviewed felt they had the tools to speak up for themselves when they entered marriage. "It's like you weren't raised with conflict resolution skills at all," observes one of the women I meet that night over dinner at Debbie Frieze's house. "So, going into marriage, I went"—she shrugs meekly—" 'okay, whatever, sure.' But I've learned. I mean, you have to learn."

Helen, a forty-four-year-old arts administrator and mother of three, nods. "It just kills me. If you were a musician or an artist or an athlete, and if you kept coming to the same point in your work and not being able to figure it out, would you just turn around and avoid it, and walk away from it? If you are trying to get better at anything else, you look at the problem, you think, 'Okay, should I go over it? Should I get new tools? Should I call a new resource? Should I do some reading? What do I have to change in this mix to get rid of this obstacle and move beyond?' We all do it all the time, problem-solve all sorts of things, but we aren't prepared that that's what marriage is. That it's a series of running into obstacles that you will then problem-solve together."

Helen pauses a moment, reflecting. "I think that the most important thing is to try to remain friends, and that's hard, because 'friends' is really different from being married. With your friends, when something has gone south, you kind of renegotiate and figure things out, and you work it out together and you figure it out together."

We are sitting around Debbie's kitchen table, eating bread and soup, and drinking no small quantity of wine. Everyone is a little loose, so I take the opportunity to bring up another aspect of marriage.

"How important is sex to you?" I ask.

"It's not very important to me," Helen says. "It's more important because of knowing that it's important to my husband."

"Me too," says Susannah, forty, grinning. "Maintenance."

The other women laugh. "Yes," Helen says. "Sometimes you think, 'Oh, what a mood. Boy, I know what would fix this.' But given the choice of having sex or reading my novel . . ."

"Oh, yeah," interrupts Susannah, "I always want to say, 'Mind if I read while we do this?' "

Helen grows serious. "I'm not terribly worried about it though," she says. "I mean, it flows, it changes, it will go, it will be back."

"I worry about it sometimes," Susannah confides. "It can be a big bone of contention. Right now we're okay, but . . ." She trails off.

Maybe it's not surprising, given how problematic sexual pleasure could be for women, that by midlife, desire was often pushed to the periphery. In fact, the first ever national study of sexual dysfunction to include women (which didn't take place until 1999) found that lack of interest in sex was their number one complaint.[29] As I traveled the country, interviewing women, I began to feel like a naif for asking about it, as subtly silenced myself as the voice of desire had been within them. Yet, I wasn't willing to let sexuality slide off my radar. According to psychologist Judith Wallerstein, developing a "richly rewarding sex life" is the central task of a good marriage, essential in maintaining stability and "replenishing emotional reserves." The area of greatest contrast between those who were happily married and those who were divorcing, she found, was that in the latter group couples had often endured years of celibacy.[30]

Why were women resigned to low desire? Some, doubtless, had never discovered their sexual potential or were incompatible with their mates. Others were simply exhausted: The physical demand of infants nursing at their breasts or toddlers tugging at their arms, which had depleted them during the Crunch, had been replaced by the equally draining psychological demands of mother-managing school-aged children. "One of the many things that has not changed in most families is that there is only one person in the family who always knows where everybody is," Helen says. "You could poll anybody else from the family and nobody knows. But *you* know, and you walk around with that all the time. It's amazing. It's just—brain space." She grins. "I guess it's that space that men use for sports."

"Or sex drive," says someone else.

"Sex is a really good example," Helen says, nodding. "I mean, for me, going away for a weekend is great, because it can be sexually liberating. But it always takes twenty-four hours until I get to the place where, 'Oh, my gosh, am I going to have my own brain now? Am I going to have my own body? Am I really going to just be myself?' And then I can be a sexual being."

Helen's point was important: Sexual desire invariably returned when a woman felt like "myself," when she surfaced from the roles of wife and mother. One woman told me her sex life with her husband improved when she became an avid bicycle racer, particularly when he began to share the pursuit: It fostered their relationship as adults, separate from their role as parents, and that, in turn, rekindled eroticism. Nearly everyone talked about how much easier it was to be sensual when they could get away with their husbands for a weekend. And, unsurprisingly, for couples who can remain emotionally connected, marital satisfaction—including sexual fulfillment—tends to bounce back when kids leave home:[31] That's the time when a woman shucks the Good Mother for good, when the power balance in marriages has been renegotiated, when women feel the most "myself." If sex is vital to a happy marriage, independent identity for women appears to be the key to good sex. Rediscovering sensuality can, in turn, be the catalyst for further autonomy. In her provocative book *The Erotic Silence of the American Wife*, Dalma Heyn found that women who've had extramarital affairs repeatedly described a sense of reconnection to a person they felt they'd lost—themselves.[32] It was a telling discovery, quite separate from whether that resulted in a return to the marriage or its destruction.

Divorce Is a Happy Word

Unlike for Judy Winkler and Debbie Frieze, whose separations revived stalled marriages, renegotiating the terms of relationships didn't always work. Sex lives couldn't always bounce back, friendship faltered—sometimes abusive behavior surfaced—and marriages failed. Although divorce is more common today than ever (about half the women I interviewed during their forties were divorced), women whose marriages had broken up seemed no less prone to self-recrimination: Recall that in the Promise years women believed they were wiser than their mothers had been about marriage, more equipped to make "better" choices. Often they viewed their higher education as armor against a bad decision. But that can make the collapse of a marriage all the more humiliating. "You feel like even more of a failure now if you're admitting that you need to get out, because you should've known better," says Judy Winkler.

Sometimes that stigma encouraged women to stay in bad or abusive marriages longer than they should have. "I'd convinced myself that if I was a better wife, a better person, it would be okay," says Ricki, forty-two, a schoolteacher whom I met with Judy. Ricki's husband was depressive and emotionally abusive, but she stuck by him for eighteen years. To get out of the marriage, she gave up alimony, their jointly owned property—all economic rights beyond child support for her two daughters. She's also lost a number of friends who feel awkward including an "extra" woman in their gatherings. Still, she says, it was worth it. "To me, divorce is a happy word," she says. "Growing up, I thought it meant the end of the world. Now I see divorce as a success, as something I worked hard for. And I got it. I earned it."

An emotionally close, meaningful marriage is physically and psychologically beneficial for both women and men, particularly as they age.[33] Often, even after several years of impasse, a relationship can rebound and a couple can still reap its rewards. But here's the rub: In a long-term, unhappy marriage, women suffer more. They're more likely to be in ill health or clinically depressed than either unhappy men or happy people of either sex.[34] It's part of the price of the Perfect Wife: Women carry the emotional weight of a marriage, preserving the peace at the expense of their own well-being until it becomes intolerable. They are also, ultimately, more likely than men (who are always healthier when married than single[35]) to finally call it quits. In the anthology of essays *Women on Divorce*, it becomes clear that by the time they do, their sense of self has been nearly obliterated. "I have asked myself a hundred times: How did it come to the point where I lost the right to set reasonable limits and boundaries, to satisfy needs of my own?" reflects writer Diana Hume George. "How can I reconcile the me I know—strong, autonomous—with the woman who was so silenced, so afraid? The process of self-erasure in a relationship happens in small, almost imperceptible increments."[36] And Penny Kaganoff, one of the book's editors, muses, "I was losing myself inch by inch, and I knew I had to leave my husband or disappear completely."[37]

If marriage can encourage women to suppress the self, divorce, however painful the process, seems to do just the opposite: Women routinely expressed a stronger sense of identity in its wake.[38] "I've found things that I truly love to do instead of doing things that my husband or my family thought I should like to do," says a forty-three-year-old twice-divorced lawyer. "I have hobbies and interests and things; I have great joy in the ways I spend my time."

Even women who were abandoned by their husbands described a surge of renewal. Natalie, forty-three, who works at a nonprofit agency in Washington, D.C., had been married twenty-one years when her husband left her and their two sons for another woman. A year later, when I talk with her, she says she still loves him and feels a great void. Even so, a part of herself has reemerged since he's been gone. "I was independent and did all this stuff before we lived together," she says. "Then you become part of a team, and there's sort of this yin-yang, and you begin to doubt that you can do certain things. Now suddenly he's not here. And I'm taking care of the leaking ceiling, and I'm rushing my son to the emergency room when he woke up one morning not being able to breathe. I'm doing it all. And there's strength in that, there is, but there is still a hole."

The youngest among the women I interviewed wanted to marry (and believed their unions would last forever). They rarely questioned the worth of the institution or its relevance to them as individuals. Twenty years later many similar women, now divorced, would never wed again. Over the last three decades the rate of remarriage after divorce dropped by forty percent, a trend driven by economically independent women who no longer see marriage as their best option.[39] What's more, by the mid-1990s, only 38 percent of spouses said they were "very happy" in their marriages—a historic low.[40] So, somewhere between the dreams of young women and the realities of those in midlife, there is an enormous disconnect. The experience of older women is neither passed along nor learned from. "For some reason we keep getting funneled in this narrow way," says Delia, forty-seven, in Los Angeles, "and we buy in to this ridiculous notion that once you get through that funnel, that's when life begins." Delia is a dramatic-looking woman: over six feet tall, dressed in black, with a mane of dark hair. She is in the midst of divorcing her husband of twenty years, who is also her business partner. "But if one out of every two marriages fails, then there's something about it that doesn't address our potential." She sighs and waves her cigarette in the air. "We're just not honest enough with young women about how they can design their own worlds and their own lives."

IN *COMPOSING A LIFE*, Mary Catherine Bateson writes about the value of continued redefinition in individual lives, the lessons it holds for both women and men in modern times. "We must invest time and passion in specific goals," she writes, "and yet at the same time acknowledge that these are mutable."[41] Marriage is mutable. Professional life is mutable. Motherhood is mutable. All the more reason for women to do what so few seem to: take the long view of their own interests, where they're separable from others, and plan strategically for the next twenty—thirty, fifty—years of their lives, particularly given that they will likely spend a significant part of it on their own. Just this piece of knowledge—that no matter how she balances her life, a woman will spend key portions of it without a mate—may change the emphasis women place on their choices, putting a different spin on the role of friendships with other women, on the trade-offs between career advancement and family responsibilities, on the importance placed on their own earning capacity in the second half of life (including on those "baby steps" among the most traditional women). The question is not just "what I want for myself now," but "what will I need for myself in years to come." Ideally that's something women would begin asking at twenty-two; by midlife, it's essential.

The sense that their beauty is fading, described earlier, is, perhaps, the ultimate example of mutability. At the same time, according to Terri Apter, the anxiety over appearance at midlife is often a sign of growth: It's part of recognizing the disjuncture between others' expectations and an internal understanding of oneself. Judging aging women as unattractive, she believes, is a way to dismiss their increased personal power, to neutralize them.[42] Part of the challenge of this generation (which, at it happens, will look younger and healthier longer than any in history) is to take that renewed inner strength and turn it outward, to create a complex, competent sexual femininity that doesn't rely on youthfulness: to repossess the physical self on a woman's own terms.

"But, see, here's where your definition better change," says Sob Sister Kim Beaulieu in Minneapolis, sitting forward in her chair. "Looking good doesn't have to mean looking young. It's as simple as that. You can look good and feel good about yourself and be, I think, attractive to other people—those who know you as well as those who don't—but you *don't look young*. And that requires an attitude adjustment. And that's critically important."

She leans back, folding her arms and adds: "It's a train you better get on or you'll be hit by it."

"What train?" I ask.

"Acceptance of aging," she says. "I find myself looking at women and noticing my own reactions when someone says, 'Isn't she attractive,' and I think, 'Is she? How old is she?' And being affirmed when the person is sixty, fifty, even forty-five. You have to actively practice that. Because we weren't taught to feel that way."

Whether they were single or married, mothers or not, women

were, indeed, looking in the mirror as they entered midlife, reconsidering the internally reflected self as well as the one in the glass on the wall. At its best, this was a liberating process, allowing them to reclaim lost parts of themselves: to assert autonomy; to reconceive connections to family, work, and community; to quiet the voices of conflict that had swamped them during an earlier stage, and to become, finally, more authentically themselves. During the Reconsideration, women asked new questions about the meaning of work, the nature of marriage, the sources of satisfaction. For Wendy Echoldt, whom I met in Washington, D.C., and Roseanne Peretti who had recently moved to New York from Oakland, California, the task as single women was to satisfy their need for connection, to create a feminine identity that was dependent on neither husband nor children. For Denise Littleton, a lawyer and board member of a corporation in Maryland, asking "What do I want now for myself" meant reevaluating her career path, finding work that felt true to her as a woman, a mother, and an African American. It also meant bringing some of the power she'd gained in the workplace back into the home.

Chapter 11

Single and Forty: God Forbid?

WENDY ECHOLDT PICKS ME up early one morning in her forest green Miata convertible and we weave through traffic toward her office in Washington, D.C. It's a single woman's car: There's no backseat begging for a baby carrier, and the leather interior would never survive sticky little fingers. Wendy, who is forty-one, wears a long light-blue Ungaro blazer that flatters her hourglass figure, a black skirt that hits midcalf, and sensible pumps. Even with her thick, auburn hair wrapped into a bun, she is an attractive woman. Her eyes are a deep blue, courtesy of colored contact lenses ("people ask me if these eyes are 'really mine,' " she says, grinning. "I say, 'Sure they are. I bought 'em!' "). There is a gold band on the ring finger of her left hand, set with a large ruby encircled by diamonds.

The ring was a gift to herself, a nod to Wendy's conviction that she is permanently single. It wasn't an easy conclusion. As a girl, growing up in a small West Virginia town, she had assumed that her life would be like her mother's: After college she would marry a reasonably well-to-do man who would father her children, and, ideally, buy her a beach house. Since her income would be incidental to the support of her family, she imagined that she'd, "figure out what I wanted to do with my life, not what I had to do for a living, which is a very different thing."

It would be nice to be able to say that Wendy eventually recognized the folly of marrying your dream instead of earning it, that she discovered her hidden talents and catapulted herself to a kind of career success that didn't leave time or inclination for a husband and children, but that's not what happened. After college she knocked around a bit, then worked in a jewelry store while she considered her options. Around the time she turned twenty-five, though, Wendy began to gain weight and struggled with depression. No one was unduly concerned—her friends assumed she was just pining after a college beau who'd gone to Phoenix and married someone else. A year later, when she moved to Washington to be near her sister and look for a better job, the doctors she consulted dismissed her as just another young woman faltering under big-city pressures. So Wendy kept gaining weight, and the bigger she got, the more invisible she seemed to become, especially to men.

"I would go to a bar with my girlfriends and guys wouldn't talk to me," she remembers. "They would politely excuse themselves and go over to the really pretty girl at the end of the bar, or even a marginally cute girl at the end of the bar who didn't weigh 180 pounds. I wasn't used to that happening. I mean, not that I expected them to come over and go, 'Oh, my God, you are beautiful.' But at some point in the evening people used to talk to me. As I got heavier and heavier, people didn't—men or women. If you were large, you didn't exist."

It turned out that Wendy's condition wasn't psychological. She had a benign tumor on her adrenal gland which also affected her thyroid. By the time she was treated and had lost the weight, she was thirty-five. Like many women who've suffered a severe blow to their self-esteem—in the wake of a nasty breakup, for instance, or because of a troubled family life, or warped body image—she was hungry for the smallest crumb of male attention. She tumbled into a relationship with a charming, handsome man who, she says tersely, "didn't care about me at all, which doesn't mean he wasn't a nice person." After three turbulent years she summoned the courage to throw him out for good. Now, she says, although she'd like to fall in love—who wouldn't?—she's no longer expecting it.

"I realized I'm not good at relationships," she tells me. "I'm not good at picking men who care about Wendy. I'm good at picking men who care about themselves. You know, you have to wade through an entire stadium full of self-absorbed, egotistical losers before you find one reasonably normal human being who doesn't already have a spouse, or more baggage than he could ever carry, let alone drag, or a mother who lives next door—the list is endless. You just get to the point where it doesn't seem worth the effort."

Wendy makes a quick left turn into the parking lot beneath her office building and waves to the attendant. Perhaps she missed her chance at finding love, she reasons, but she wasn't about to let professional success pass her by as well. During her illness Wendy worked as a bookkeeper for the National Organization for Women. ("They were probably the only organization in Washington that would hire a depressed 230-pound woman," she cracks.) Once she'd recovered, though, she realized that crunching numbers wasn't enough for her. She wanted to shine. "I found myself all of a sudden shouting 'Me! The girl in the back! I can do that!' " she says, waving her hand in the air. "If I made it through the last ten years, just get out of my way and watch."

We step off the elevator and walk into the tasteful teal reception area of the trade association for pharmaceutical companies, where Wendy is vice president of finance and operations, which means she oversees all money matters—budgets, investing, financial statements—as well as runs the office. Lately she's moved into emerging technology as well, building the association's Web site and planning a technology expo. for an upcoming conference. "That's what I love about this job," she says, "it's not like I just do one thing. I'm always doing something that's new for me and for other people." Wendy talks with possessive pride about "our members" and "our goals." "My job is who I am," she says. "It's what I do. It's like when women say, 'I'm Susie's mom' or 'I'm so-and-so's wife.' " She pauses for a beat, gesturing around the lobby. "Well, I have a job."

Breaking *The Rules*

Most of the never-married women I spoke with had, like Wendy, expected to marry and have children. Some had become involved in long relationships that never quite gelled. Some never found the "right guy." Others had, at some point, simply changed their minds, deciding that professional commitments and committed relationships were irreconcilable. But however they got there, single women in their forties, more than any other group, have come to represent both the promise and the punishment of women's choices: Like those who wait to have children until thirty-five (or later), they are held up to young women as evidence of expanded options but also wielded as their potential penalty.

A few months before meeting Wendy, I'd had a conversation in New York with five women in their twenties, including Abbey Green. When I asked them about the essential difference between their lives and their mothers', the answer was instantaneous. "It's choices," Leslie, twenty-nine, had said confidently. "When my mother was my age, she was married with two children. I can do what I want: have a career, get married or not, have children or not."

Yet, an hour later, when I asked how they would feel if

they were still single at forty, they looked horrified. And not just horrified—fearful.[1] "That's just not an option," Leslie had said firmly. "Do we have to have this conversation?" another woman added. "I don't want to think about it." And Abbey went so far as to rap her knuckles against the table. "God forbid," she said, shaking her head. "God forbid."

For these women, initially so self-assured, the vision of single life began to metamorphose around the age of thirty from choice to threat, from liberation to desperation, from a symbol of defiance to one of deviance. Some have gone so far as to call it the eleventh commandment: "Thou shalt not be single, over thirty, and happy."[2] Yet, if women can't see single life as a viable alternative with its own set of costs, rewards, and challenges, then they remain as controlled by marriage as previous generations, equally vulnerable to making choices negatively—out of fear instead of authentic desire. They just have an extra few years before anxiety descends. The phenomenal popularity of the book *The Rules* preys on such worries, urging women to see their marital status rather than the quality of their lives as the true measure of happiness. Meanwhile, a pop culture trendlet has recently emerged which depicts single women in a marginally more nuanced way. Books like *The Girls' Guide to Hunting and Fishing* and *Bridget Jones' Diary*, as well as television shows like *Ally McBeal*, portray an exquisite tension between pluckiness and panic. But glamorous desperation has its upper limits: the protagonists are all comfortably under thirty. HBO's *Sex and the City* has been lauded for pushing the edge of the single-girl envelope—its main character is a shocking thirty-four.

This popular image of anxious, midlife single women doesn't jibe with studies that consistently rate their health and well-being as comparable to or better than their married peers.[3] Nor does it fit with the way single women I spoke with actually described their lives. "Last year an old boyfriend wrote me, telling me all about his life, his wife, and kids," says a forty-year-old film editor in Los Angeles. "And I wrote back, saying, 'If I knew at twenty-two that I'd be single at forty, I would've thought, 'Oh, my God, that's horrible! I'll be lonely and my life will be meaningless and I won't have amounted to anything. I won't have achieved this thing you're supposed to achieve.' But the truth is, I've achieved so many other things I didn't expect. And I have lots of friends and plenty of money and my life is really good.

"This idea gets implanted that if you're over thirty-five and single, you're miserable," she continues. "But, I was meeting all these new people and really enjoying my job, and having all these incredible experiences. It was like I was having a rebirth. So, I can't look back and say that because I didn't achieve this thing that was imposed on me, I'm lesser in some way." She pauses, considering. "But, I have to admit, when I wrote to him and said, 'Look, my life is great,' and it didn't feel like a lie, it surprised me."

"Sometimes it's lonely," concedes a forty-one-year-old software developer in San Francisco. "It's as if I'm standing outside a walled town full of families and children, trying desperately to get in. And once in a while someone throws me a scrap of meat over the wall. But then, on the other hand, walls can keep people in as well as out. And sometimes I feel like, as much as I'm kept out, the women in the town are kept in, and they are standing there, looking out at me through the cracks, wishing that they could go off too, and wander in the hills." That interplay between loneliness and solitude was a common theme among single women I spoke with: The former may be an undeniable, occasionally painful, part of their lives, but the latter was surprisingly enriching.[4]

Many women, like Wendy, enthused about professional success, but I'd expected that: Single women excel in the workplace and earn more than their married peers.[5] What was unexpected, and potentially more relevant to young women wrestling with the eleventh commandment, were the ways those women had incorporated traditional feminine values into nontraditional lives. Whether they were like Wendy, who might've preferred a different outcome, or like Roseanne Peretti, who, when first I met her among a group of women in California, told me, "I'd like to put a positive spin on being single," these women had found depth and meaning in connection with others, in community. The bonds they'd formed with family and friends, the creative ways they'd found to nurture the next generation, contradicted the fearful assumptions of younger women. Perhaps, then, if the satisfactions of solo life were better understood, women would feel freer to resist the pressure to lower their standard for happiness rather than risk being alone.

When the Ring Doesn't Fit

Roseanne Peretti rolls her eyes and, for the third time in a half hour, gets up to answer a frantic knock at the door. She has promised the two young boys who live down the hall from her in Windsor Terrace, Brooklyn, that she'll help them make a surprise dinner for their mother's birthday tonight, and, although it's barely noon, they're eager to get started. "You know what, Youseef?" she says to the chubby thirteen-year-old who is bouncing impatiently on the balls of his feet. "This is going to come off perfectly, so you can relax. I know you've done a lot of planning, but it's going to be fine."

Roseanne is tall and solidly built, with black hair and ruddy skin that is just beginning to wrinkle around her bright blue eyes. Her smile is easy and conspiratorial, and she has a gently wisecracking style. She moved here from Oakland, California, nine months earlier to take a job as an account executive for a costume jewelry company; a few months shy of her fortieth birthday, she thought it was time to experience the world beyond her hometown.

Unlike the young women I'd interviewed in New York, and unlike Wendy Echoldt, Roseanne never aspired to a traditional life. Even as a girl she felt different, as if she weren't subject to the same rules as everyone else. Maybe it was because, similar to Emily Sorenson, she was the fourth in a family of eight kids, with the middle child's conflict between easy anonymity and the drive for distinction. Maybe it was because she was a natural reader, discovering the local women's bookstore when she was still in grammar school. Certainly the times played a part: Roseanne came of age in the San Francisco Bay Area in the mid-1970s. Feminism was ascendant. *Roe* v. *Wade* had just been decided. It was a brief period where young women, at least some of them, felt fully entitled to their sexual impulses: They were free to be the agents, not just the objects, of desire.[6] For Roseanne, that sexual confidence was key to a developing a broader sense of self-determination. "As a teenager I felt okay saying 'Yes, I am going to have sex and my diaphragm is in my purse and if it's going to happen, I'm going to make that choice,' " she says. "And that made me feel like I had more control and more freedom in general."

Roseanne was an iconoclast, suspicious of the status quo. Rather than go straight to college, she rented an apartment with friends a few blocks from her parents' house. She worked in her father's construction company, flipped burgers, and cleaned houses to pay her bills, but her real priority was having fun: haunting thrift stores and flea markets, clubbing until the wee hours, meeting new lovers. There were more serious boyfriends too (Roseanne fell in love twice during her twenties) but when I ask about her most significant relationship of that period, she pointedly ignores the implication that I'm asking about men. Instead, she tells me about her elderly grandmother who lived next door to her. No man has had the impact on her or her choices that her grandmother did. For four years, tending to her grandma, who was wasting away from Parkinson's disease, dominated Roseanne's life. During the week she monitored the in-home attendants. On the weekend Roseanne herself took over, and, as her grandmother deteriorated, bathed her, diapered her, dressed her, fed her, took her on outings to a nearby park. "Taking care of her like that was something really great that I could give her, and I was very happy to do it," Roseanne says. "And I learned a lot. I learned about the circular nature of life, and the process of aging and deterioration. And also, that it's really important that women learn how to take care of themselves. Because eight chances out of ten, even if you stay married, which she did, your husband is going to die before you, and you'd better know what you're going to do then."

If the sexual freedom of her early years gave Roseanne a sense of control over her destiny, nursing her grandmother left her with something else—a broadened vision of what caretaking meant. Later, as it became less likely she would have children of her own, Roseanne would recall this relationship as a template of different ways to nurture, to reap the rewards of family and community. At the time, though, as her grandmother's death approached, Roseanne felt burned out. She was twenty-seven years old. She was still cleaning houses for a living. And she was lonely. It was time, as she put it, to "conform." So, she traded her rebel-girl lifestyle for an entry-level sales job with a lingerie company—she figured she was good with people and it was a career that wasn't dependent on a BA. She also married her boyfriend, a mechanic and aspiring musician. They'd been living together for several years before Roseanne's grandmother died; they even owned a house together. So, when he proposed, she accepted, not so much because she loved him (although she did) as because it seemed the logical next step. Despite her countercultural leanings, she couldn't imagine another way to strengthen their commitment.

"We were clearly really in love and in a deepening relationship," she says, "and we were somehow propelled along this path that was inappropriate for us. You know how it is when you've been together for a while. People ask, 'Well, when are you going to get married?' Obviously, I went into it thinking it was for life, otherwise why bother. But it only lasted three years."

Several of the midlife single women I met, like Roseanne, had wed briefly around age thirty. Like her, they had viewed themselves as independent, self-sufficient, even rebellious. Yet, there was something deep within them that recoiled at the idea of remaining single. They felt a certain inevitability about marriage, especially if their boyfriends were pushing it. As Katie, a divorced forty-year-old actress whom I met among a group of single women in Los Angeles, said, "My ex-husband was really into me. He seemed to love me so much. And I don't think I wanted to be thirty and not be married. That scared me."

Elise, a journalist who married at twenty-eight and divorced three years later, agreed. "I try to go back and figure out why I got married, and I don't know," she said. "Maybe I needed to get it out of the way. It was almost a passive choice. I just sort of kept putting one foot in front of the other. He wanted to get married, and so we got married."

Neither Elise nor Katie felt "in love" with their husbands, nor did they feel especially passionately toward them. They thought that was how marriage was supposed to be: that by becoming the Good Wife and suppressing their own needs, they would experience a more mature form of love. "I had this idea that I was getting a jump on the game," Katie said. "All the research I'd read says you lose your sexual attraction eventually, so you should marry someone you like being around. And I liked being around him. We were friends." Listening to Elise and Katie, I recall the uneasy mix of high and low expectations of marriage among the women in the Promise years, the clash between romantic dreams and utilitarian goals. Elise's comment that marriage was something that she had to "get out of the way" before continuing on with her life was particularly striking: The women I spoke with who'd married, even for just a few years, seemed more content with remaining single as they aged, as if they'd established their "normalcy," and now could more freely choose their futures.

Looking back, Roseanne doesn't think her partnership with her husband ever really coalesced. "We didn't develop the ability to make goals as a couple," she says. "That was what I expected to be different about marriage. In retrospect, I wish we'd talked more about what our expectations were, or even talked enough for me to realize that he had no interest in compromising to share our lives—he wanted us to be living more on parallel tracks. So, we were entangled, but we weren't really together, and I think that's what made the relationship fail."

Just before the divorce was finalized, Roseanne asked her husband why he'd been so eager to marry. He told her he'd been afraid that if they didn't, he'd lose her. Roseanne shakes her head. "I just wish that there had been a way for us to say 'I'm really in love with you and I want to be with you for a long time, but I don't need to live with you or marry you,' " she says. "But I just didn't see those kind of alternatives then."

Big Girls and Little Girls

Wendy Echoldt's office is moderate sized with a small conference table and the same teal color scheme as the reception area. She has hung two lush, impressionist-style paintings of ballet dancers on the walls, which she bought as a reward to herself for landing this job. Behind her desk there is an eight-by-ten photograph of her niece, Olivia, as an infant in a ruffled dress, baldheaded with a wet, toothless grin. Two shelves against the wall hold more pictures of Olivia, as well as a shot of Wendy, dressed in leather, on a Harley. They are the only glimpses she allows her colleagues of her life outside of this room.

Wendy flips on her computer, checks her e-mail, her voice mail, and her on-line horoscope, then begins preparing for the technology expo. she's planning. "We definitely need big, soft chairs there," she says, smiling. "These are all fat, middle-aged white guys." Wendy is joking, but in reality that's a pretty fair assessment of her clients. When she travels to various conferences in swanky hotels, she's usually the only woman among one hundred fifty men. During the first two years of her job she couldn't get through one without being asked on a date, usually by men who were already married. One of the association's members asked her over a business dinner if she'd take down her hair so he could touch it. Another grabbed her and kissed her. She's tried to counter further unwelcome advances by neutralizing any hint of sexuality on the job, by burying the playful, warm side of her personality. "I never wear a skirt that shows my knees or a jacket that shows my hips," she explains. "I don't want to look cute. That's why I wear my hair in a bun. I know it's severe, but I find it reminds people of their second-grade teacher, the one who'd whack you with a ruler if you misbehaved."[7]

I'd assumed that Wendy's run-ins with sexism would make her especially sympathetic to the concerns of women in her office. Instead, her intense commitment to the job actually seems to separate her, particularly from those who have children. She believes she has a greater stake in professional satisfaction than they do, because she'll never have a mother's option to leave or cut back. It's not that she sounds resentful exactly, although there is some of that; it's more that she sounds surprisingly like the "fat, middle-aged white guys" she pokes fun at, making the same assumptions they often do about the commitment level of working mothers. It's a complicated issue, particularly when she's proven right. "One of the women here is pregnant with her second child," she says. "Her husband has a company that's hitting its stride. My prediction: She'll have the baby and not come back from maternity leave. For her, whether she's happy or fulfilled in this job is unimportant. She can leave. Those things are *real* important to me."

Several times during our conversations, Wendy explains that there are two ways of being a woman in the business world: You can be a "big girl" or a "little girl." Sometimes that distinction seems fair enough—big girls take responsibility for themselves, little girls try to flirt their way to the top. Big girls trade on competence, little girls play on helplessness. But at other times the boundaries can seem amorphous, vaguely reminiscent of the age-old split between the "good girl" and the "bad girl."

To be fair, though, the judgments among women in Wendy's office flow both ways. When she introduces me to a group of employees chatting around the coffeemaker, one, who is visibly pregnant, looks at me quizzically. "I don't understand," she says. "What are you writing a book about?" I tell her I'm writing about how women negotiate life choices. She looks over at Wendy for a moment, still puzzled. "Oh," she says, smiling in comprehension, "you mean you're writing about the different ways people manage offices?"

"I thought that was really telling," Wendy says when we return to her desk. "I don't think it would even occur to the people I work with that I could be interesting. It was a huge revelation when I brought in the picture of me on that motorcycle. Even my boss had a fit. He said, 'Do you have leather clothes? Are you some kind of biker chick?' "

She sips her coffee pensively. "I don't think the younger staff here has a clue who I really am," she continues. "Some of them probably think I go home at the end of the day, sit on my couch in my suit, cross my feet at my ankles, fold my hands, and wait until morning, when I can go back to work."

Like Parenthood on Prozac

"Olivia is the most delightful child," Wendy says. We're zipping through traffic in her Miata again, on our way to baby-sit the delightful Olivia for a couple of hours while her parents attend a church function. "She's relentlessly happy," she continues. "And why shouldn't she be? She has three adults who absolutely adore her."

Wendy was thrilled when her sister, Pam, became pregnant at the age of forty—thrilled to be able to dote on a child in the family, and also absolutely thrilled that it wasn't her. Not that Wendy hadn't considered motherhood: Right around her thirty-fifth birthday she came down with a chronic case of baby fever. "I couldn't even look at children," she remembers. "It was so hard. And I was chasing this man who didn't love me. And I was like, 'We can have a child, we can have a child, we can have a child.'" She winces at the memory. "But, you know," she says, "it passed. Kind of like a head cold." A few years later, when her gynecologist suggested that she consider freezing some eggs "just in case," Wendy turned him down. "I said, 'Doc, if it's gonna happen, it's gonna happen. I'm not going to push it.' Some choices you just have to live with. I can live with this one."

Olivia was another story. When Olivia first lisped "Wenty," which is what she and everyone else in the family continue to call her, Wendy jokes that she spent two weeks changing her investments to make her niece the sole beneficiary. When she discusses major decisions about Olivia's upbringing, she always uses the inclusive "we" instead of "they:" what *we* think about her education, her future, her talents. Olivia may be her sister's child, but she is an integral part of Wendy's life. This is her opportunity to pass along a legacy of creativity, to give and receive unconditional love, to help a little person grow. In interview groups around the country, women often spoke of the importance of "aunties" in their lives, whether they were blood relatives or just close family friends. This was even more marked among African American women. During adolescence especially, those "second mothers" gave them someone to confide in, to escape to, even to provide an alternative model of what women's lives could be.[8]

"I want to say this has given me the chance to have a child," Wendy says, "but I don't have to do the hard stuff. I'm not there in the morning when Pam and her husband are trying to get out of the house, and they both can't be getting dressed because someone's got to keep at least a half an eye on the kid. I don't have to take off work when she's sick or to put braces on her teeth. So, it's not really like being a parent. It's more that sort of part-time, parentlike experience without the pain. Like parenthood on Prozac."

Pam lives in Virginia in an expensive Colonial house in a quiet neighborhood. Inside, it looks like Christmas Day just after the presents have been unwrapped. The den is strewn with all manner of childhood paraphernalia: an easel with crayons and paints, videos, toy trains, a zoo full of stuffed animals, an assortment of Disney figurines. Wendy heads straight to the den to check on Olivia, who has just awakened from her nap. "Oh, my love bug," Wendy croons, scooping her up and cradling her, afghan and all, against her shoulder. "Oh, give me a big snuggle." Olivia is nearly three, a sweet-tempered child with blond, curly hair and dark brown eyes. Wendy rocks her niece, stroking her back as she makes her way upstairs to change the little girl's diaper and read until she is ready to see a visitor.

When they come back Olivia is holding Wendy's hand and prattling enthusiastically. She wants to watch *How the Grinch Stole Christmas*. She wants Auntie Wenty to sit on the floor and take down her hair so she can play with the long, auburn ponytail, the one Wendy hides from her male colleagues. As they watch the video, with Olivia explaining the finer points of her Thomas Train collection, I wonder how many of Wendy's coworkers would recognize her, surrounded by toys, her legs splayed, her hair wild, with a cardboard crown on her head and several stuffed animals securely in her lap. If, as she indicated, some of her young employees think of her as the Grinch whose heart is three sizes too small, here, with this child who bears no small resemblance to Sally Who, her heart seems just about to burst out of her ribs.

Family Is Where You Find It

Roseanne had given Youseef a few dollars and told him to go to the
store for soda and come back in an hour, but he's knocking on the door
again within fifteen minutes, and this time he's brought his eleven-
year-old brother, a skinny, gap-toothed boy named Mahmet. They look
at Roseanne with such pleading, puppy-dog eyes, so desperate to start
preparing for the party, she relents and we give up our conversation. Roseanne installs the boys at the tiny kitchen table to blow up
balloons while she ropes her housemate, John, who is a chef, into helping her frost the birthday cake. Youseef jokes happily with Roseanne
as they work, and John takes frequent breaks to wrestle with Mahmet, whose energy seems boundless. It's not a scene one sees too
often these days: a man and a woman with two children spending a
leisurely afternoon making a festive meal with a homemade cake. A
stranger happening by would think they were the essence of domesticity, a Hallmark moment of family harmony—except, of course, that the
adults are not actually related to one another or to the children.

Roseanne's involvement in others' lives goes way beyond
Wendy's. Despite her iconoclasm, she was actually one of the most
conventionally feminine women I met, in that she values caretaking
and community over everything else in her life. At first that seemed incongruous: On one hand, she was a sexual adventurer, a free spirit,
disinterested in a live-in relationship. On the other, she spoke most
proudly of the lifelong multigenerational ties she'd formed not only
with her siblings' children but with neighbors, with friends' children,
with the elderly. Like some of the women that psychologist Mardy Ireland interviewed for her study of childlessness, Roseanne identified
strongly with the maternal, yet she had found ways to nurture without
having a baby herself.[9]

Even now when Roseanne discusses her new job, her central
complaint sounds like that of the most conflict-ridden mothers I spoke
with: She spends up to three weeks a month on the road, and that pre-
vents her from baking, sewing, being with children, and participating

in family life. It just so happens that for Roseanne, the families she's committed to aren't her own. "My job just doesn't give me the time to be as involved as I'd like," she says. "Like, a friend of mine who lives two blocks away has a four-month-old baby. I know that if I were here more, I'd just call her and say, 'Come over and drop the kid off. Go for a walk. Go do your shopping. Go get some exercise.' People need that support. It makes a huge difference. I know from my own childhood how important it was for my mother that my grandmother could help her with childcare. And it was equally important to me to be able to go someplace outside the family, where I could feel very special and very loved."

Like Wendy, Roseanne has gone through periods where she wanted children of her own. At times, she says, the desire has seemed almost physical. But when, at thirty-five, she became pregnant accidentally with a man who wasn't interested in having a family, she opted against single motherhood. "Ultimately, I didn't feel like my own desire to have a child was a good enough reason to do it when he didn't want to," she said. "And I guess it's like with my grandmother: I felt there were a lot of other ways to exercise that maternal energy that might be both better for me and also for the world at large.

"I actually think that I'll have the most time to have children when I'm in my late forties or fifties. And I could adopt a child. I could raise a foster child. I could become a Big Sister. Any of those options would satisfy me. Maybe it's my destiny to raise other people's children, and that's okay. For me, it's about the experience of nurturing and guiding. It isn't really about giving birth."

Sister to Sister

After dinner with Olivia's parents, Wendy's brother-in-law takes his little girl down to the basement for their nightly father-daughter putting practice (Olivia has a set of plastic golf clubs scaled to the size of a three-year-old). Pam, meanwhile, begins to clear the table. The sisters look nothing alike: Pam is fine-boned and narrow-faced with oversized glasses and dark, permed hair that hangs to her jaw. She wears a long, flowered dress that is less fashion-conscious than Wendy's tailored business suit. Pam had an ulterior motive for inviting me here tonight. She is an executive at an insurance company and has her own take on the pressures women face in the workplace. It is clearly a favorite topic: Pam talks quickly, the words pouring out, her voice impassioned. "For one thing," she says, closing a pizza box, "in the upper echelon, where I am, there are only women without children. I'm the only working mother in my division. My boss, who is a man, just can't comprehend how you could be a mommy and still work. All the other men have stay-at-home wives too. But I expected that, and, even though I try, I know they probably won't change their attitude until their daughters or their granddaughters come into the workplace.

"But, you know," Pam continues, "whatever tension there is between the men and the women, it's triplicate between women and women. *That* I wasn't as prepared for. The tension between elite women and their secretaries. Or the tension between childless women and mothers. The women are even less understanding than the men. The men at least have kids. And they take time off. The women work like killer bees."

I ask Wendy how she feels about what her sister is saying. After all, it was only that afternoon she was telling me with a dollop of irritation that working mothers were less attached to their jobs than childless women. But before she can answer, Pam jumps in. "Yeah, what do you think, Wendy? Who'd be more understanding if a woman had to leave because of a sick kid, you or Jim?" Jim was a vice president at Wendy's company who recently left to take another job. He has five children and a stay-at-home wife.

Wendy is silent for a moment. "On the baby thing in general?" She pauses again then shrugs. "Probably Jim. We have a young female attorney who took off six months for maternity leave. I would've been much less tolerant about it than he was. I would've been saying, 'If we can be without her for six months, maybe we don't need her.' Meanwhile, he's saying to her, 'Will that be enough time?' "

Pam nods. "You see?" she says, pointing triumphantly. Her very own sister. They stare at each other for a moment across this divide. If they were two women who worked together rather than having grown up side by side, where would their sympathies lie? Who would be the big girl in this scenario? Who would be the little one? "It's not like I don't realize how hard it is," Wendy says thoughtfully. "If a mother takes off more than once in a blue moon, she's looked at as not being a vital part of the team. Jim may be a parent, but he *never* left early. He *never* missed functions or even a senior staff meeting because the kids were sick. His wife did not work." She pauses again. She may recognize the pressures working mothers face, but she can't relate. "I guess being single and not having kids basically lets me live like the men in the office and not the women."

We leave Pam at ten o'clock after Wendy makes plans to see Olivia again on the weekend. Wendy is going home to relax, read, and go to sleep. She won't get up until 8:30 or so the next day—as she says, she doesn't "do well" in the morning. Pam, however, still plans on picking up the house. "I want it clean before the car pool arrives for Olivia tomorrow," she says, laughing. "I wouldn't want those children to see the house dirty!" She'll be up by six to do a few more chores and spend some time with Olivia before her mother comes and relieves her so she can rush off to work. Meanwhile, she turns toward the kitchen sink. "It's not like the dish fairy is going to clean these for me," she says as Wendy heads out to her sports car.

As we head toward the highway, I recall the interview group where I first met Wendy. She was the only woman there who was single and childless. "And it's really okay," she had insisted when she introduced herself. "It's not bad at all. When the electricity went out Monday night, I had beer and chips for dinner out on the front steps, looking at the park across the street, and I was happy with that. I didn't have to worry that someone else might want food and might want me to fix it. I didn't have to explain anything to anyone."

Another woman in the group interrupted her. "I just can't believe you're for real," she said. "I can't believe you really feel that way."

I ask Wendy if she remembers that, and she nods. "Yeah," she says, "she said, 'I can't believe you are really happy.' That stuck with me. People have very standard ideas of what you ought and ought not to be." We drive for a moment in silence. "And, well, I'm *not* happy every day," she continues. "Some days are just plain icky. But some days are wonderful." She turns her eyes from the road a second and looks at me. "Just like for anyone else."

Sex and the Single Girl

The biggest challenge in Roseanne's unconventional life is how, as a single midlife woman, to cultivate affairs of the heart. She doesn't want to live with a man again; after her divorce she was wary of her tendency to lose her identity in intimate relationships, describing them as "time away from myself," but she doesn't want to give up love or sex. She dreams of finding a compromise between what she calls an "escalating commitment" and the "fuck-of-the-day club:" creating the kind of relationship she didn't have the courage to establish with her ex-husband. But it's never been an easy balance to achieve. "It's really difficult when your expectations are outside the norm," she says. "How do you communicate that? How do you find the appropriate type of person? I haven't quite figured out how to do it."

Seeking sexual satisfaction within or outside of a relationship posed a dilemma for most of the single women I interviewed. They struggled with feeling less marketable as they aged, and, like Roseanne, wondered what the alternatives were to conventional relationships, particularly if they were economically self-sufficient. One woman fantasized about having a lover with whom she could have a regular weekly dalliance. Another pointed out that the taboo against dating younger men makes women more dependent on stable relationships for sex. A third joked that she must've been a camel in another life, since she could go so long in between lovers. "But I *want* to have regular sex in my life," she wailed, summing it up. "I think I deserve sex in my life. I don't want to be fifty and happily single but not having sex."

Wendy Echoldt, too, has found romance difficult. Recently, for the first time in years, she met an attractive man while at a technology conference in Jamaica; he neglected to tell her, however, that he was separated, not divorced, from his wife. They still flirt on the phone, and occasionally have lunch, but she's not willing to let it go any further. "I don't want to be somebody that he dates on the road back to being a functioning human being again," she said, sighing.

Roseanne's imperfect solution has been a four year involvement—longer than her marriage—with a married man whom she met at a health club in Oakland. He had pursued her avidly for months before convincing her to act on their mutual attraction. She expected they'd have a one-night stand that would "get him out of my system," but, to her surprise, the relationship has endured—and there is some evidence that such arrangements have become more common.[10] When Roseanne lived in California, they would meet before work in the morning or at lunchtime. Now that she's moved across country—a decision which she did not allow the affair to influence—they talk on the phone daily and tryst on business trips. The appeal, Roseanne says, is that her lover is completely devoted to her pleasure. He's attentive, a good listener, a passionate sexual partner. As a successful business owner, he's also been a valuable mentor.

It sounds perfect, I say, except for the part about the wife. Doesn't Roseanne ever feel guilty? "You know," she responds, "I don't. I don't know much about their relationship and I don't ask. I'm not a doormat. Maybe he's getting something from me that he's not getting there, I don't know. I'm not sure that there is anything wrong with their marriage."

Several of Roseanne's girlfriends who have over the years been in similar relationships duped themselves into thinking the men would someday leave their wives. She has no such illusions; in fact, she says the idea alarms her. If her lover's wife ever confronted her, Roseanne claims she would deny the affair. She considers the limits his marriage places on her romance as an advantage. It makes him safe, providing both intimacy and distance from it:[11] She won't have to face the issue of marrying him herself, since he already has a wife. As a mistress, she doesn't feel responsible for fulfilling all his emotional needs, or, perhaps more significantly, for suppressing her own. And because she's "not one of his responsibilities," she says, the affair stays "alive, dynamic, and very hot."

Roseanne talks about her relationship as yet another kind of liberation, a corollary to her expansive views about sexual empowerment, nurturing, and community. It also, she admits, shows how truly difficult it is to find a suitable relationship at her stage in life. "It's not that I don't think it would be possible to have this with a single man," she says, "but it's not so easy to duplicate. It's that mojo, ju-ju love connection that happened when this man and I met. You don't come across that too often."

Still, I find myself resisting. It's hard to see how a relationship with a man who is deceiving his wife—at least—can be anything but exploitative. Roseanne admits that it is "essentially not okay" to be involved in a relationship that's based on a lie. She agrees it's a choice that most people would condemn and says she would never encourage other women to follow her lead. Nonetheless, she insists, the relationship satisfies her. Certainly it excludes her from neat classification. But Roseanne has always resisted the usual roles. At any rate, life rarely allows tidy conclusions: Marriages go belly-up, plans of happily-ever-after turn sour, the trifecta of successful career, eternal romance, and perfect children eludes. If Roseanne were a fictional character, I would happily leave out this plot twist because her affair makes me uncomfortable. But she's a real person with all the complexity that entails. Even if one rejects her conclusions, it still may be that the ability to find love and create community where none naturally exists is the most important gift of all.

BACK IN ROSEANNE'S kitchen there is a knock and the boys begin to panic: They're sure that it is their mother and their surprise will be spoiled. Roseanne looks through the peephole and gives the all-clear— it's just their grandfather, who lives with the family. He says something to Youseef through the door in Arabic and Mahmet bursts out laughing. "He thinks you two are *married*," he says, gasping for breath. Then he pauses expectantly, the question hanging in the air. In fact, the boys aren't sure about John and Roseanne's relationship themselves. Roseanne waggles her eyebrows at him. "Well, wouldn't you like to know?" she says, and goes back to her cake. She prefers to leave it ambiguous: She thinks it's good for the boys to be thrown a little off balance, to suspect there may be ways of living besides their own.

Their grandfather, a tiny man with wizened brown skin, pushes his way in and looks around the kitchen at the balloons and the newly frosted cake and the oven from which the mouthwatering smell of roasting chicken and lamb waft. He throws an arm around Roseanne and turns to me, smiling. "This is the best person in America," he says in Arabic with the boys translating. "The best!"

Chapter 12

Who Said It Would
Be Easy?

DENISE LITTLETON HURRIES DOWN the hall of her office in suburban Maryland, a few minutes late for a meeting. Her short, brown hair is styled in loose, summery curls. Behind the wire-rim glasses that slide down the bridge of her nose, her eyes are amber, framed by thick lashes and gracefully arched eyebrows. At forty-one, her golden-brown skin is still smooth and dewy. She wears a brown linen dress and jacket, with low-heeled bronze mules. When she smiles, the gap between her front teeth lends her a mischievous air.

"In the last few years, I've become more myself at work," she said. "The clothes I wear. My choice of words. All of that. I used to feel so very different from everyone else. And I felt like the prototype of what I was supposed to look like, walk like, act like was a white male."

Denise turns right, into the office of the head of corporate relations. She's the last one to arrive, but the best chair at the table—the high-backed, ergonomically correct one that's usually behind the desk—is still vacant. It's clearly the power seat, and Denise slips into it, casually greeting the four men and two women who've already gathered. For the past year Denise has been vice president of legal affairs and corporate secretary of a multibillion-dollar hospitality services company that was spun off from a larger conglomerate where she'd worked for the previous thirteen years. The spiffy title, along with a salary boost, was part of the lure, and the corporate secretary post, which she's held at both companies, is a career plum: She is not only the first African American and the second woman on her corporate board, she is one of the few black women in the entire country to hold such a position.[1] But Denise says her true triumph was negotiating the role she's in right now: creating the company's new charitable foundation which will provide hunger relief, particularly to children. "This is not a conventional role for a corporate attorney," she explained. "And usually, the people who are most highly valued in corporate America are the ones who bring in the money. This is giving *out* the money. So, before I pushed for this spot, I talked to the CEO and satisfied myself that he was behind this project one hundred and fifty percent. That it would have resources, not just lip service."

The meeting is brief, focused on getting the foundation up and running: someone from accounting talks about how to automatically deduct employee contributions from their paychecks; someone else reports on filing for not-for-profit status. A publicist weighs in on when to unveil the project to the press. As each person speaks, he or she reflexively turns toward Denise. She says very little, mostly nodding approvingly, occasionally reminding colleagues to tend to an easily forgotten detail, such as opening a bank account, or filing paperwork.

"I've dreamed of being in an executive position, where I can make a difference in areas that are important to me," she says as the meeting breaks up. "And community service has always been a part of my life. I would be willing to do it outside of my normal, regular hours to fulfill that need, but to be able to do it as part of my job . . ." Denise grins. "It allows me to test the waters to see if I really like it, to see if I want to maybe move into this capacity full-time."

She returns to her own office, downloads her e-mail, and calls her mother, who is spending the day with Denise's daughters, to remind her about ten-year-old Jessie's orthodontist appointment. Then she checks in with her husband, Calvin, who owns a property management company. While they discuss who will run errands, who will make dinner, who will pick up eight-year-old Rory, I examine Denise's display of family photos. There is a studio shot of one of the girls as an infant, a white headband around her bald pate; a shot of Calvin in a tux, tall and strikingly handsome, darker than Denise, his hair and beard close-cropped, with wide, brown eyes and a sweet smile. There's also a frame that Denise hasn't yet filled: It still holds the picture that came with it, of a white guy and his blond daughter. Denise covers the mouthpiece of the phone and gestures at it with her chin. "That's the diversity in my office," she says, and laughs.

Calvin offers to pick up Rory, then take both girls to swim practice. "Great!" Denise responds, pumping her fist and mouthing "yes" to me. That means she'll have a free evening. "What a guy!" They sign off, and she turns her attention to organizing the agenda for the upcoming board of directors meeting. With a little concentrated efficiency she'll leave the office today by four; since it's Thursday, and one of her conditions for accepting this job was working a four-day schedule, that's when her weekend will officially begin.

IT WOULD BE easy to make Denise's life sound perfect: It is, after all, pretty close to what the younger women I interviewed wanted—and expected—to attain. She has achieved not only success but a sense of authenticity as a woman and an African American in a white, male world—*and* she does it four days a week, for a six-figure salary. She has a loving marriage to a man who's also a fully engaged parent; she has time to spend with her two daughters, who are each bright and happy. Although she hesitates to say it (after all, aren't women supposed to feel bad no matter what—perennially inadequate, perpetually frazzled), she's deeply delighted with how things have turned out. "I feel like, 'How dare I claim this,' " she says, looking around her office as if she might get busted. "But, you know, in many ways I feel like I really did it."

Yet if Denise has fulfilled the promise of "you can be whatever you want to be," her experience also reveals how glib that slogan truly is, how daunting the obstacles still are for women in assembling the pieces of a satisfied life, and what an enormous role chance plays in doing it. She will be the first to tell you that none of what she's achieved—not the job satisfaction, not the good marriage, not the two children, not the lovely home in the upscale neighborhood—not one single bit of it came easy. Sometimes, along the way, rather than living The Dream, she's felt trapped in a nightmare. "I may have the elements there," she says, "but it's a struggle, and it's *been* a struggle. I've had to work really, really, really"—she looks at me pointedly and says it again for emphasis—"*really* hard to get here."

Walk Like a Man, Talk Like a Man

Denise would never describe herself as powerful. Like many of the women I interviewed at the peak of their careers, she considers herself influential, a leader, even ambitious. But powerful? Denise grimaces. "That word bothers me," she says as we cruise along the highway toward her home after work. "Maybe because it's not a coveted female characteristic. It's like asking, 'How competitive are you?' which is something that a friend of mine and I fight about all the time. She thinks I'm more competitive than I'm willing to admit. She says,

'Denise, you wouldn't be where you were if you weren't competitive.' And I've decided she may be right."

From an early age Denise grappled with the contradiction between her drive for success and her identity as a woman and an African American. Was the goal power or balance? Assimilation or reformation? Achievement or satisfaction? Often she uses the phrase "to whom much is given, much is expected." To her it symbolizes the double-edged nature of her opportunities. Denise's parents grew up in a segregated world: Her grandfather and father were lawyers for the federal government, educated at all-black schools; her mother, the daughter of a doctor, worked her way up from secretary at a black university to associate editor of an academic journal there. They had high expectations of their daughter. As a younger woman Denise felt both proud and obligated to make choices that would justify their sacrifices, showing a black woman could excel in a newly integrated world. Like Shay Thomas, Denise attended a largely white private high school across town from her all-black neighborhood. She went to Duke University, then Harvard Law. She worked for one of the largest companies in the nation, and before that for a prestigious law firm. But also like Shay, Denise found navigating those worlds complicated, often confusing. She, too, has had to "prove" her competence so continuously that eventually she came to doubt it herself.

"I was on the honor roll at Duke," she says, "but somehow I still felt I was lesser, that I wasn't as smart as my white friends. I was never mentored. I don't think a professor knew my name the whole time I was there. They didn't care. And it was the same at Harvard. I was just a number to them and, unfortunately, I didn't know to try to—" She breaks off, shakes her head angrily, her lips tight. "Well, why *would* I seek them out? Why *would* I try to start a relationship with them? There seemed to be this network there, this tradition, that had been working for a long time. And I wasn't a part of it."

Denise cultivated two strategies to cope with that exclusion, which she'd call upon repeatedly in the decades ahead: She buried herself in her studies, and she sought out the support of female friends. She developed life-long relationships among the few other black women at law school, including Candace Young, with whom she would later work. "We first bonded crying in a bathroom," Denise recalls, smiling. "It's like"—she widens her eyes and shouts—"what are we doing here? This is miserable!" They've been as close as sisters ever since, sharing a friendship that's been restorative, though occasionally complex.

Denise talked once a week to Calvin, too, who was still in North Carolina and was grappling with his own conflicts. He'd grown up on a military base in Europe, where he felt more American than black. It wasn't until he came back to the United States for college that, as he says, he felt race drop on him like "a heavy, wet coat," never to lift again. Calvin and Denise shared their pain, comforting and encouraging each other, and they laughed a lot. Denise made it through Harvard, and by her final year, they were engaged.

Denise originally planned to make her career on Capitol Hill, perhaps focusing on child advocacy. But the reality was, she had loans to pay, and, by the time she graduated, Ronald Reagan—hardly a proponent of children's rights—was president. Besides, as a Harvard grad and a pioneer of sorts she felt pressure to build a legal career in a corporate firm, where she could break down barriers to power. So, she joined a tony Washington, D.C., firm. It was the "right" thing to do, even if it felt wrong. "I hated it," she says. "But law firms are really the best place to develop your skills. And I did learn a great deal, but you have to balance that against how they treat you."

Like all new associates, Denise was worked to exhaustion, but she also felt the weight of being the sole black woman among eighty lawyers, and one of just a handful of women. Sometimes she was subjected to overt racism—there was the partner who would speak to her in "black English" despite her own flawless diction and wax nostalgic for the Negro spirituals his grandfather's servants used to sing—but usually, as would be the case throughout her career, the effect was more subtle, more insidious.[2] "I felt like I couldn't be what I was supposed to be," she recalls, "which was a white male. And on one hand, I felt deficient, like something was wrong with me. I understood that I had just not been brought up in that environment, but I felt like this is what I should strive to be like. So, I would shy away from unnecessary meetings, lunch, social activities . . ." Those are all the informal networks that build careers, I comment.[3] She nods. "When I was in a situation that I couldn't avoid, I played the game real well," she adds. "But it always felt like a game. And it always felt so unnatural."

Listening to Denise, I remembered the young women I'd interviewed who'd grown discouraged by jobs where they felt like they had to put on a false self—a male self—each morning before going into work. I remembered Shay Thomas and her friends who felt their presence was questioned every day in medical school. I remembered Emily Sorenson holding her own in the all-male manufacturing industry despite feeling like she "was never considered to be one of them." "Fit," according to psychologist Christina Maslach, who studies job burn-out, is the most important predictor of an employee's contentment.[4] But that's a tricky concept: In order for women and minority men to "fit," to truly have equal opportunity in the workplace, how much should they have to adapt to the prevailing environment, and how much should it expand to accommodate them? "You get weary after a while," Denise says. "And angry at times. But I think the biggest impact is that you really begin to doubt yourself and your work. You begin to internalize what they project onto you, and it becomes really, really hard to fight that. So, you're never at peace, you're always questioning."

Denise comforted herself with the knowledge that what she was doing was temporary. Her identity was far more grounded in her prospective motherhood than in her career. She and Calvin planned to have children (they wanted four) and then she would quit her job to be a stay-at-home mom. So although she was surprised when, at twenty-seven, she got pregnant—she and Calvin had been married just a few months, and Denise was living with her parents while he finished his MBA in Philadelphia—she was also thrilled. "Cal would have graduated by the time the baby was born," she says. "He was going to get a great job. And, this could work. This was going to be the thing that would get me out of this awful path I was on in my career."

"I'd Failed My Husband.
I'd Failed My Family. I'd Failed Myself."

"It was just one of those delightful first pregnancies," Denise says softly as she tugs absently at a curl on her forehead, staring off into the middle distance. "We were talking to the baby and reading to the baby. We had the little outfits and the room was all set up. You know, everything that you do."

We are sitting in Denise's dream house, a tasteful three-story brick home in an upper-middle-class, largely white neighborhood. The Littletons moved there two months ago, but already—unlike her office, which, although she's been there a year, is largely unadorned—the décor reflects Denise's personality. A table in the entryway overflows with framed family photographs, and another showcases the girls' ceramics projects. Works by black artists grace the walls. A collection of African carvings lines the mantle in the den, across from the overstuffed couch where Denise is curled up, dressed in jeans and a neatly pressed shirt, her bare feet tucked beneath her. Over her shoulder the sun dapples the leaves in her lush backyard. She glances at me with a sad smile. "It was probably my fortieth week of the pregnancy when I got concerned that something wasn't right, because the baby wasn't moving as much as she had been. The doctor listened to the heartbeat and assured me that everything was fine."

Four days later she and Calvin went to the hospital, expecting to deliver a healthy child. But this time, when the nurse listened for a heartbeat, there was none. They did an ultrasound. Nothing. A resident took Calvin into the hallway to break the news: The baby had died. "When Calvin came in and told me, he literally fell on the floor crying," Denise recalls. "I guess I kind of went into shock. I stood up and helped him. I said, 'This is going to be okay. It didn't work this time, but it will work next time. It will be okay.' "

She remained detached, almost businesslike, as her doctor explained that she'd still have to go through labor. Part of her, the part that would later feel this loss so acutely, just shut down. After the delivery, she and Calvin held their daughter, whom they named Zoë. "I'm so grateful we had the time with her," Denise says, "but it sort of began and ended." They looked at her perfect little fingers and toes, examined every part of her. She had Denise's amber eyes. They never would find out, for sure, what had gone wrong.

Denise finally started to cry the following morning, and her tears went on for months. "Calvin was very sad, but he was able to keep going," she says. "He had a job to go back to. He had structure." For Denise, however, life simply stopped. She was supposed to be home with the baby. She was supposed to be a mother. "I just didn't know how I was going to make it," she says. "There I was, still bleeding, producing milk, and there was no baby." She forced herself to go back to work, but for months she would come home, get into bed, and cry. Her deepest sense of herself as a woman was thrown into question. "The one thing I always knew was that I wanted children," she says. "And now I didn't know if I was going to be able to have them. I felt that I had failed Calvin. I felt that I had failed my family. I had failed myself. I had failed this child whom I was supposed to protect and nurture for life. I *killed* her for Pete's sake."

In her misery, Denise couldn't tolerate staying in a job she hated, so she accepted an in-house position at an international corporation in the hospitality industry. Although she hadn't imagined herself as someone for whom career would be especially important, she discovered that work gave her days shape, and a badly needed sense of control. Just as for women who have children, work made her feel more balanced. She also began to regain her professional confidence. "I went there, and did what I was trained to do, and I did well at it," she says. "And—surprise, surprise—they liked me." Which is not to say that her misgivings entirely evaporated. Despite the company's commitment to diversity, Denise was still the only black woman in a seventy-five-person department (there were about ten women altogether). "Once, during a sensitivity training session, I drew a picture of myself alone in a boat," she recalls. "There was all this water around me and there were sharks in the water, and also some friendly fish. But I was totally by myself. Alone." Denise's biggest ally was her secretary, who was herself the only black woman on the support staff. A few years later, Candace, Denise's best friend from law school, was hired by the company as well; while hardly a critical mass, their friendship at least lessened Denise's isolation.

She may not have always been fully comfortable, but Denise was satisfied with her contribution at work. And she was earning good money. But work was the only thing she felt was going well. Months went by and she didn't get pregnant. After two years she had a miscarriage, and the following year she had another. Friends began having children, and while she was happy for them, her despair deepened, and she no longer felt she could turn to them for support. As for many infertile women, the quest to get pregnant became both all consuming and wholly defining for Denise, eventually distancing her from the people who loved her most. Even her marriage to Calvin began to falter. The two barely spoke, rarely went out, and made love only when Denise thought she might conceive. "At some point neither he nor I knew whether our marriage was going to survive this," Denise says. "And to be honest, at some point I didn't *care* whether our marriage survived." Her faith in God had guided her through dark times before—it had helped her persevere in school when she felt unwelcome, kept her going in the face of hostility at work—but now that was wavering too. Denise felt truly alone in her grief. She found refuge in a support group for women who'd had stillbirths, as well as in her friendship with Candace. "In my hardest and most confusing moments, she was one of the few people I could talk to," Denise recalls. "She understood that I just needed someone to listen compassionately and not feel pressure to fix it for me."

Denise and Calvin sought marriage counseling too, and slowly their relationship began to recover. "There was a lot that wasn't working, but we always cared about each other," she says. "I think that's how we got through it. And nothing will break us apart now. Nothing. Losing a child really tested our relationship. It brought out the best in us and it also identified the worst. We know what that is now. And we know how to endure."

According to psychologist Laura Carstensen, who studies long-term marriages, it's typical for even the most satisfied couples to experience a significant, rough patch—as long as five years—where spouses dislike each other, where they barely speak, where they hover on the verge of divorce. Frequently couples handled the period badly, not communicating the way self-help books say they should. Spouses weren't empathic, they quarreled, they blamed, they withdrew. Women, whose physical and mental health are more at risk in an unhappy marriage than men's, found these fraught times particularly difficult. Couples who make it through, however, generally say bad times bound them more closely.[5] That was true for Denise and Calvin.

I ask her what the best part is about her marriage these days. Denise smiles, and for the first time in several hours, it's an expression of pure joy. "The best part is he's my friend," she says. "He's my buddy. He knows me and I know him. I mean, I can tell you that we have very similar values and all that kind of stuff. But what brought us together is what has kept us together, and that's that we're friends."

Getting Up, Tumbling Down, and Doing It Again

Ten-year-old Jessie bursts in to the kitchen. Her grandmother has just dropped her off, and she's hoping to squeeze in a snack before swim practice. She rummages in a cupboard, emerging with a box of microwave macaroni and cheese. Jessie has Calvin's large, dark eyes and a wide smile covered in metal. Her hair, which is thick and curly with reddish highlights, is pulled into a haphazard ponytail. She wears a white miniskirt and T-shirt, her toenails painted silver. She impatiently watches the meal cooking and seems ready to eat it straight from the pot when Denise looks up and catches her.

"Unh-unh," Denise says.

"I'm just stirring," says Jessie, all innocence, reaching for a bowl.

Denise smiles skeptically, as Jessie sits down at the table. "Bless the food," she reminds her, and Jessie says a quick grace.

Denise was not, as permanently infertile women are, forced to redefine femininity, to come to terms with it as something separate from childbearing. I wonder a bit who she would have become if she hadn't been a mother, what other sources of meaning as a woman she might've found, but Denise can't imagine it. When she was thirty-one, four years after Zoë's death, she gave birth to Jessie with the help of fertility drugs. She conceived Rory the old-fashioned way just over a year later.

Denise is quick to tell me that she loves being a mother— she still wishes she could've had another child or two—yet, having a baby didn't turn out to be the panacea she'd thought it would be. Like most women, she imagined caring for an infant as a manageable task: She'd feed it, it would nap, she'd have time to cook, read and exercise. Instead, Jessie was a demanding, active baby who nursed constantly. Reading? Exercise? Denise didn't even have time to complete a thought. And after being part of a team at work, she felt surprisingly isolated. It was confusing. Having a child—really, achieving motherhood—had been so integral to her sense of self; it was supposed to make her whole. She felt guilty that she didn't love every minute of it. "I thought it would all come naturally and it just didn't," she told me. "I realized, 'I don't know what I'm doing with this baby.' I mean, I adored her. I remember feeling like I didn't know I could love anybody this much. But it took a good year to adjust, even with that strong desire and that passion to have a child."

Even before Jessie was born, Denise had abandoned the idea of staying home full-time. Work had been such a crucial counterweight when her personal life had imploded, she didn't want to give it up. On the other hand and Denise's vision of motherhood was that of a primary caretaker, having those expectations, she wouldn't go back to her pre-baby schedule. No one in her department had ever worked part-time before, but her boss agreed to let Denise try a three-day schedule. It was the best compromise she could imagine—she was even allowed to phone in for a staff meeting that was held on one of her days off, rather than coming to the office—although, inevitably, her feelings were still mixed. Often, she felt "mommy-tracked": out of the loop, unable to take on high-profile projects, ineligible for opportunities to advance. That hurt, even though cutting back had been her decision. "I'd had a real sense of accomplishment and pride that I didn't get much of anymore," she says. "I was working on more routine, lower visibility projects. On the other hand, when I was home with Jessie, I didn't think about work. It felt like the right choice, but in a lot of ways, it also felt like a schizophrenic life."

The Littletons seemed back on track: They had two children, good jobs, and Denise had the flexibility she'd wanted as a mother. In many ways they were the prototypical contemporary couple, simultaneously progressive and traditional, with all the attendant tensions and rewards. Then, when Rory was just four months old, Calvin was fired from his $125,000-a-year job as a director of sales at a high-tech company. He was told they were reorganizing his department, and, although his job performance had been exemplary, there was no longer a place for him there. He offered to take a pay cut but was refused: He just didn't seem to belong, they said. Race was never mentioned, but, Calvin said, the insinuation was clear.[6] "I believed that if I went to Duke and overcame, and if I went to Wharton and overcame, that when I got out there I would be recognized for who I was," he would tell me one afternoon as we sat in Denise's home office.

Calvin saw Zoë's death as an assault on Denise's femininity. This new salvo, he felt, was a direct hit on him as a man. The Littletons share many household and childcare tasks relatively equally, but they each have deeply held beliefs about masculine and feminine identity. Denise's sense of herself as a woman centers on motherhood: on having given birth to her daughters, on their connection as females, and on the pleasures and burdens of mother management. For his part, Calvin's manhood has been connected to supporting his family. Whether he worked or not, whether he made more or less money than Denise, Calvin has always paid the family bills; her income goes to savings. If Denise lost her job, it might've hurt her pride, but she may also have seen it as a welcome opportunity to spend more time with her children, to be the Good Mother she feels she can never fully be when she's working. But unemployment is one of the few things that can make a man feel like a Bad Dad; Calvin was devastated. "I was not confident," he said. "I was very confused. I had been thrown off my life course. I wondered whether I could ever be successful in America or if I'd always run into the same wall."

Suddenly Denise, who had once expected to be a traditional mom, was the family's sole breadwinner, with an infant, a child who was barely two, and a husband who'd taken a body blow to his ego. This was not the way it was supposed to be, she thought. She went back to a full-time work schedule, leaving Rory with her mother or Calvin, and taking Jessie to her company's day-care center. Interestingly, she told virtually no one at work what had happened, including her boss. The traditionalist in her didn't see her ability to rally for her family as a point of pride. "I guess I still think women aren't supposed to be the breadwinners," Denise admits. "And I think people would have looked down on me and my family." One day, stressed and exhausted, she fell down the stairs at work, with Jessie in her arms; Denise nearly broke her leg protecting the child. "It was a metaphor for what had happened in our lives," she says. "I was doing fine. I was walking down the steps holding my child, and all of a sudden I started tumbling and, to this day, I can't tell you how. It felt like that was what had happened with our lives. We were doing fine. We had finally had these children. He had a good job. I had a job I was comfortable with. Boom! All of a sudden we just tumbled."

As it turned out, Calvin found another position within three months, at a smaller, minority-owned company, but at a much-reduced salary. A few years later he started his current business. The company has been a success—his income now matches Denise's—but it started out as a gamble. Once Cal was working again, Denise felt secure enough to cut back down to four days a week, but still she worried. She fretted that she wasn't being the mother she *should* be. And she feared that, on a part-time basis, her superiors wouldn't find her contribution worthwhile. When, in the spring of 1992 she was called into her boss's office, Denise was sure she was going to be fired. "It was that whole impostor thing again," she says. "I thought, 'They finally found out I'm a fraud.' " Instead, she was appointed corporate secretary to the company's board of directors. Denise was an excellent lawyer: competent, thorough, a good team player. And those qualities doubtless played into the choice to appoint her. But she also knew that she wasn't the next person in line for that job. "The company was making a concerted effort to promote women and minorities," she says, "and I applaud them for that. Although the last thing I ever wanted was to be in a position because I was a female and minority. I wanted to be there because I deserved it and because of my skills and what I could add."

Once again opportunity came with a bittersweet edge. People who'd been passed over for the job were livid, and they let her know it. "I guess it pays to be the right color at the right time," one commented. The atmosphere got so bad that Denise began locking her office door when she wasn't there, to protect against sabotage. Meanwhile, for the first time friction developed between her and Candace, who was also black, also female, and who wasn't offered the post even though she had always worked full-time. Denise once more felt isolated, different. Her boss promised to help her grow into her new role—finally she would have the mentor she'd lacked—he even agreed to let her stay on her four-day schedule, a clear signal that the "mommy track" wouldn't hamper her career in the long run. The problem was, that although like Emily Sorenson's company, Denise's regularly appears on lists of the best corporations of working mothers, her part-time arrangement depended on her boss's goodwill. Two years later, when he retired, the new general counsel had different ideas. "Our department had been very family oriented," Denise says. "But when this new leadership came in, that was not on their radar screen." Denise's salary was frozen until she returned to full-time status. Her new boss was still interested in mentoring her, but only if she upped her hours and logged more travel—the very things she was trying to avoid. "There was a part of that that seemed really appealing to me," Denise admits. "I could've worked full-time, and weekends too, and been a superstar. I could volunteer to be a part of projects and activities for the exposure and the experience. And I felt that the company was behind me, and supported me, and believed in me."

What would you have liked about that? I ask. "Power," she says. I raise an eyebrow and she laughs. "Yeah, I know," she says, raising a hand to stop me before I can comment—the very thing she'd claimed earlier she didn't care about. But as it turns out, she did care, and she felt its absence. "I could've gone a lot further in my career, but I didn't think I could and still be the mother I wanted to be," she explains. "It would've required being on call twenty-four hours a day. So I had to carve out my niche and stay there, and that came with some disappointment." If the choice was between power and family balance, Denise said, she'd have to choose the latter, whatever the price—but it turned out to be steeper than she'd imagined. Over the next several years, she began to feel stagnant, put out to pasture. She'd been at the company for over a decade: She'd been treated well, promoted, accommodated, and, in return, she felt deeply loyal. She also could see that she was quickly sailing toward a backwater. She was nearly forty years old and began asking the salient question of midlife women: What do I want for myself now? Yes, to whom much is given much is expected, but at a certain point her life and her choices had to be her own. Denise began putting feelers out, but it wasn't easy to find an elite position that she could enter part-time. Calvin urged her to simply quit if she was unhappy, but she resisted. "I knew that wasn't the right answer," she said. He urged her to come work with him, but that didn't seem right either.

Then, in 1998, her company spun off one of its subsidiaries. A close colleague was going to run the legal department there and offered her a job. It would be a smaller, less prestigious corporation and there was no guarantee, over the long run, that it would prove financially viable. In five years, she might find herself out on the street. As it was now, she was the rare black woman to reach the inner sanctum of corporate America. It was what her parents and community had dreamed for her, all that she'd been programmed to achieve. The greatest gift of that success, though, may be the room it gives a woman to put together a life on her own terms, to demand what she wants from a position of strength—from power. "I finally decided that the reason I went to these schools, and the reason I got these degrees, is so that I could be happy," Denise says. "So I could have choices. I couldn't be afraid of the risk." She took the job.

Becoming Herself

Denise and I stroll through a concrete plaza that links her office park to the mall where we're eating lunch. To our right there's a small lake, the water lapping against a cement embankment, where one can feed the ducks or rent pedal boats by the hour. On a busy Thursday, however, there are no takers. It's been a year since Denise began working here, and if the key to satisfaction is fit, then she's finally found it. Out of fourteen lawyers in her department, three are black and half are female—which means Denise no longer feels compelled to be on every committee, acting as the Jiminy Cricket of diversity. Interestingly, the fact that the company is half owned by Europeans has been helpful, too. "Being black is not the only big cultural difference," she says. "I'm less of an oddity. And that was part of what was really exciting to me—to be in a culture where you were forced to look at all those differences, all those issues regarding fit."

Although it's involved some compromise, working part-time won't permanently derail her career here or diminish the value placed on her contribution. She can pursue her foundation work, typically the domain of women or minorities, without worrying that it's a step down or that she'll be seen as weak. Although there are some glass-ceiling issues in the company—where aren't there?—it doesn't feel so much like an old-boy network. "They know who I am here," she says. "They know that I don't know sports and I'm not going to learn sports. I'm not saying that it wasn't okay where I was before, but I just felt so very different." It was, I suggest, almost as if she had to prove herself on white male terms before she could comfortably assert her own.

Denise nods. "That's exactly right," she says. "And, although it's hard for me to see how this could have happened given the experiences I've had, I wish that I could have had the confidence to just go into the community-service piece from the beginning." I ask what had stopped her. "I felt like I was supposed to do something different," she says, picking at her sandwich and fries. "I was supposed to use these talents, these degrees, this knowledge in more nontraditional roles for black people and women, and not go into fields that we had been in already, which would be like human resources."

In many ways that other route would've been easier, Denise says, the path of less resistance. Perhaps she would have been happier along the way, even felt a greater sense of meaning in her work. But, she admits, she also would've always wondered if she had been up to this challenge, if she had been stopped by fear. And there have been advantages to her achievements. "There's a great deal of pride that comes with being a corporate officer for a major corporation," she says. "I have access to a boardroom. I've seen how all of that works. And I'm well compensated. Make no bones about it—one of the reasons I've put up with what I have is because of the money. I never expected to accumulate what my husband and I have accumulated." She pauses for a moment, nibbles thoughtfully on a French fry. "I'm not sure that I'd tell many women to follow in my footsteps though, which is interesting." The institutional support, she believes, while improving, is still not fully there, and the impact on the soul from the internal contradictions and self-doubt is still too great.

Denise carries the battle scars of her experience but also the satisfaction of having nudged the culture just a little closer to a point where women are allowed to be more fully themselves in the workplace. "I feel like I have blazed the trail, particularly those who want to try to combine their career with part-time work, and for other black women," she says. "And, since I've been in this environment, I've seen a lot of change in assistance given to people struggling with family issues. That makes me feel like I've made a difference. And that feels good." She nods thoughtfully, repeating, "that feels good," as much to herself as to me.

Where the Heart Is

Highland Beach is a planned enclave of summer homes, largely owned by blacks, on Chesapeake Bay, one of several such communities left in America. It was founded by Frederick Douglass's son when whites refused him property up the beach. Denise and Calvin bought a house here a year ago and it is her sanctuary. "I go to Highland to find support and strength as a black person," she explains as we drive past the security guard at the community's entrance. "It's where I go and my family goes for sustenance." She pulls up to a quaint clapboard house with a wrap-around porch. The Littletons own the house with Candace, who was recently widowed and has a four-year-old son. Another friend, Shelley, owns a place down the street, and Denise's cousin Monica's family has the house next door.

Candace has beaten us here today, as has Monica, who leans over the picket fence to say her hellos and tell Denise about a special event at the Frederick Douglass House tomorrow: five-dollar manicures and massages. It sounds good to Denise. One part of her life she has yet to figure out is how to carve out time for herself, a few hours a week where she escapes the roles of mother, wife and worker. Just yesterday she told me she resented Calvin's twice-monthly golf games—at first she claimed it was because they wiped him out for an entire Saturday but then admitted the real reason was that he felt entitled to take time for himself and she didn't. "I guess it wouldn't make me so angry if I had something to do too. But I feel like I'm already away from the girls so much." She's tried, sometimes with an almost comic determination, to find her own hobby, but somehow she's never made it through the series of lessons—tennis, horseback riding, tap dancing—that she's signed up for. On her Fridays "off," she usually runs errands and does housework; the rest of the time, between work and motherhood, her own needs tend to get pushed to the side. It's a common lament: Women, as journalist Melinda Marshall has pointed out, prioritize toward those who they can least bear to disappoint, and that is very rarely themselves.[7]

As the women chat, a group of children begins to gather in front of Denise's house: cousins, friends, strangers, along with a few white children who live here year round. It's a damp day, and gray, but that doesn't stop the kids from begging to go down to the beach. Denise and Candace ramble to the shore with them, settling in on beach towels to supervise. Candace comments that Shelley is already at the store buying food, and the women laugh at their own well-deserved laziness. There's always someone being a better mother, a better wife, but for the moment, they can let it go.

In *Divided Lives*, a portrait of three high profile working mothers, journalist Elsa Walsh found a strong sense of community was one of the key components of a woman's satisfaction.[8] That's what Denise has at Highland. Her closest friends gather there: These are the women who saw her through the dark days after Zoë's death, whom she turned to when Calvin lost his job. They are also the ones, over the years, who helped keep her professional compass steady, reminding her that she was qualified for and entitled to success no matter what anyone else said.

Denise's friendship with Candace has been especially vital. They were classmates in law school, colleagues at work; they understood more viscerally than anyone the pressures of each other's lives. But as for many women, it was often easier to share their troubles than to celebrate their successes, particularly when it shifted their status relative to one another. According to psychologists Luise Eichenbaum and Susie Orbach, who have studied female friendship, women seek equivalence with one another: one friend becoming different—by marrying, having a child, staying home rather than working, getting a promotion—can provoke envy, competitiveness, or feelings of abandonment that destroy relationships.[9] Denise and Candace, who not only worked together but were the only two black women in their department, inevitably were compared, and the potential for jealousy and insecurity loomed large. When Denise was appointed to the corporate board, their relationship snapped. Denise accused Candace of petty jealousy. Candace responded that she felt duped: Denise had expressed vulnerability in their friendship but downplayed her achievements, acted needy but masked her competence. "I'd had some pretty hard years," Denise explained, "so I wasn't talking about all the successes at work, how I had done really good on a project or something like that. Candace and I had really come together a lot around our difficulties—I mean, we first became friends crying in a bathroom. But I think there was a sense of competition that we had been unwilling to acknowledge."

It's not surprising that Denise initially resisted recognizing their rivalry: As she herself said earlier, competitiveness, like power, conflicts with her notions of femininity. It is feminine to support authority, masculine to take charge; it is feminine to be a "team player," masculine to compete. And it is particularly antifeminine to compete with other women, especially a friend. Rather than admit such negative feelings, psychologist Lillian Rubin found, women will suppress them to maintain the friendship, even if, conversely, that's what causes them to drift away.[10]

"At the time, Candace made it clear to me that she was going to say her piece," Denise told me, "but that it was okay for me to disagree, and we didn't have to come to a consensus about it immediately. That wasn't easy for me, but she was right: We had to keep working on it, and looking at it, and coming back to it. I think it's unusual that our friendship survived. But it was like with Calvin: Our goodwill got us through. We'd been there for each other in so many instances leading up to this. And in some ways, going through that has allowed us to be more real with each other."

It begins to drizzle, and Denise volunteers to take the children back home. Candace and I stroll toward a small dock that extends into a marsh. The strains of a Louis Armstrong tune wafts over from some other family's picnic up the street. A red-winged blackbird flies out from the rushes. Candace sits on a bench. She is an ample woman with green eyes, reddish hair and freckles dotting her pale skin. She wears a T-shirt from a fund-raiser for the Jackie Robinson Foundation. She looks back at the intersection from which Denise has just disappeared. "I've really seen her grow," she says, "I've watched Denise become her own woman at work and in her marriage. When they were first married"—she pauses a moment, then grins—"I can't believe I'm going to say this, but Calvin treated her as less than an equal. He was kind of bossy, and I think she acquiesced to that. But as they went on, and she became the sole breadwinner for a while and rose in the corporation—it wasn't just the job, but that was part of it—I think that they've changed drastically to a marriage of "—she pauses again, searching for the right word—"equals," she continues. "Really a marriage of equals."

Both Denise and Calvin had mentioned that they felt she'd changed, in some intangible way over the last few years of their marriage, that the dynamic between them had shifted. Denise described it as finding her own voice, as becoming more herself. It was a midcourse correction that was subtler than those of some of the women I spoke with, but significant nonetheless. It was as if she has completed a circuit: With the strength derived from her community Denise pushed for authenticity at work, creating a new definition of power there. She then infused her marriage with the authority and confidence she'd gained in the workplace, creating a roomier definition of femininity at home.[11]

BACK AT THE house, several families have gathered on the porch for Chinese food and pizza. The women sit at one table, looking at pictures from Monica's recent trip to the Virgin Islands. "Everyone was in those thong bathing suits," Monica says, waving a hand in the air. "There were people in thongs who had no business being in thongs. I mean *no* business." Denise leans back in a wicker chair, smiling: She carries herself more loosely here, laughs more easily. Kids scamper in and out, calling all the grown-ups "aunt" and "uncle" even if they're not related by blood. Someone puts some old disco tunes on the stereo. I gaze through the screen door at Jessie and Rory, who are playing in the yard with their friends. Denise comes up behind me. "I'm glad you got to see this," she says quietly. "This is where my children have their childhood."

Before I visited Denise, I'd asked her over the phone what advice she would give her daughters as they grew up. Her answer was immediate.

"You can't have it all," she'd snapped. But, I'd said, it seemed to me that she did. Denise had fallen silent for a long time. Women are so used to enumerating their failures, I thought, while waiting for her response. Why was it so hard to acknowledge their successes? "Maybe so," she finally said. "But I didn't expect to have to strategize and think and plan and juggle so very much. I guess I expected it to be a lot easier."

Who said it would be easy? I'd asked.

"That's right," she'd agreed ruefully. "Who said it was going to be easy? I guess some of the fairy tales did."

Standing in the fading daylight, I remind her of that conversation. "I guess I wish my daughters didn't have anything to prove," she says. "I don't want them to be where I was and feel like, 'I have to do this. I have to prove that I can compete with these people.' I want them to know their worth and know their strengths and feel really good about using them in an area that will be fulfilling to them. And if they do want to go into corporate America, I just want them to be a little better equipped to maneuver it than I was."

What would that involve? I ask. "Frankly," she says, "a tad sense of arrogance. Feeling very certain about what they can contribute, that who they are is good enough. Knowing that there will be situations that are uncomfortable, and situations that are painful, and situations where people may not believe that they can do what they can do. But I want them to know, inside, that they can. And I want them to go ahead and do it without fear.

"I wasn't sure that I could do that," she continues. "I really wasn't. And in many ways I'm thrilled at where I ended up. I just wish that I could have started my career with the same level of confidence I have now. I spent a lot of years doubting myself, my capabilities, my intellect, my intuition."

We watch as two teenage boys saunter across the lawn to flirt with Denise's eighteen-year-old niece, Tamika, a college student at Spellman. Earlier Tamika had told me that she, too, plans to enter the business world. Her voice brimmed with expectation, but listening to her, my own feelings were mixed: How much still has to change in the workplace and family life in order for Tamika to achieve Denise's level of satisfaction without the devastating trials? It remains so difficult for women to strike a happy balance of public and private goals, to write a new set of rules that would allow us to realize the long stalled promise of change. I wonder, if I talk to Tamika in twenty years, what will have become of her hopes and dreams?

Behind me, the song changes to the Jacksons' "Never Can Say Goodbye." Someone turns a light on deep inside the house. Denise's voice shakes me out of my reverie. "I don't have it all," she says thoughtfully. "But I do have what works for me. And I guess that's good enough."

Afterword:
Thriving in a Time of Flux

O N A RAINY FALL afternoon my phone rings. "Peggy!" says a familiar voice. "It's Abbey Green."

It has been over two years since I've spoken with Abbey, though I've thought about her frequently. I'd felt an especially visceral connection with her during our interviews: So often she'd reminded me of my own younger self. Last I'd heard, Abbey had left New York to attend graduate school in the Midwest. Now, she tells me, she's working in the marketing department of an Internet company, a place that fosters the kind of open, visionary management style of which she once dreamed. I mention that I'm just a few weeks shy of finishing my book. "Really?" she says with characteristic enthusiasm. "Well, what did you find out?"

I hesitate briefly. What could I tell Abbey—or any of the women I met—that could help them in making future choices, challenge their thinking, inspire them to effect change? The nature of flux is that it is dynamic, ever-shifting; that's what makes this moment in history both exciting and frustrating—and nearly impossible to sum up. Women's lives have become a complex web of economic, psychological, and social contradictions, with opportunities so intimately linked to constraints that a choice in one realm can have unexpected consequences (or benefits) ten years later in another.

After four years of talking to women, though, a few things have become clear. The first is fundamental: There's a critical connection between sexual agency and a lifelong sense of self. As Abbey herself attested, it's imperative that girls feel a strong sense of sexual self-determination from the outset, that they understand that sex is not about pleasing boys or competing with friends but ought to grow from authentic desire, feelings of intimacy, mutual respect, as well as an innate right to pleasure. "It's absolutely key to esteem issues for me," she had insisted when we first met. "If you're comfortable with your body, you're comfortable with yourself. If you feel like you deserve all this pleasure in bed, you start to feel like you deserve it other places too." Like Abbey, many of the young women I interviewed had struggled to overcome dehumanizing early experiences, encounters which teach them that men's desires supersede their own.[1] As they grow older, that lesson fuels a more general reluctance to articulate (and in some cases, to even recognize) their own needs, particularly in their relationships with men and children.

For most of the young women I met, part of the Promise was attaining a marriage of equals, one in which intimacy and responsibility—both in and outside the home—were reciprocal. They believed that the most satisfying life would be one in which independence combined with interdependence, in which they contributed to the world through work as well as nurturing their families. Yet, the images of the Perfect Wife and the Good Mother cast surprisingly long shadows over their lives. Even as they dreamed of equality they were tracking themselves into lower-paying, more flexible jobs than their male peers under the assumption that, when the time came, it would be up to them to make most of the sacrifices at home. They viewed that strategy as pragmatic, a compromise between dueling expectations, but, in addition to potentially decreasing their engagement with work, it ensures that they will have less leverage in negotiating chores and childcare, that their future husbands will feel less accountability at home, and, over time, that the prospect for the kind of partnerships they envision will be vastly reduced.[2]

The fact remains that in order for women to fulfill their potential as individuals, separate from their roles as wives and mothers, men—at least more men—have to take on full responsibility at home. Some do. The couples I met who had avoided the Near-Peer slide, such as Emily and Dan Sorenson in Chicago, were more satisfied with the balance of their lives than anyone else I interviewed.[3] Those couples had several things in common. The wives earned at least half of their family's income. The husbands had flexible jobs, worked regular hours, or were self-employed—the same circumstances that typically free women to handle emergencies, stay home with sick kids and, generally, devote more time to family life. Often something unexpected had happened—the woman needed to travel for her job, for instance, or a man was temporarily downsized—that had disrupted traditional gender roles, allowing the husband to develop his own sense of parental authority.

Sometimes among these couples the men had faced the kind of no-win trade-offs that typically befall women: Men in dual-career marriages receive fewer promotions than their single-earner peers. (They also take a salary hit—a "Daddy penalty"—earning up to nineteen percent less for the same job.[4]) Still, just as for women who make similar compromises, the payoff is a closer relationship to their children.[5] Nor does father-nurturing subtract from mothering: The amount of time women spend with their children remains the same regardless of how much time Dad puts in.[6] Men who share childcare more equally also report more positive feelings about their wives' employment and the wives themselves are less likely to be depressed.[7] "Dan likes that we're both experiencing things and we're both trying to balance similar things," Emily told me. "And I think we don't tend to take each other for granted as much as we might otherwise. You start living in separate worlds if one is staying at home and one is working. So while it's difficult sometimes, it balances our marriage. Not to say your finances dictate the balance of power in your marriage, but it sure has a big influence, don't you think?"

I thought of what Emily had said when I read an article in *The Wall Street Journal* about how young women, much like the ones I'd met, were preparing for motherhood years in advance, "armed themselves to the teeth" by laying the groundwork for flexible careers.[8] Unsurprisingly, few young men were doing the same. The writer seemed to be admiring the women's savvy in avoiding "the painful work-family conflicts of older women." Yet, anticipating the Near-Peer slide and reinforcing the Good Mother mythology may be precisely the wrong tactics: It appears that the more roles are reversed, the less stressful family life will become. Perhaps, then, all those well-intentioned seminars on work-life balance that are offered to young women in college and graduate school should be rethought: We all might be better off if they were targeted at men.

MEN MAY HAVE to do more, but women also have to let them. Mother management among the women I interviewed kicked in early. Recently I joked with a friend that every time she felt the urge to correct her husband's handling of their newborn, every time she was about to snatch the baby from him because Mother Knows Best, she should consider whether she wanted to *have* to do that when the child is ten. Stepping in made her feel a rush of competence, but it also reinforced that he was just her sidekick, not really responsible for their child's basic needs.

Micromanaging family life makes women feel in control, makes them feel like Good Mothers. It's also a very real source of power in a world where women can still feel powerless. That's not so easy to give up, but until we're free from the Good Mother's psychological grip, with its unattainable standards and sweet sense of authority, we can never fully address the external barriers to a more satisfying life. Perversely, though, as women's opportunities have grown outside of the home, Perfect Mother martyrdom seems to have grown more extreme, even glorified. For instance, there's the e-mail I received last March, telling the story of a couple watching TV. "I'm going to bed," the wife says, then proceeds to perform a long list of household tasks: throwing a load of clothes in the wash, setting out the breakfast dishes, checking the kids' homework, feeding the dog. Every few minutes her husband looks up and says, "I thought you were going to bed." "In a minute," she replies, then continues with her chores. This goes on and on. The punch line? Eventually the husband says, "I think I'll go to bed too." And he does. The letter ended with the suggestion: "Send this to five phenomenal women in celebration of women's history month." I was stunned. Since when is it "phenomenal" for a woman to resign herself to such imbalance? Since when is it cause for celebration?

It's a simple equation: if you're doing it all, you do not have it all. Mother management, driven by the fear of being judged by others as well as by their own harsh internal judgment, reinforces both the Near-Peer slide and the Second Shift. It also makes children—how they dress, how they comport themselves, how mentally healthy they appear—a reflection of a mother's self-worth, an extension of her identity. Giving up mother management is no small challenge. To do it requires that women get down in the psychological mud and wrestle with their deepest convictions about female silence and deference, about motherly self-denial and identity. It requires the courage to stand up to society censure and a great deal of faith that an alternative is possible. It also requires banishing, once and for all, the Good Mother.

EVEN WHEN TRADITIONAL roles seem the most desirable—or the most practical—course, they can be undertaken with egalitarian ideals in mind. That's especially important for women who decide to stay home full-time. The couples I met who had made the most conventional choices were least likely to discuss their implications. Periodically during my research, I recalled an early conversation in New York with a twenty-seven-year-old, pregnant financial analyst who was planning to quit her job after her child was born. "I don't worry about divorce," she'd told me defiantly. "If that came about, it would be so horrible, let the whole world fall in on me. If it's compounded by the fact that I don't have a career, who cares." It was such an extreme response, and, given the statistics on divorce and widowhood, so foolhardy.

Perhaps more than anyone, women who follow the most traditional path need to clarify their roles with their spouses in advance: How, while staying home, can they still strive for intellectual and economic equality as partners, and how will they assure some equity in parenting? The women I spoke with who were home full-time complained just as much—perhaps more—than working women about lack of time as a couple, lack of time for themselves, unfair division of labor, and a stagnant sex life. Given that, it seems imperative for a woman to consider before committing to at-home motherhood how she can adapt traditional patterns to have a stronger sense of autonomy within them. Aside from the childcare, how much housework will she be expected to do? How much will her husband do? How will she build skills for eventual reentry into the workforce? If they agree that her domestic labor contributes as much to their partnership as his wage-earning, would he expect to hand over half of his income, his pension, his company stock options, even his business to her if they divorce? (According to a *Business Week*/Harris Poll of households earning $100,000, the answer is no, perhaps offering the most honest assessment of men's beliefs about women's unpaid labor. Only 41 percent felt that an estate should be divided evenly when one spouse has generated most of the wealth; most believed the higher earner deserved the larger slice of the pie.[9]) Over the short term, how will a couple assure that the woman has free time, that she has room for self-development? "What do I want for *myself* now?" was the typical question of midlife—but, really, women need to ask it all along the way, for their own well-being as well as for the good of their relationships with husbands, children, employers, and friends.

WOMEN CAN'T LEAD fuller lives until men are equal partners in the home, but men can't be true partners at home until there's further change in the workplace. Most of the employers I visited, like women's husbands, were more accommodating than in generations past, but, they, too, hadn't come far enough. Three of the women I profiled—Emily, Denise Littleton, and Mira Brodie—worked for corporations that have been cited by publications such as *Working Woman* and *Working Mother* as among the most supportive of women. Despite that, they had each encountered barriers to advancement, and believed that the only way to reach the uppermost tiers of their professions was to conduct themselves as men traditionally have—but without the luxury of a stay-at-home spouse. Some, like Mira, were willing to remain single and childless if that's what it took. That's a valid choice when freely made, and it may well be the right one for her, but it shouldn't be a prerequisite of success. When I first met Mira, she argued that the workplace wouldn't really change until there was a critical mass of women at the highest levels of power. She's right: According to a Families and Work Institute report, having a few token women in top positions doesn't affect the culture of an institution. It's not until women fill half or more of upper-level jobs that companies become more likely to provide near-site day care, elder care resource and referral programs, and that options such as flextime can be pursued without penalty.[10] But here's the rub: Until those humanizing factors are in place, women will have a hard time achieving the numbers necessary to make change. That's partly why, although women have flooded formerly male-dominated professions for decades, they make up only 13 percent of law partners, 26 percent of tenured professors, and 12 percent of corporate officers.[11]

That means that until men fully understand what it means to straddle two worlds, women who pursue "life balance" will continue to sacrifice career advancement. Take the case of Lewis Platt, who was, until recently, CEO of the Hewlett-Packard Company. Under his leadership, HP became known as a bastion of enlightened, egalitarian thinking. Why? Because Platt's wife, who had stayed home with their daughters, died of cancer in 1981. Until then, according to *The New York Times*, he felt that women essentially created their own problems.[12] Juggling a demanding job as a single parent, though, he had a conversion experience. When he became CEO, Platt not only instituted but *encouraged* HP employees—from upper-level executives on down, men as well as women—to use flexible scheduling, share jobs, work from home, and take sabbaticals, all without sacrificing advancement opportunities. The turnover rate among women at the company, which had been twice that of men's, is now the same,[13] and women are well seeded along the pipeline to top-level positions. It's no coincidence that when Platt moved on to become the company's chairman in 1999 (he subsequently left the corporation), he was replaced by a woman, one of just three female CEOs of Fortune 500 companies. Platt's story shows that radically redefining the workplace—the very meaning of work—is possible, although his example is not without irony: Do women really have to *die* in order for men to see the light?

I thought about Platt during a recent conversation with an old high school buddy who is now an AIDS researcher at a prestigious university, married, with one child. "So many of my female colleagues really struggle to balance everything," he told me. "I really feel for them. A lot of them just drop out once they have kids."

"Well," I snapped back, "my goal is to make it just as hard for you as it is for them." He laughed. "No, I'm serious," I said, glaring. He'd irked me, so my response wasn't quite what I'd meant. My goal, really, was for men to reckon with the same conflicts as women do, as well as have the same choices: They should be as willing and able as women to choose low-paying, personally fulfilling professions, to marry a high-earning spouse and be primary caretakers of their children. As for those women who were forced to choose between work and family obligations, what if they could have made progress toward finding a cure for AIDS? Until that level of transformation happens, there will continue to be a loss of talent and a tremendous social cost to the contradictions we all face.

WOMEN DON'T NEED corporations or even men to change to expand their own vision of what it means to be female. The lives of the single and childless women were especially valuable in that regard. Recall that Roseanne Peretti, the divorced account executive in Brooklyn, had consciously created meaningful multigenerational ties to community, family, and children. Her experience (which was not unique among the never-married, divorced, and childless women I interviewed) illuminated the opportunities for nurturing, creative expression, social contribution and self-development outside traditional boundaries. It also belied a culture that depicts single women, even the glamorous ones, as emotionally stunted, desperate, or victims of their own ambition. In fact, research consistently shows that single women grow happier as they age and are more independent, more assertive, and more interested in personal growth than their married peers.[14] Nor does childlessness affect a woman's long-term well-being: Childless couples are as happy as parents who have good relationships with their children—and happier than those whose relationships are distant.[15]

Most young women I met agreed that a woman could lead a full life without a husband and children, but they weren't eager to try it. As long as marriage and motherhood feel compulsory, though, they risk compromising themselves in their choice of partners, in their decisions about when and whether to have children, and in how those children are cared for. They will also be encouraged to act against their own best interests when trying to balance their needs with their families', and they'll be less equipped to hang on to an essential sense of self in the largely selfless relationship of a parent to a child.

The gap between the relative contentment of midlife single women and younger women's perceptions of them was alarming—particularly since, with a lower marriage rate, later marriage, divorce, and widowhood, today's women will spend more of their lives alone than in any previous era. Perhaps young women should look more closely at the statistics on women's health in marriage and their satisfaction in divorce, not to dissuade them, but to inspire them to find an approach to marriage—its beginning, its middle, and its potential end—that would be more flexible, airier, that would leave more room for a female self that is both distinct and connected.

The need for women to share such experience with one another, to talk across lines of age and circumstance, came through most emphatically in my interviews. Women tended to cluster with those most like themselves—working mothers with working mothers, single women with single women, forty-year-olds with forty-year-olds. That's not surprising: In an unstable time, someone else's choices and accommodations can feel like a reproach. My own hunger for that kind of honest, multigenerational discussion was part of what drove me to write this book. When I began, I was tormented by a deeply personal question: Should I have children? I ended up answering so much more. I'm a different woman than I was four years ago—more open, more optimistic, less judgmental of others and of myself. Talking with younger women like Abbey, Mira, and Shay, for instance, I reflected on how I, too, had struggled with the contradictions of the Promise, and how that confusion shaped my subsequent choices. Too often, I realize, I made decisions based on what I *didn't* want to be rather than what I hoped to become.

In retrospect, I suspect I was searching for my own perfect role model among the mothers I met, someone whose life could act as a blueprint to guide me through the Crunch. I didn't find her, but that turned out to be okay: Each conversation gave me new ideas about how I'd like to define, or perhaps redefine, motherhood for myself, and that was far more valuable. The single midlife women I met, both those who were never married and those who were divorced, were a revelation. They inspired me to contemplate how I've changed since becoming a wife, the parts of myself I needed to relinquish to truly share my life with Steven, and the parts, perhaps, I shouldn't have. Along with the childless women, they taught me that there are many ways beyond motherhood to build a meaningful, connected life. As the months have gone by and I have not yet become pregnant again, I have had some dark days, but, overall, I've retained my equanimity. I have the single and childless women I interviewed to thank for that. The relationships they had with siblings' and friends' children, their volunteer work, and the advantage they took of their freedom gave me a true alternative to which I can aspire.

Reporting this book was not always easy. Sometimes I bumped up against my own biases; sometimes I confronted my own regrets. As a result of that process, though, I feel more prepared to consciously construct the life I want and better able to accept the times when I fall short of that mark. I'm grateful to have had the opportunity to learn so much from my interviews but also a little disheartened: I wish such conversations were the norm in women's lives, that they didn't have to be so artificially and elaborately created. I hope, someday, they can be.

There are so many interviews I'd still like to do, so many questions I'd like to ask. I wonder how caring for sick and aging parents will affect women's choices, how it will shape the next phase of their lives. Is there a "Good Daughter" icon that correlates to the Good Mother and Perfect Wife? I would've liked to have pressed further on issues of widowhood too, which need to be front and center of the next feminist agenda. How is it that, after a lifetime of being caretakers themselves, elderly women are more likely than men to be neglected by their families?[16] How can we better protect ourselves from poverty? In the end, there is no single path to a textured, satisfying life—nor should there be. But there are decisions we can make more consciously, strategies we can employ more usefully, consequences we can understand more fully as we assemble the pieces of our professional and personal dreams. Through that process women can move a little further, come a little closer, to reaching the promise of our half-changed world.

Notes

INTRODUCTION

[1]Alan L. Otten, "Male Professions Are Much Less So," *The Wall Street Journal*, November 15, 1993, p. B1; Nina Bernstein, "Study Says Equality Eludes Many Women in Law Firms," *The New York Times*, January 8, 1996, p. 9; Jackson Park, "Married . . . with Anxiety," *Elle*, July 1997, p. 68; Lois Smith Brady, "Why Marriage Is Hot Again," *Redbook*, September 1996, p. 122; Diane E. Lewis, "Disenchanted Women Give Up Careers," Minneapolis *Star Tribune*, April 6, 1998, p. D7; Sue Shellenbarger, "Women Indicate Satisfaction with Role of Big Breadwinner," *The Wall Street Journal*, May 11, 1995, p. B1; Pamela Stock, "Single & Loving It," *Mademoiselle*, October 1996, p. 144; Aimee Agresti, "I Couldn't Stand Being Single," *Mademoiselle*, February 1999, p. 30; Leslie Dreyfous, "Children: To Have or Have Not," the *San Francisco Chronicle*, March 20, 1991, p. B3; Lynn Smith, "A Dream Denied," the *Los Angeles Times*, October 12, 1994, p. E1.

[2]Frank Rich, "Hillary Clinton, R.I.P.: Hollywood Dumps the New Woman," *The New York Times*, November 29, 1995, p. A23.

[3]U.S. Bureau of the Census, Statistical Abstract of the United States: 1998 (118th edition), Washington, D.C., 1998, pp. 409, 417; Joanna L. Krotz, "Why Can't a Woman Be Paid Like a Man?" *Working Woman*, July–August 1999, p. 92; Daniel E. Hecker, "Earnings of College Graduates: Women Compared with Men," Monthly Labor Review, March 1998, available on-line; http://stats.bls.gov/opub/mlr/1998/03/contents.htm; Reynolds Holding, "Women in Law: Status Report on the Glass Ceiling," *San Francisco Chronicle*, April 11, 1999, p. 6; Eileen Alt Powell, "Fast Track Off Limits to Women," *The San Francisco Examiner*, November 17, 1999, p. B1. Kate Zernike, "MIT Women Win a Fight Against Bias: In Rare Move, School Admits Discrimination," *The Boston Globe*, March 21, 1999, p. A1; "Smart Stats," *Glamour*, February 1997, p. 106.

[4]Terry A. Lugaila, "Marital Status and Living Arrangements: March, 1997 (Update)," *Current Population Reports P20–506*, Washington, D.C.: U.S. Bureau of the Census, June 1998, p. 1.

[5]Ruth Sidel, *On Her Own: Growing Up in the Shadow of the American Dream*, New York: Viking, 1990, p. 17.

[6]In her classic work, *The Hungry Self: Women, Eating & Identity*, New York: Perennial Library, 1986, psychologist Kim Chernin explores the ways a troubled relationship with food expresses the essential problems of being female in women's lives, particularly at moments in the culture when women attempt the type of social and self-development that has traditionally been the province of men.

[7]Daniel J. Levinson with Judy D. Levinson, *The Seasons of a Woman's Life*, New York:

Alfred A. Knopf, 1996, p. 16–20; Terri Apter writes that women work out their ideals about marriage and maternity between twenty-five and forty; during that period the clash between their affiliative and expansive needs create deep fissures in their lives. *Secret Paths: Women in the New Midlife.* New York: W. W. Norton, 1995, p. 31.

[8]Hazel Marcus, professor of psychology, Stanford University, personal interview. Markus spoke as a member of the MacArthur Task Force on Successful Mid-life Transition, which found that a college education gives women even more than men an agentic self: a sense of opportunity, control, and confidence. According to one study of 1,502 women between the ages of 18 and 55, 95 percent of those who were college graduates felt they were doing at least fairly well, compared with only 3 percent of women who had not completed high school. The Families and Work Institute, *Women: The New Providers* (Whirlpool Foundation Study, Part One), New York: The Families and Work Institute, 1995, available on-line: http://www.whirlpoolcorp.com/whr/ics/foundation/New Providers1.pdf.

[9]Gail Sheehy, *Passages,* New York: Bantam, 1976, p. 23.

[10]In 1997 the median age of first marriage reached 25 years for women (26.8 years for men); about 35 percent of women 25 to 34 had never married; for blacks alone the figure was 54 percent. Lugaila, "Marital Status and Living Arrangements," p. 1; University of Pennsylvania demographer Philip Morgan, personal interview.

[11]Daniel B. Wood, "Young Women Exercise Options," *The Christian Science Monitor,* May 24, 1994, p. 9; Lewis, "Disenchanted Women Give Up Careers to Stay Home."

CHAPTER ONE

[1]Anne Machung, "Talking Career, Thinking Job: Gender Differences in Career and Family Expectations of Berkeley Seniors," *Feminist Studies,* 15, 1 (Spring 1989): 35–58. See also Rhona Mahony, *Kidding Ourselves: Breadwinning, Babies, and Bargaining Power,* New York: Basic Books, 1995, pp. 2–5.

[2]Patricia McBroom, *The Third Sex: The New Professional Woman,* New York: Paragon House, 1992, pp. 27–30.

[3]Terri Apter, *Working Women Don't Have Wives: Professional Success in the 1990s.* New York: St. Martin's Griffin, 1993, p. 210. Apter cites a survey of senior executives in which over half the women polled were never married, divorced, or widowed and fewer than 40 percent had children. See also Jean Lipman-Blumen, Todd Fryling, Michael C. Henderson, Christine Webster Moore, and Becky Vecchiotti, "Women in Corporate Leadership: Reviewing a Decade's Research," special report, Wellesley, Mass.: Center for Research on Women, 1996, p. 78. In journalism, a 1996 survey of Washington correspondents found that half the women were unmarried and two thirds did not have children. Mark Fitzgerald, "Survey: D.C. Women Equal in Newsroom, Not Out," *Editor & Publisher Magazine,* November 2, 1996, p. 15.

[4]Sixty percent of boys do. This difference remains consistent throughout their lives. Edward O. Laumann, John H. Gagnon, Robert T. Michael, and Stuart Michaels, *The Social Organization of Sexuality: Sexual Practices in the United States,* Chicago: University of Chicago Press, 1994, p. 84.

[5]Thirty-five hundred Americans were randomly sampled for a poll on sexual behavior in the United States. In Marcia Douglass and Lisa Douglass, *Are We Having Fun Yet?: The Intelligent Women's Guide to Sex,* New York: Hyperion, 1997, p. 3.

[6]Karen Bouris, *The First Time: Women Speak Out About "Losing Their Virginity,"* Emeryville, Ca.: Canari Press, 1993; and Karen Bouris, *The First Time: What Parents and Teenage Girls Should Know About "Losing Your Virginity,"* Emeryville, Ca.: Canari Press, 1994.

Bouris reports on a poll in which two thirds of young women but fewer than half of young men wished they'd waited to have sex until they were older. *The First Time*, 1994, pp. 3–4. In psychiatrist Shirley Feldman's study of attitudes toward first sexual experiences, feelings about sex, and notions of commitment among eighteen to twenty-four-year-olds, most women expressed regret about the circumstances of their first intercourse and would advise a younger woman to wait until it was "really right." Shirley Feldman, senior research scientist in child psychiatry, Stanford University, personal interview. Similarly, in her study of postsexual-revolution culture, psychologist Lillian Rubin found that only 10 percent of women reported positive first experiences. Interestingly an equally small number of men described their first time as pleasurable, but the men went on subsequently to enjoy sex more. *Erotic Wars: What Happened to the Sexual Revolution?* New York: Farrar, Straus & Giroux, 1990, p. 42.

[7]Both Feldman and Rubin found that positive first experiences for women usually occurred in the context of an "important" relationship. Among Rubin's subjects, the relationship was often with a slightly older man. Feldman, personal interview. Rubin, *Erotic Wars*, p. 42.

[8]Douglass and Douglass, *Are We Having Fun Yet?* p. 3

[9]Germaine Greer, cited in Naomi Wolf, *The Beauty Myth*, New York: William Morrow, 1991, p. 154

[10]Susan Faludi, *Backlash: The Undeclared War Against Women*, New York: Crown, 1991, p. 9.

[11]Daniel J. Levinson with Judy D. Levinson, *The Seasons of a Woman's Life*, New York: Alfred A. Knopf, 1996, pp. 25–26.

[12]Ibid., pp. 117–141.

[13]In 1997 the median age of first marriage reached 25 for women (26.8 for men), an all-time high. Terry A. Lugaila, "Marital Status and Living Arrangements: March 1997 (Update)," (Current Population Reports P20-506), Washington D.C.: U.S. Bureau of the Census, June 1998, p. 1. Between 1970 and 1993 the number of unmarried women between 25 and 34 tripled. U.S. Bureau of the Census, "Statistical Facts for Women's History Month," March, 1995.

[14]"Prince Charming Who?" *Jane*, September–October 1997, p. 82. The poll, conducted by Yankelovich Partners, queried 1,000 women between the ages of 18 and 34. The women also said they believed the perfect age for a woman to marry is 26; the average age at which their mothers married was 20.

[15]Lillian B. Rubin, *Intimate Strangers: Men and Women Together*, New York: Harper Colophon Books, 1983, p. 8.

[16]Lauren Dockett and Kristen Beck, *Facing 30: Women Talk About Constructing a Real Life and Other Scary Rites of Passage*, Oakland: New Harbinger Publications, 1998, p. 18.

[17]Stephen Smith, "Fear Turns to Obsession," MSNBC News, available on-line: http://http://www.msnbc.com/news/124391.asp#BODY, August 1, 1999.

[18]Ibid. Infertility is more prevalent among poor women and women of color as well.

[19]Machung, "Talking Career, Thinking Job," p. 37.

[20]Kim DaCosta, "Marriage and Motherhood: A New Perspective on Commitment, Sacrifice and Self-Development," unpublished master's thesis, University of California at Berkeley, 1995.

[21]Machung, "Talking Career, Thinking Job," p. 57.

CHAPTER TWO

[1]Male managers continue to believe that successful managerial traits are more likely to be held by men in general than by women in general. Rosalind C. Barnett, "Women in

Management Today," Working Paper No. 249. Wellesley, Mass.: Center for Research on Women, 1992, p. 24.

[2]Patricia McBroom, *The Third Sex: The New Professional Woman*, New York: Paragon House, 1992, and personal interview.

[3]Sarah Hardesty and Nehama Jacobs, *Success and Betrayal: The Crisis of Women in Corporate America*, New York: Franklin Watts, 1986, pp. 31–32.

[4]See Jean Lipman-Blumen, Todd Fryling, Michael C. Henderson, Christine Webster Moore, and Rachel Vecchiotti, "Women in Corporate Leadership: Reviewing a Decade's Research," special report, Wellesley, Mass.: Center for Research on Women, 1996, p. 77; Kathleen Hall Jamieson, *Beyond the Double Bind: Women and Leadership*, New York: Oxford University Press, 1995, pp. 1–6.

[5]Lipman-Blumen et al., "Women in Corporate Leadership," p. 76.

[6]Patricia Sellers, "Women, Sex & Power," *Fortune*, August 5, 1996, p. 56.

[7]Lipman-Blumen et al., "Women in Corporate Leadership," p. 71. Corporate leaders rate mentoring second only to education as having had a significant impact on their success, but a 1993 study by Catalyst, a nonprofit organization dedicated to advancing women in business, found that women were at a disadvantage in finding mentors both because of a lack of women in senior positions who could take on that role and because men, concerned that their attempts to initiate a mentoring relationship might be misinterpreted as romantic (and possibly legally actionable) overtures, are reluctant to mentor women. Catalyst, "Mentoring: A Guide to Corporate Programs and Practices," New York: Catalyst, 1993. Those findings were reconfirmed in the *1999 Catalyst Census of Women Corporate Officers and Top Earners*, New York: Catalyst, 1999; and Catalyst, *Women of Color in Corporate Management: Opportunities and Barriers*, New York: Catalyst, 1999.

[8]Lipman-Blumen et al., "Women in Corporate Leadership," p. 71.

[9]Hochschild uses the term "backstage wealth" to describe the support available to men and women as they pursue their work outside the home. Arlie Hochschild with Anne Machung, *The Second Shift: Working Parents and the Revolution at Home*, New York: Viking Penguin, 1989, pp. 253–256.

[10]Felice N. Schwartz noticed a similar phenomenon among MBA candidates she interviewed. While women removed wedding bands before interviews, some men actually *borrowed* rings—the perception that they would need to support a family indicated greater stability and stronger commitment to a job. *Breaking with Traditional Women and Work, the New Facts of Life*, New York: Warner Books, 1992, p. 10.

[11]Further, while more companies now offer maternity leave, women often encounter negative attitudes from bosses and coworkers when they return to work. Lipman-Blumen, et al., "Women in Corporate Leadership," pp. 78–79. Felice Schwartz notes that employers are often men who frequently have stay-at-home wives themselves, which can affect their perception of female employees. *Breaking with Traditional Women and Work*, p. 37.

[12]McBroom, *The Third Sex*, pp. 8–9.

CHAPTER THREE

[1]Korn/Ferry International, "Diversity in the Executive Suites: Good News and Bad News," available on-line: http://www.kornferry.com/diversit.htm; November 1997; Rona Dogar, "It's a Woman's World," *Newsweek*, May 11, 1998, available on-line: http://search.newsweek.com; "14 Reasons for Men to Be Nervous," *Glamour*, September 1996, p. 168.

[2]Karen Bouris, *The First Time: What Parents and Teenage Girls Should Know About "Losing*

Your Virginity," Emeryville, Ca.: Canari Press, 1994, pp. 3–4. A National Opinion Research Center poll of 3,500 Americans found that for one quarter of women first intercourse was forced. Marcia Douglass and Lisa Douglass, *Are We Having Fun Yet: The Intelligent Women's Guide to Sex,* New York: Hyperion, 1997, p. 3.

[3]Rhona Mahony, *Kidding Ourselves: Breadwinning, Babies, and Bargaining Power,* New York: Basic Books, 1995, pp. 144–145.

CHAPTER FOUR

[1]Women of color are paid less than white women, are less likely to say they can find mentors, and are more pessimistic about their chances for advancement. However, overall, gender affects managers more than race: men of color, in general, are doing better in corporations than women of color. "Fact Sheet: Women of Color in Corporate Management: Opportunities and Barriers," New York: Catalyst, July 1999, available online: http://www.catalystwomen.org/press/mediakit/factswoc3.html; "Advancement Opportunities Lacking, Say Corporate Women of Color," New York: Catalyst, February 1998, available on-line: http://www.catalystwomen.org/press/release0210.html; "Catalyst Study Finds Women of Color Under-Represented in the Managerial Workforce," New York: Catalyst, October 1997: available on-line, http://www.catalystwomen.org/press/release1022.html.

[2]U.S. Bureau of the Census, *Statistical Abstract of the United States: 1998* (118th edition), Washington, D.C., 1998, p. 41. Blacks comprise 12.5 percent of the population. Central Intelligence Agency, *The World Fact Book, 1999,* available on-line: http://www.odci.gov/cia/publications/factbook/us.html.

[3]Audrey Edwards, and Craig K. Polite, *Children of the Dream: The Psychology of Black Success,* New York: Doubleday, 1992, p. 138.

[4]Muriel Whetstone, "Why Professional Women Should Consider Blue-Collar Men," *Ebony,* March 1996, p. 25.

[5]David Andrew Price. "A Good Man Is Hard to Find," *The Wall Street Journal,* February 21, 1995, p. A25; National Center for Educational Statistics, "Postsecondary Education." *Digest of Educational Statistics,* available on-line: http://nces.ed.gov.pubs99/digest98/index.thml, 1999, table 264.

[6]Terry A. Lugaila, "Marital Status and Living Arrangements: March 1997 (Update)," (Current Population Reports P20-506, Washington D.C.: U.S. Bureau of the Census, June 1998, p. 2.

[7]Debra Dickerson, "She's Gotta Have It: The Search for Black Men," *The New Republic,* May 6, 1996, p. 13.

[8]Ibid.

[9]Audrey Chapman, *Entitled to Good Loving: Black Men and Women and the Battle for Love and Power,* New York: Henry Holt and Company, 1995, p. 45.

CHAPTER FIVE

[1]In 1997, 19.7 percent of women aged 30 to 34 were never married. Terry A. Lugaila, "Marital Status and Living Arrangements: March 1997 (Update)," (Current Population Reports F20-506), Washington, D.C.: U.S. Bureau of the Census, June 1998, p. 2. Between 1970 and 1993 the number of unmarried women between 25 and 34 tripled. U.S. Bureau of the Census, "Statistical Facts for Women's History Month," March 1995.

[2]Phyllis Rose, *Parallel Lives: Five Victorian Marriages,* New York: Vintage Books, 1983, pp. 7–8.

[3]Betty Carter and Joan K. Peters, *Love, Honor & Negotiate: Building Partnerships That Last a Lifetime*, New York: Pocket Books, 1996, p. 88.

[4]Dalma Heyn, *Marriage Shock: The Transformation of Women into Wives*, New York: Villard, 1997, p. 77.

[5]Laura L. Carstensen, Jeremy Graff, Robert W. Levinson, and John L. Gottman, "Affect in Intimate Relationships: The Developmental Course of a Marriage," in *Handbook of Emotion, Adult Development, and Aging*, Carol Magai, ed., San Diego: Academic Press, 1966, pp. 241–242; Laura Carstensen, professor of psychology, Stanford University, personal interview.

[6]Arlie Hochschild with Anne Machung, *The Second Shift: Working Parents and the Revolution at Home*, New York: Viking Penguin, 1989, p. 57.

[7]Carter and Peters, *Love, Honor & Negotiate*, p. 9; see also Pepper Schwartz, *Peer Marriage: How Love Between Equals Really Works*, New York: The Free Press, 1994, p. 53.

[8]Philip Blumstein and Pepper Schwartz, *American Couples: Money, Work, Sex*, New York: William Morrow, 1983, pp. 55, 76; Schwartz, *Peer Marriage*, p. 1.

[9]Rhona Mahony, *Kidding Ourselves: Breadwinning, Babies, and Bargaining Power*, New York: Basic Books, 1995, pp. 4–5.

[10]University of Pennsylvania demographer Philip Morgan, personal interview; Michael Specter, "Population Implosion Worries a Graying Europe," *The New York Times*, July 10, 1998, p. A1. Although the figures do not distinguish between voluntary and involuntary childlessness—and one might question whether "voluntary" can legitimately include women who feel they've had to choose between motherhood and professional aspirations, since men are rarely forced into such decisions—the numbers are high enough that it is safe to assume the rates are socially driven and not a result of infertility.

[11]Jeanne Safer, *Beyond Motherhood: Choosing a Life Without Children*, New York: Pocket Books, 1996, p. 76.

[12]Grace Baruch, Rosalind Barrett, and Caryl Rivers, *Lifeprints: New Patterns of Love and Work for Today's Women*, New York: Signet Books, 1983, pp. 106–107.

[13]Ingrid Connidis and Julie McMullin, of the University of Western Ontario, studied nearly 700 Canadian men and women over age 55. Katherine Griffin, "Childless by Choice," *Health*, March/April 1996, p. 99. See also Safer, *Beyond Motherhood*, p. 122.

[14]Kim DaCosta, "Marriage and Motherhood: A New Perspective on Commitment, Sacrifice and Self-Development," unpublished master's thesis, University of California at Berkeley, 1995, p. 18.

[15]Karen Houppert, "The Parent Trapped," *Newsday*, January 24, 1999, p. B13. Houppert reviews Maushart's book, *The Mask of Motherhood: How Becoming a Mother Changes Everything and Why We Pretend It Doesn't*, New Press in which Maushart reports, among other things, that women are five times more likely to suffer mental illness in the first year of motherhood than at any time in the life cycle.

[16]Philip Cowan and Carolyn Pape Cowan, "New Families: Modern Couples as New Pioneers," in *All Our Families: New Policies for a New Century*, Mary Ann Mason, Arlene Skolnick, and Stephen D. Sugarman, eds. New York: Oxford University Press, 1998, pp. 173, 180; Carstensen et al., "Affect in Intimate Relationships," p. 230; Barbara Kantrowitz and Pat Wingert, "The Science of a Good Marriage," *Newsweek*, April 19, 1999, p. 57.

[17]Joan K. Peters, *When Mothers Work: Loving Our Children Without Sacrificing Ourselves*, New York: Addison Wesley Longman, 1997, p. 2.

[18]Schwartz, "Peer Marriage," p. 114; Peters, *When Mothers Work*, p. 197; Cowan and Cowan, "New Families: Modern Couples as New Pioneers," pp. 180, 184.

[19]Schwartz, *Peer Marriage*, pp. 2, 162. See also, Rosalind C. Barnett and Caryl Rivers, *She Works/He Works: How Two-Income Families are Happier, Healthier and Better Off*, San

Francisco: HarperSanFrancisco, 1996, p. 199; and Peters, *When Mothers Work*, p. 10. These couples are also often called "transitional" in their gender ideology or marriage. Hochschild, *The Second Shift*, pp. 15–17; Mahony, *Kidding Ourselves*, p. 106.

[20]See, for instance, Hochschild, *The Second Shift*, and Mahony, *Kidding Ourselves*.

[21]Schwartz, *Peer Marriage*, p. 111.

[22]Carter and Peters, *Love, Honor and Negotiate*, p. 16; Cowan and Cowan, "New Families," p. 181.

[23]Dianna Waggoner, "For Working Women, Having It All May Mean Doing It All," *People*, September 4, 1989, p. 51.

[24]Peters, *When Mothers Work*, p. 82; Barnett and Rivers, *She Works/He Works*, pp. 226–227.

[25]Terri Apter, *Secret Paths: Women in the New Midlife*, New York: W. W. Norton, 1995, pp. 19–20. In addition to its psychological ramifications, mother management can have a profound impact on a woman's physical health: In one Canadian study, the combination of high job stress and disproportionate family responsibilities resulted in significant and persistent increases in the blood pressure for white-collar college-educated women. Unlike men, whose blood pressure drops in the evening, women's elevated pressure persisted at home after working hours. Center for the Advancement of Health, "Office Stress, Large Family Responsibilities Put Women at Risk," Publicity Release, March 22, 1999, available on-line: http://www.cfah.org.

[26]A 1997 Roper Poll found that the number of Americans who were highly satisfied with their jobs dropped to the lowest figure since the poll began in 1973. The decline was most pronounced among executive and professional workers and baby boomers aged 30 to 44, with the steepest plunge reported among women. Katherine Griffin, "What I Do for Love," *Working Woman*, December 1998, p. 38. Eighty-four percent of women in another, 1995 Roper Poll agreed that "regardless of changes that may have occurred, women still face more restrictions in life than men do." "Women Less Optimistic than Men," *About Women on Campus*, Spring 1996, p. 4.

[27]Nancer H. Ballard. "Equal Engagement: Observations on Career Success and Meaning in the Lives of Women Lawyers," Working Paper No. 292, Wellesley, MA: Center for Research on Women, 1998; see also, Sue Woodman, "On the Run From the Law," *Ms.*, November/December, 1995, p. 38.

[28]U.S. Bureau of the Census, *Statistical Abstract of the United States: 1998* (118th edition), Washington, D.C., 1998, p. 409.

[29]Diane E. Lewis, "Disenchanted Women Give Up Careers to Stay Home," Minneapolis *Star Tribune*, April 6, 1998, p. D7. See also, Joann S. Lublin, "Some Adult Daughters of 'Supermoms' Plan to Take Another Path, *The Wall Street Journal*, December 28, 1995, p. A1.

[30]Andrew Delbanco, "Consuming Passions," *The New York Times Book Review*, January 19, 1997, p. 8.

[31]An international Gallup Poll found that 48 percent of Americans believed this model was best, greater than in most of the 22 countries surveyed. "Americans Support Traditional Sex Roles More Than Those in Most Other Countries," *About Women on Campus*, Summer 1996, p. 12.

CHAPTER SIX

[1]Mark Fitzgerald, "Survey: D.C. Women Equal in Newsroom, Not Out," *Editor & Publisher Magazine*, November 2, 1996, p. 15. By contrast, 22 percent of men were unmarried, and 40 percent did not have children. The median annual income for reporters as a group was $60,000, but while the midpoint for women was in the $40,000 to

$60,000 range, for men it was between $60,000 and $80,000. Additionally men made more outside income: 15 percent were earning $25,000 or more for speaking fees or talk shows, while 20 percent of the women earned less than $1,000 from those sources.

[2]Howard Kurtz, "Bosses' Words Irk Journalists; Newspaper Executives' Comments Seen As Disparaging Women," *The Washington Post*, May 21, 1998, p. C1; Hannah Brown, "Mother Lode of Trouble," *New York Post*, available on-line: http://208.248.87.252/052298/2807.htm, May 22, 1998; Hannah Brown, "Joyce Purnick Is Wrong, You Can Have It All," *New York Post*, available on-line: http://208.248.87.252/052298/2808.htm, May 22, 1998.

[3]Claudia Dreifus, "Ms. Behavin' Again," *Modern Maturity*, May–June, 1999, p. 50.

[4]Mardy S. Ireland, *Reconceiving Women: Separating Motherhood from Female Identity*, New York: Guilford Press, 1993, pp. 39–40.

[5]Ibid., p. 91.

[6]Ibid. p. 42.

[7]Laura Carstensen, professor of psychology, Stanford University, personal interview; Grace Baruch, Rosalind Barnett, and Caryl Rivers found that whether or not a woman had children had no significant impact on her well-being. *Lifeprints: New Patterns of Love and Work for Today's Women*, New York: Signet Books, 1983, pp. 106–107.

[8]Rhona Mahony, *Kidding Ourselves: Breadwinning, Babies, and Bargaining Power*, New York: Basic Books, 1995, pp. 113–114.

CHAPTER SEVEN

[1]Melissa Ludtke suggests a more accurate term would be "single mothers by *second* choice." *On Our Own: Unmarried Motherhood in America*. New York: Random House, 1997, p. 110.

[2]Ludtke writes that the "New Great American Dream" is the "great career, the great husband, and the children whose care mother and father share." *On Our Own*, p. 111. See also Jane Mattes, *Single Mothers by Choice*, New York: Times Books, 1994, pp. 4–5;

[3]During the same period, the percentage of out-of-wedlock births to teenagers ages 15 to 19 declined from 39.5 percent to 30 percent. U.S. Bureau of the Census, *Statistical Abstract of the United States: 1998* (118th edition), Washington, D.C., 1998, p. 81. The percentage of women who gave birth out of wedlock who held professional or managerial jobs rose from 3.1 to 8.3. The typical woman who conceives via donor insemination has a graduate degree and earns a median income of $55,800. Ludtke, *On Our Own*, p. 31.

[4]Dan Balz, "Quayle Revisits Old Theme in Speech About U.S. Values," *The Washington Post*, September 9, 1994, p. A4.

[5]Ludtke, *On Our Own*, p. 123; *All Things Considered*, radio interview with Melissa Ludtke, Washington, D.C: National Public Radio, January 12, 1998.

[6]Mardy S. Ireland, *Reconceiving Women: Separating Motherhood from Female Identity*, New York: Guilford Press, 1993, pp. 42–43.

[7]Kim DaCosta, "Marriage and Motherhood: A New Perspective on Commitment, Sacrifice and Self-Development," unpublished master's thesis, University of California at Berkeley, 1995, pp. 2, 18.

[8]Additionally a 1994 *New York Times*/CBS poll found that the majority of teenage girls would consider becoming a single parent if they didn't marry. Ludtke, *On Our Own*, p. 122.

[9]Lawyers in for-profit firms earn 59 percent more than those in nonprofit firms. Robert H. Frank, "What Price the Moral High Ground?" Economics Department,

Cornell University, undated manuscript, cited in Rhona Mahony, *Kidding Ourselves: Breadwinning, Babies, and Bargaining Power*, New York: Basic Books, 1995, p. 148.

[10]Psychologist Diane Gottlieb, in Joan K. Peters, *When Mothers Work: Loving Our Children Without Sacrificing Ourselves*. New York: Addison Wesley Longman, 1997, p. 174.

CHAPTER EIGHT

[1]Kathleen Gerson, *Hard Choices: How Women Decide About Work, Career, and Motherhood*, Berkeley: University of California Press, 1985, p. 213.

[2]Betty Carter and Joan K. Peters, *Love, Honor & Negotiate: Building Partnerships that Last a Lifetime*. New York: Pocket Books, 1996, p. 4; Pepper Schwartz, *Peer Marriage: How Love Between Equals Really Works*, New York: The Free Press, 1994; Philip Cowan and Carolyn Pape Cowan, "New Families: Modern Couples as New Pioneers," in *All Our Families: New Policies for a New Century*, Mary Ann Mason, Arlene Skolnick, and Stephen D. Sugarman, eds., New York: Oxford University Press, 1998, pp. 180, 184; Joan K. Peters, *When Mothers Work: Loving Our Children Without Sacrificing Ourselves*, New York: Addison Wesley Longman, 1997, p. 10. Rhona Mahony, *Kidding Ourselves: Breadwinning, Babies, and Bargaining Power*, New York: Basic Books, 1995, pp. 106–109.

[3]Mahony, *Kidding Ourselves*, p. 148.

[4]When asked how much time is "reasonable" for men to take off after a child is born, 63 percent of executives, human resources directors, and CEOs said none. Catalyst, "Fact Sheet: Father's Day 1999," available on-line: http://www.catalystwomen.org/press/factsfathers99.html, 1999.

[5]Carolyn Ambler Walter, *The Timing of Motherhood: Is Later Better?*, Lexington, Mass.: Lexington Books, 1986, p. 55.

[6]Schwartz, *Peer Marriage*, pp. 165–166.

[7]From 1991 to 1993 the percentage of stay-at-home dads dropped from 20 to 16, which is roughly what it was for the entire decade between 1977 and 1988. Beth Freking, "Men Find It's Tough to Be a Stay-at-Home Dad," Minneapolis *Star Tribune*, July 15, 1996, p. E3.

[8]Schwartz, *Peer Marriage*, p. 165.

[9]Gerson, *Hard Choices*, pp. 130, 217.

[10]Terri Apter, *Working Women Don't Have Wives: Professional Success in the 1990s*, New York: St. Martin's Griffin, 1993; Kerry Hannon, "A Woman's Special Dilemma," *U.S. News & World Report*, June 13, 1994.

[11]Peters, *When Mothers Work*, p. 13.

[12]Ibid., p. 131; Schwartz, *Peer Marriage*, pp. 148–150.

CHAPTER NINE

[1]Deborah Tannen, *Talking 9 to 5, How Women's and Men's Conversational Styles Affect Who Gets Heard, Who Gets Credit, and What Gets Done at Work*, New York: William Morrow, 1994, pp. 30–42.

[2]Tannen, pp. 67, 123; Jean Lipman-Blumen, Todd Fryling, Michael C. Henderson, Christine Webster Moore, and Rachel Vecchiotti, "Women in Corporate Leadership: Reviewing a Decade's Research," special report, Wellesley, Mass.: Center for Research on Women, 1996, p. 77.

[3]Lipman-Blumen et al., pp. iv–v.

[4]Korn/Ferry International, "Diversity in the Executive Suites: Good News and Bad News," available on-line: http://www.kornferry.com/diversit.htm, November 1997.

[5]Tannen, *Talking 9 to 5*, pp. 32–39.

[6]Catalyst, *1998 Catalyst Census of Women Corporate Officers and Top Earners*, New York: Catalyst, 1998; "Fact Sheet: 1999 Catalyst Census of Women Corporate Officers and Top Earners," available on-line: http://www.catalystwomen.org/press/factscote99 .html, November 11, 1999. Men hold nearly 94 percent of all line-officer positions— those with profit-and-loss responsibility—that are traditionally prerequisite to promotion to the uppermost ranks of executive leadership; Lipman-Blumen et al. found that in 1993 the median weekly earnings for male executives, administrators, and managers was $791, compared to $528 for females in comparable roles. "Women in Corporate Leadership," p. iii. Meanwhile male students role-playing as supervisors routinely gave higher raises to male subordinates than to female, indicating unconscious discrimination persists into a younger generation. Tannen, *Talking 9 to 5*, p. 31.

[7]Patricia Beard, "What's a Mother to Do?" *Elle*, April 1998, p. 138.

[8]Rosalind C. Barnett and Caryl Rivers. *She Works/He Works: How Two-Income Families Are Happier, Healthier and Better Off*, San Francisco: HarperSanFrancisco, 1996, pp. 98–99, 106–107.

[9]Beard, "What's a Mother to Do?" p. 140; A comprehensive multiyear study of 6,000 children whose mothers worked during the first three years after giving birth showed they were not significantly different from those with unemployed mothers; working mothers' children were slightly less compliant and scored slightly lower on academic achievement and vocabulary tests, but those differences disappeared by the time the children were seven. Barbara Vobejda, "Children of Working Moms Get Along Just Fine," *San Francisco Chronicle*, January 28, 1999, p. A3. A poll of 1,000 children in grades three through twelve also found that having a working mother was never once a predictor of how children rated their mothers' parenting skills. Ellen Galinsky, "Do Working Parents Make the Grade?" *Newsweek*, August 30, 1999, p. 52.

[10]Galinsky, "Do Working Parents Make the Grade?" p. 54. Only 10 percent felt they had too little time with their mothers, versus 15.5 percent who felt that way about their dads. Children with employed moms were no more likely to feel neglected than children with at-home moms and felt equally supported by their mothers. What all children wanted, regardless of whether their mother was at home or working, was more focused, less rushed time with both parents.

[11]One study of 746 married women found that those who stopped working to care for children reported 30 percent more distress over a three-year period. Another study found that stay-at-home wives with happy marriages had relatively low levels of depression, but the least depressed were employed wives with happy marriages and flexible jobs. Julia Lawlor, "Goodbye to the Job. Hello to the Shock," *The New York Times*, October 12, 1997, p. BU11. Barnett and Rivers also found that women's psychological stress increases when they drop out of the workforce or cut back to less than twenty hours per week, and they are more likely to be depressed than their employed counterparts. Women with multiple roles, they concluded, are healthier than those with fewer roles. *She Works/He Works*, p. 28; Joan K. Peters, *When Mothers Work: Loving Our Children Without Sacrificing Ourselves*, New York: Addison Wesley Longman, 1997, p. 3; Rosalind C. Barnett, "Women in Management Today," Wellesley, Mass.: Center for Research on Women, Working Paper No. 249, 1992, pp. 13–14, 15–16.

[12]Anne Roiphe, *Fruitful: A Real Mother in the Modern World*, New York: Houghton Mifflin Company, 1996, p. 154.

[13]Rhona Mahony, *Kidding Ourselves: Breadwinning, Babies, and Bargaining Power*, New York: Basic Books, 1995, pp. 105–106.

[14]Pepper Schwartz, *Peer Marriage: How Love Between Equals Really Works*, New York: The Free Press, 1994, p. 6. Catalyst, "Fact Sheet: Two Careers, One Marriage: Making It Work in the Workplace," available on-line: http://www.catalystwomen.org/press/ facts2c.html, January 1998. Both men and women want informal flexibility on the job

when family needs necessitate: freedom to arrive late, leave early, or work from home. Further, dual-income couples tend to view their careers as equally important, but when one spouse's career is primary, money is the determining factor. Men were more likely both to say they see the couple's careers as equal (58 percent versus 49 percent of women) and to say their own careers are primary (33 percent, versus 6 percent of women).

[15]The Families and Work Institute, "Executive Summary," *The 1997 National Study on the Changing Workforce*, New York: The Families and Work Institute, 1997, available on-line: http://www.familiesandwork.org/summary/nscw.pdf, p. 6. Meanwhile the amount of workday time employed married mothers spent on chores has decreased by 36 minutes.

[16]Women continue to do 81 percent of the cooking, 78 percent of the cleaning, and 87 percent of the shopping. Ibid.

[17]Lipman-Blumen et al., "Women in Corporate Leadership," p. x; Barnett, "Women in Management Today," pp. 15–16; Mahony, *Kidding Ourselves*, p. 150. A study of 746 married professional and blue-collar women found that those who reduced their hours and worked part-time or as freelancers reported ten percent more symptoms of distress over a three-year period than those who worked full-time. Lawlor, "Goodbye to the Job." Further, the definition of "part-time" has crept up to 40 hours a week. "Full-time part-timers" often find themselves doing the same job they've always done but in fewer hours, for less money, fewer benefits, and lower status—and doing more household chores. Reed Abelson, "Part-Time Work for Some Adds Up to Full-Time Job," *The New York Times*, November 2, 1998, p. A1.

[18]Barnett calls them "low control" versus "high control" jobs. Low control jobs, like cooking, cleaning, and family laundry are hazardous to mental health. High control ones, which can be put off until another time, have little or no impact on health. *He Works/She Works*, pp. 179–189. See also Hochschild, *The Second Shift*, pp. 43–45, regarding the tendency of couples to create a mythology of equality around the tendencies for women to do (the much more constant) "inside" work while men to do "outside" work.

[19]Equity means that "two individuals are receiving equal relative gains based on the overall balance of rewards and costs in a relationship." Nancy B. Kaltreider, Carolyn Gracie, Carole Sirulnick, "Love in the Trenches: Dual-Career Relationships," in *Dilemmas of a Double Life*, Northvale, N.J.: Jason Aronson, Inc., 1997, p. 125; Schwartz found that "peer couples" based their relationships "on a mix of equity (each person gives in proportion to what he or she receives) and equality (each person has equal status and is equally responsible for emotional, economic, and household duties)," *Peer Marriage*, p. 2.

CHAPTER TEN

[1]As quoted in Ravenna Helson, "The Self in Middle Age," in *Multiple Paths to Midlife Development*, Margie E. Lachman and Jacquelyn Boon James, eds., Chicago: University of Chicago, 1997, p. 23.

[2]Daniel J. Levinson, with Judy D. Levinson, *The Seasons of a Woman's Life*, New York: Alfred A. Knopf, 1996, p. 372; Terri Apter found women asking precisely the same question, "What do I want out of my life now?" *Secret Paths: Women in the New Midlife*, New York: W. W. Norton, 1995, p. 63. Maggie Scarf describes "middlescence" as "a second upsurge of identity issues" similar to the teenage years. *Unfinished Business: Pressure Points in the Lives of Women*, New York: Ballantine Books, 1980, pp. 452–453. In *Women of a Certain Age: The Midlife Search for Self*, psychologist Lillian Rubin found that

at midlife, issues of identity come "roaring" to the fore. Reissue, New York: Harper & Row, 1990, p. 42. The MacArthur Foundation Research Network on Successful Midlife Development found that both women and men show gains in areas of personal autonomy as they age, but that women gain in larger increments. Erica Goode, "New Study Finds Middle Age Is Prime of Life," *The New York Times*, February 16, 1999, p. D6.

[3]Levinson, *The Seasons of a Woman's Life*, pp. 375–377; Apter, *Secret Paths*, p. 120; Sarah Hardesty and Nehama Jacobs, *Success and Betrayal: The Crisis of Women in Corporate America*, New York: Franklin Watts, 1986, p. 3. A 1996 Roper Poll found that fewer than one third of women got "great personal satisfaction" from their jobs, and that women were less optimistic than men about opportunity in the workplace. "Body/Mind Flash," *Self*, January 1996, p. 25.

[4]Nancy B. Kaltreider, " 'To Love and to Work': Balancing Priorities Throughout the Life Cycle," in *Dilemmas of a Double Life*, Nancy B. Kaltreider, ed., Northvale, N.J.: Jason Aronson, Inc., 1997, p. 13.

[5]Peter Passell, "Hurdles Are Still High for Women Who Want a Career and a Family," *The New York Times*, September 7, 1995, p. D2. Among women college graduates, 33 percent reached this level of "success" but only 17 percent managed to have both a successful career and children.

[6]Deborah L. Jacobs, "Back from the Mommy Track," *The New York Times*, October 9, 1994, p. F1.

[7]Jonathan Curiel and Tanya Schevitz, "New Role for Moms—Family Chauffeur: Errands, Shuttling Kids Falls to Women," *San Francisco Chronicle*, May 6, 1999, p. A21.

[8]For example, see Tamar Lewin, "Taming the Wild Adolescent," *The New York Times Magazine*, April 5, 1998, p. 98.

[9]"Women Less Optimistic About Work Than Men," *About Women on Campus*, Spring 1996, p. 4; Stuart Silverstein, "Differing View of the Executive Ceiling," *Los Angeles Times*, February 28, 1996, p. D1; Rosalind C. Barnett, "Women in Management Today," Wellesley, Mass.: Center for Research on Women, Working Paper No. 249, 1992, p. 17.

[10]Joanne Martin, professor of organizational behavior, Stanford University, personal interview.

[11]L. K. Cartwright and P. Wink, "Personality Change in Women Physicians from Medical Student Years to Mid 40s," *Psychology of Women Quarterly*, 18, pp. 291–308, 1994. In Helson, "The Self in Middle Age," p. 30.

[12]Levinson's women, for instance, had become simultaneously more engaged by their work and more detached from it: more focused on their own goals regardless of whether they were ignored or opposed by others. *The Seasons of a Woman's Life*, p. 374.

[13]Mary Catherine Bateson, *Composing a Life*, New York: Atlantic Monthly Press, 1989, p. 4.

[14]A 1995 Families and Work Institute study showed that 85 percent of women and 67 percent of men reported wanting to work less than full-time or not at all. A third of women said they would prefer to stay home, but so did 21 percent of men. *Women: The New Providers* (Whirlpool Foundation Study, Part One), New York: The Families and Work Institute, 1995, available on-line: http://www.whirlpoolcorp.com/whr/ics/foundation/NewProviders1.pdf.

[15]There are 8.5 million women-owned businesses, employing 24 million people and generating $3 trillion in sales. Betsy Wiesendanger, "Labors of Love," *Working Woman*, May 1999, p. 43. However, a significant gender gap remains in earnings: The average annual receipts of women-owned businesses are $15,418 vs. $44,697 for men. Jean Lipman-Blumen, Todd Fryling, Michael C. Henderson, Christine Webster Moore, and Rachel Vecchiotti, "Women in Corporate Leadership: Reviewing a Decade's

Research," special report, Wellesley, Mass.: Center for Research on Women, 1996, p. iii.

[16]Lipman-Blumen et al., "Women in Corporate Leadership," p. 32.

[17]There is some evidence that women are more likely than men to use power to achieve organizational goals rather than enhancing their own political strength. Ibid., p. 32.

[18]Patricia McBroom, The Third Sex: The New Professional Woman, New York: Paragon House, 1992, pp. 15, 103–104.

[19]Sue Shellenbarger, "Woman's Resignation from Top Pepsi Post Rekindles Debate," The Wall Street Journal, October 8, 1997, p. B1.

[20]Helson, "The Self in Middle Age," p. 29.

[21]Apter, Secret Paths, p. 86.

[22]Ravenna Helson, professor of psychology, University of California at Berkeley, personal interview.

[23]Terry A. Lugaila, "Marital Status and Living Arrangements: March 1997 (Update)," Current Population Reports P20-506, Washington, D.C.: U.S. Bureau of the Census, June 1998, p. 1; Laura Carstensen, professor of psychology, Stanford University, personal interview.

[24]Kerry Hannon, "A Woman's Special Dilemma," U.S. News & World Report, June 13, 1994, p. 93; "Women Emerge in Benefits Debate," San Francisco Chronicle, September 13, 1999, p. A6.

[25]Carstensen, personal interview.

[26]Apter, Secret Paths, p. 240. See also, Levinson, Seasons of a Woman's Life, p. 391.

[27]Barbara Kantrowitz and Pat Wingert, "The Science of a Good Marriage," Newsweek, April 19, 1999, p. 52; Judith Wallerstein and Sandee Blakeslee, The Good Marriage: How & Why Love Lasts, New York: Warner Books, 1996, p. 17; Carstensen, personal interview.

[28]Kantrowitz and Wingert, "The Science of a Good Marriage," p. 56; Sherry Suib Cohen, "You Talk. He Listens. A True Story," McCall's, April 1999, p. 52.

[29]Forty-three percent of women have sexual difficulties. Thirty-one percent lacked interest in sex, about a quarter were unable to achieve orgasm, and 23 percent said sex was "not pleasurable." Edward O. Laumann, Anthony Paik, and Raymond C. Rosen, "Sexual Dysfunction in the United States: Prevalence and Predictors," Journal of the American Medical Association, February 10, 1999, in Claudine Chamberlain, "When the Lovin' Is Lacking: What's Not Happening in U.S. Bedrooms," ABC News, February 16, 1999, available on-line: http://abcnews.go.com/sections/living/InYourHead/allinyourhead_29.html.

[30]Wallerstein and Blakeslee, The Good Marriage, p. 192.

[31]Philip Cowan and Carolyn Pape Cowan, "New Families: Modern Couples as New Pioneers," in All Our Families: New Policies for a New Century, Mary Ann Mason, Arlene Skolnick, and Stephen D. Sugarman, eds., New York: Oxford University Press, 1998, pp. 173, 180; Laura J. Carstensen, Jeremy Graff, Robert W. Levenson, and John M. Gottman, "Affect in Intimate Relationships: The Developmental Course of Marriage," in Handbook of Emotion, Adult Development, and Aging, Carol Magai, ed., San Diego: Academic Press, 1996, p. 230; Carstensen, personal interview.

[32]Dalma Heyn, The Erotic Silence of the American Wife, New York: Turtle Bay Books, 1992, p. 190.

[33]Carstensen et al., "Affect in Intimate Relationships," pp. 241–242.

[34]Carstensen, personal interview; Robert W. Levenson, Laura L. Carstensen, and John M. Gottman, "Long-Term Marriage: Age, Gender and Satisfaction," in Psychology and Aging, 8, 2 (1993), pp. 301–313.

[35]Robert W. Levenson, Laura L. Carstensen, and John M. Gottman. "The Influence of Age and Gender on Affect, Physiology, and Their Interrelations: A Study of Long-Term

Marriages," *Journal of Personality and Social Psychology*, 67, 1 (1994), p. 66; Robert W. Levenson et al., "Long-Term Marriage," p. 301.

[36]Diana Hume George, "The Gender Wars," in Penny Kaganoff and Susan Spano, eds., *Women on Divorce: A Bedside Companion*, New York: Harcourt Brace 1995, p. 87.

[37]Penny Kaganoff, "Other Uses for a Wedding Gown," in Kaganoff and Spano, *Women on Divorce*, p. 31.

[38]In an open-ended question about how divorce had affected their lives, 72 percent of women in one large-scale study mentioned positive growth in their sense of self, and 95 percent cited a positive effect on their career and/or education. Only a third mentioned a negative effect—finances, relationships with children, strain—as the main one. Eighty percent of those who said divorce was a major turning point said it was a turning point in a positive direction. Grace Baruch, Rosalind Barnett, and Caryl Rivers, *Lifeprints: New Patterns of Love and Work for Today's Women*, New York: Signet Books, 1983, p. 234.

[39]Jane Gross, "Divorced, Middle-Aged and Happy: Women, Especially, Adjust to the 90's," *The New York Times*, December 7, 1992, p. A14.

[40]"Marriage Rate in U.S. Drops to Record Low: Far Fewer Spouses Say They're 'Very Happy,'" *San Francisco Chronicle*, July 2, 1999, p. A1.

[41]Bateson, *Composing a Life*, p. 9.

[42]Apter, *Secret Paths*, pp. 69, 76–77.

CHAPTER ELEVEN

[1]10.7 percent of white women aged 40 to 44 have never married, and an additional 14.1 percent are divorced. Among black women, 25.4 percent in that age range have never married and 19 percent are divorced. Terry A. Lugaila, "Marital Status and Living Arrangements: March 1998 (Update)," *Current Population Reports*, P20-514, Washington, D.C.: U.S. Bureau of the Census, July 1998, pp. 1–2. Eighty percent of never-married women aged 40 to 44 are childless, U.S. Bureau of the Census, *Statistical Abstract of the United States: 1998* (118th edition), Washington, D.C.: 1998, p. 85.

[2]Carol W. Anderson and Susan Stewart with Sona Dimidjian, *Flying Solo: Single Women in Midlife*, New York: W. W. Norton, 1994, p. 16.

[3]A number of studies have showed that single women's health and psychological well-being exceed single men's and is comparable or exceeds that of married women. See, for instance, Anastasia Toufexis, "When the Ring Doesn't Fit . . ." *Psychology Today*, December 1996, p. 55; Jean Potuchek, "The Lives of Single Women: The Meaning of Singleness," audiotaped lecture, Wellesley, Mass.: Center for Research on Women, 1996. Grace Baruch, Rosalind Barnett, and Caryl Rivers, *Lifeprints: New Patterns of Love and Work for Today's Women*, New York: Signet Books, 1983, p. 263; and Susan Faludi, *Backlash: The Undeclared War Against American Women*, New York: Crown, 1991, pp. 15–18. The same holds true in comparing married childless women to mothers. Baruch et al., *Lifeprints*, pp. 106–107; Katherine Griffin, "Childless by Choice," *Health*, March/April 1996, p. 99; Jeanne Safer, *Beyond Motherhood: Choosing a Life Without Children*, New York: Pocket Books, 1996, p. 122.

[4]For further discussion, see Marcelle Clements, *The Improvised Woman: Single Women Reinventing Single Life*, New York: W. W. Norton, 1999, and Carolyn Knapp, "The Merry Recluse," *Salon*, available on-line: http://www.salonmagazine.com/mwt/feature/1998/07/cov_27feature.html.

[5]Faludi, *Backlash*, p. 36.

[6]For an exploration of girls' sexuality in the 1970s, see Sharon Thompson, *Going All the Way: Teenage Girls' Tales of Sex, Romance & Pregnancy*, New York: Hill and Wang, 1995.

[7]According to a 1995 Catalyst survey, many women executives would agree with

Wendy's strategy: They say adopting a style that neither threatens nor attracts men was key to their success, second only to exceeding performance expectations. Kristin Downey Grimsley, "From the Top: The Women's View," *The Washington Post*, February 28, 1996, p. C1. In Hollywood too, a woman executive "must be impeccably professional, sharper, and savvier than your male counterparts. And you must take sex entirely out of the picture." Jenny Hontz, "More Than Meets the Eye in Tarses-Bashing," *Daily Variety*, July 23, 1997, p. 15.

[8]See Rosalie Riegle Troester, "Turbulence and Tenderness: Mothers, Daughters, and 'Othermothers' in *Brown Girl, Brownstones*," in *Double Stitch: Black Women Write About Mothers & Daughters*, Patricia Bell-Scott, Beverly Guy-Sheftall, Jacqueline Jones Royster, Janet Sims-Wood, Miriam DeCosta-Willis, and Lucie Fultz, eds., Boston: Beacon Press, 1992, pp. 163–172.

[9]Mardy S. Ireland, *Reconceiving Women: Separating Motherhood from Female Identity*, New York: Guilford Press, 1993, p. 39.

[10]Victoria L. Rayner, "Many Single Women Prefer Married Men," *USA Today Magazine*, August 1996, p. 4.

[11]Such clearly delineated relationships have been called "encapsulated intimacies." Anderson et al., *Flying Solo*, pp. 201–213.

CHAPTER TWELVE

[1]Women of color comprise just 1.3 percent of all corporate officers and 11.2 of female corporate officers in America's top five hundred corporations. Catalyst, "Fact Sheet: 1999 Catalyst Census of Women Corporate Officers and Top Earners," available online: http://www.catalystwomen.org/press/factscote99.html, November 11, 1999.

[2]A 1992 Bar Association survey of minority associates in New York City law firms found that 61 percent of African American lawyers felt their work experiences were "clearly different from those of non-minority lawyers" at their firms. 9.5 percent of Asians and none of Hispanics felt that way. Only 20 percent of African American reporters said they were judged the same way as nonminority lawyers compared to 89 percent of Hispanics and 76 percent of Asians. Sixty-one percent of blacks thought their firms had a poor "commitment to the retention of minority lawyers," as did 67 percent of Hispanics and 29 percent of Asians. Ellis Cose, *The Rage of a Privileged Class: Why Are Middle-Class Blacks Angry? Why Should America Care?* New York: HarperCollins, 1995, p. 85.

[3]Women of color face a "concrete ceiling" at work, thicker than the one made of glass. In a survey of 1,700 women-of-color managers and professionals at thirty leading companies, only 34 percent were satisfied with their opportunities for advancement. Forty-seven percent felt a lack of influential mentors was a barrier (as opposed to 29 percent of white women who felt that way); 40 percent cited lack of informal networking opportunities; 29 percent cited a lack of adequate role models within their companies who were members of their racial/ethnic group; and 28 percent cited lack of high-visibility assignments. Nearly 40 percent felt there had been no change in advancement opportunities for women of color in the past five years. "Fact Sheet: Women of Color in Corporate Management: Opportunities and Barriers," New York: Catalyst, July 1999, available on-line: http://www.catalystwomen.org/press/mediakit/factswoc3.html; "Advancement Opportunities Lacking, Say Corporate Women of Color," New York: Catalyst, February 1998, available on-line: http://www.catalystwomen.org/press/release0210.html.

[4]Christina Maslach, professor of psychology, University of California at Berkeley, personal interview.

[5]Laura Carstensen, professor of psychology, Stanford University, personal interview;

Robert W. Levenson, Laura L. Carstensen, and John M. Gottman. "Long-Term Marriage: Age, Gender and Satisfaction," in *Psychology and Aging*, 8, 2 (1993), pp. 301–313.
[6]According to Cose, elite credentials will gain blacks entrée into the corporate world, but after a few years they begin getting feedback that they're "not good team players" or are "too outspoken," ambiguous, subjective comments that are impossible to fix. The result is disappointment and a lot of turnover. *The Rage of a Privileged Class*, pp. 78–79.
[7]Melinda M. Marshall, *Good Enough Mothers Changing Expectations for Ourselves*, Princeton, N.J.: Peterson's, 1993, p. 99.
[8]Elsa Walsh, *Divided Lives: The Public and Private Struggles of Three Accomplished Women*, New York: Simon and Schuster, 1995, p. 18.
[9]Luise Eichenbaum and Susie Orbach, *Between Women: Love, Envy and Competition in Women's Friendships*, New York: Viking, 1988, p. 89.
[10]Lillian B. Rubin, *Just Friends: The Role of Friendship in Our Lives*, New York: Harper and Row, 1985, pp. 84–85.
[11]Anthropologist Patricia McBroom called women who had completed such a cycle "the third sex," indicating that they'd found a way to integrate a new, stronger definition of the feminine into the public realm while simultaneously infusing the private realm with a sense of power and authority that was once considered "masculine," *The Third Sex: The New Professional Woman*, New York: Paragon House, 1992, p. 15.

AFTERWORD

[1]See Gina Ogden, *Women Who Love Sex*, New York: Pocket Books, 1994; Caroline Ramazanoglu and Janet Holland, "Women's Sexuality and Men's Appropriation of Desire," in *Up Against Foucault: Explorations of Some Tensions Between Foucault and Feminism*, Caroline Ramazanoglu, ed., London: Routledge, 1993, pp. 239–264; and Naomi Wolf, *Promiscuities: The Secret Struggle for Womanhood*, New York: Random House, 1997.
[2]Rhona Mahony, *Kidding Ourselves: Breadwinning, Babies, and Bargaining Power*, New York: Basic Books, 1995, pp. 144–145.
[3]Philip Cowan and Carolyn Pape Cowan also found that couples on the more egalitarian end of the spectrum tend to be more satisfied than others with themselves, their relationships, and their roles as parents. "New Families: Modern Couples as New Pioneers," in *All Our Families: New Policies for a New Century*, Mary Ann Mason, Arlene Skolnick, and Stephen D. Sugarman, eds., New York: Oxford University Press, 1998, p. 181.
[4]Tamar Lewin, "Men Whose Wives Work Earn Less, Studies Show," *The New York Times*, October 12, 1994, p. A1; Betsy Morris, "Is Family Wrecking Your Career?" *Fortune*, March 17, 1997, p. 71.
[5]Joan K. Peters, *When Mothers Work: Loving Our Children Without Sacrificing Ourselves*, New York: Addison Wesley Longman, 1997, p. 112. Further, research shows that men who take paternity leave when their children are very young are more likely to be involved as the children grow older. Arlie Russell Hochschild, "There's No Place Like Work," *The New York Times Magazine*, April 20, 1997, p. 84.
[6]Peters, *When Mothers Work*, p. 83.
[7]Nancy L. Marshall and Rosalind C. Barnett, "Child Care, Division of Labor, and Parental Emotional Well-Being Among Two-Earner Couples, Working Paper No. 252, Wellesley, Mass.: Center for Research on Women, 1992, pp. 1–2, 16. Both husbands and wives report lower levels of psychological stress when men shared childcare.
[8]Sue Shellenbarger, "Today's Young Women Are Redefining Debate About Working Moms," *The Wall Street Journal*, July 15, 1998, p. B1.

9Sixty-two percent of women believed the division should be equal. Keith H. Hammonds, "He Said, She Said," *Business Week*, August 3, 1998, p. 62. Men were also far more likely to believe that stock, stock options, company pensions, and ownership of private companies should be divided according to how much each spouse actually earned rather than equally. Meanwhile, 75 percent of men and 30 percent of women believed divorce settlements favor women.

10Families and Work Institute, "Executive Summary," *1998 Work-Life Study*, New York: Families and Work Institute, 1998, p. xii, available on-line: http://www.familiesandwork.org/press/pl.html. Eighty-two percent of companies with women in half or more of top positions provide flextime, compared with 56 percent of those without women in top positions. Six times as many companies with half or more top women provide on or near-site childcare, 60 percent provide dependent-care assisted plans (compared with 37 percent with no senior women), and 30 percent offer elder care resource and referral programs (compared with 14 percent with no women in key positions). Interestingly, companies with more ethnic diversity at top levels—or even one top position filled by a minority employee—were also more likely to have family-friendly policies.

11Reynolds Holding, "Women in Law: Status Report on the Glass Ceiling," *San Francisco Chronicle*, April 11, 1999, p. 6. Women have made up about half of every law school class for the last twenty years. Kate Zernike, "MIT Women Win a Fight Against Bias: In Rare Move, School Admits Discrimination," *The Boston Globe*, March 21, 1999, p. A1; Eileen Alt Powell, "Fast Track Off Limits to Women," *San Francisco Examiner*, November 12, 1999, p. B1. Meanwhile, women are 3.3 percent of Fortune 500 companies' top earners and hold 6.8 percent of the line-officer positions—running factories, heading sales staffs, supervising accounting—from which senior management is typically promoted.

12Reed Abelson, "A Push from the Top Shatters a Glass Ceiling," *The New York Times*, Business Desk, August 22, 1999, available on-line: http://archives.nytimes.com/archives.

13Ibid. Overall, HP's turnover rate is 5 percent. The industry average is 17 percent.

14Bernice L. Neugarten, "Adaptation and the Life-Cycle," in *Counseling Adults*, Nancy K. Schlossberg and Alan D. Entine, eds., Monterey, Ca.: Brooks/Cole, 1977, pp. 34–45; Jean Potvchek, "The Lives of Single Women: The Meaning of Singleness," audiotaped lecture, Wellesley, Mass.: The Center for Research on Women, 1996. Grace Baruch, Rosalind Barnett, and Caryl Rivers, *Lifeprints: New Patterns of Love and Work for Today's Women*, New York: Signet Books, 1983, p. 263. See also Claire Etaugh, "Women in the Middle and Later Years," in *Psychology of Women: A Handbook of Issues and Theories*, Florence L. Denmark and Michele A. Paludi, eds., Westport, Conn.: Greenwood Press, 1993, p. 228; Susan Faludi, *Backlash: The Undeclared War Against American Women*, New York: Crown, 1991, p. 36.

15Baruch et al., *Lifeprints*, pp. 106–107; Ingrid Connidis and Julie McMullin, of the University of Western Ontario, studied nearly 700 Canadian men and women over age 55, in Katherine Griffin, "Childless by Choice," *Health*, March/April 1996, p. 99. See also Safer, *Beyond Motherhood*, p. 122.

16Laura Carstensen, professor of psychology, Stanford University, personal interview.

Bibliography

Abelson, Reed. "Part-Time Work for Some Adds Up to Full-Time Job." *The New York Times*, November 2, 1998, p. A1.

———. "When Waaa Turns to Why." *The New York Times*, November 11, 1997, p. D1.

Abrams, Tamar. "My Test-Tube Daddy." *The Washingtonian*, March 1994, p. 44.

Acker, Joan. "Hierarchies, Jobs, Bodies: A Theory of Gendered Organizations." *Gender & Society*, 4, 2 (June 1990): 139–158.

Agrets, Aimee. "I Couldn't Stand Being Single." *Mademoiselle*, February 1999, p. 30.

Allatt, Patricia, Teresa Keil, Alan Bryman, and Bill Bytheway, eds. *Women and the Life Cycle: Transitions and Turning Points.* London: The Macmillan Press, 1987.

Amott, Teresa, and Julie Matthaei. *Race, Gender and Work: A Multicultural Economic History of Women in the United States.* Boston: South End Press, 1991.

Anderson, Carol W., and Susan Stewart with Sona Dimidjian. *Flying Solo: Single Women in Midlife.* New York: W. W. Norton, 1994.

Apter, Terri. *Secret Paths: Women in the New Midlife.* New York: W.W. Norton, 1995.

———. *Working Women Don't Have Wives: Professional Success in the 1990s.* New York: St. Martin's Press, 1993.

Ballard, Nancer H. "Equal Engagement: Observations on Career Success and Meaning in the Lives of Women Lawyers." Working Paper No. 292. Wellesley, Mass.: Center for Research on Women, 1998.

Balz, Dan. "Quayle Revisits Old Theme in Speech About U.S. Values." *The Washington Post*, September 9, 1994, p. A4.

Bardwick, Judith M. "The Seasons of a Woman's Life." In *Women's Lives: New Theory, Research & Policy*, Dorothy C. McGuigan, ed. Ann Arbor: The University of Michigan Center for Continuing Education of Women, 1980, pp. 35–58.

Barnett, Rosalind C. "Adult Daughters and Their Mothers: Harmony or Hostility?" Working Paper No. 209. Wellesley, Mass.: Center for Research on Women, 1990.

———. "Reconceptualizing the Work/Family Literature." Audiotaped lecture, Wellesley, Mass.: Center for Research on Women, 1996.

———. "Women in Management Today." Working Paper No. 249. Wellesley, Mass.: Center for Research on Women, 1992.

———. and Grace Baruch. "Toward Economic Independence: Women's Involvement in Multiple Roles." In *Women's Lives: New Theory, Research & Policy*, Dorothy C. McGuigan, ed. Ann Arbor: The University of Michigan Center for Continuing Education of Women, 1980, pp. 69–84.

——. and Caryl Rivers. *She Works/He Works: How Two-Income Families are Happier, Healthier and Better Off.* San Francisco: HarperSanFrancisco, 1996.

Baruch, Grace K. "Reflections on Guilt, Women and Gender," Working Paper No. 177. Wellesley, Mass.: Center for Research on Women, 1988.

——. Rosalind Barnett, and Caryl Rivers. *Lifeprints: New Patterns of Love and Work for Today's Women.* New York: Signet Books, 1983.

Bateson, Mary Catherine. *Composing a Life.* New York: Atlantic Monthly Press, 1989.

Beard, Patricia. "What's a Mother to Do?" *Elle,* April 1998, p. 138.

Behbehani, Mandy. "Child-Free Women Demand Society's Respect." *San Francisco Examiner,* September 22, 1996, p. C2.

Bellah, Robert N., Richard Madsen, William M. Sullian, Ann Swidler, and Steven M. Tipton. *Habits of the Heart: Individualism and Commitment in American Life,* updated edition. Berkeley: The University of California Press, 1996.

Bell-Scott, Patricia, ed. *Life Notes: Personal Writings by Contemporary Black Women.* New York: W. W. Norton, 1994.

Bernstein, Nina. "Study Says Equality Eludes Most Women in Law Firms." *The New York Times,* January 7, 1996, p. 9.

Blumstein, Philip, and Pepper Schwartz. *American Couples: Money, Work, Sex.* New York: William Morrow, 1983.

Bouris, Karen. *The First Time: What Parents and Teenagers Should Know About "Losing Your Virginity."* Emeryville, Cal.: Canari Press, 1995.

——. *The First Time: Women Speak Out About "Losing Their Virginity."* Emeryville, Cal.: Canari Press, 1993.

Brady, Lois Smith. "Why Marriage Is Hot again." *Redbook,* September 1996, p. 122.

Brisson, Chantal. "Office Stress, Large Family Responsibilities Put Women at Risk." Washington, D.C.: Center for Advancement of Health, March 22, 1999.

Brown, Hannah. "Joyce Purnick Is Wrong, You Can Have It All." *New York Post.* On-line edition. Available: http://208.248.87.252/052298/2808.htm, May 22, 1998.

——. "Mother Lode of Trouble." *New York Post.* On-line edition. Available: http://208.248.87.252/052298/2807.htm, May 22, 1998.

Carstensen, Laura J., Jeremy Graff, Robert W. Levenson, and John M. Gottman. "Affect in Intimate Relationships: The Developmental Course of Marriage." In *Handbook of Emotion, Adult Development, and Aging,* Carol Magai, ed., San Diego: Academic Press, 1996. pp. 227–247.

Carter, Betty, and Joan K. Peters. *Love, Honor & Negotiate: Building Partnerships That Last a Lifetime.* New York: Pocket Books, 1996.

Catalyst. *1998 Catalyst Census of Women Corporate Officers and Top Earners.* New York: Catalyst, 1998.

——. *1999 Catalyst Census of Women Corporate Officers and Top Earners.* New York: Catalyst, 1999.

——. *Women of Color in Corporate Management: Opportunities and Barriers.* New York: Catalyst, 1999.

——. "Advancement Opportunities Lacking, Say Corporate Women of Color." On-line. Available: http://www.catalystwomen.org/press/release0210.html, February 1998.

——. "Catalyst Study Finds Women of Color Under-Represented in the Managerial Workforce." On-line. Available: http://www.catalystwomen.org/press/release1022.html, October 1997.

——. "Fact Sheet: Father's Day 1999." On-line. Available: http://www.catalystwomen.org/press/factsfathers99.html, June 1999.

————. "Fact Sheet: Two Careers, One Marriage: Making It Work in the Workplace." On-line. Available: http://www.catalystwomen.org/press/facts2c.html, January 1998.

————. "Fact Sheet: Women of Color in Corporate Management: Opportunities and Barriers." On-line. Available: http://www.catalystwomen.org/press/mediakit/factswoc3.html, July 1999.

————. "Mentoring: A Guide to Corporate Programs and Practices." New York: Catalyst, 1993.

Chamberlain, Claudine. "When the Lovin' Is Lacking: What's *Not* Happening in U.S. Bedrooms." ABC News, February 16, 1999. On-line. Available: http://abcnews.go.com/sections/living/InYourHead/allinyourhead_29.html.

Chambers, Veronica. *Mama's Girl.* New York: Riverhead Books, 1996.

Chapman, Audrey. *Entitled to Good Loving: Black Men and Women and the Battle for Love and Power.* New York: Henry Holt, 1995.

Chen, Renbao, and S. Philip Morgan. "Recent Trends in the Timing of First Births in the United States." *Demography,* 28, 4 (November 1991), pp. 513–533.

Chernin, Kim. *The Hungry Self: Women, Eating & Identity.* New York: Perennial Library, 1986.

Chira, Susan. "Working Mothers: How to Fight the New Backlash." *Glamour,* April 1998, p. 230.

Chodorow, Nancy. *The Reproduction of Mothering: Psychoanalysis and the Sociology of Gender.* Berkeley, Cal.: University of California Press, 1978.

Chow, Claire S. *Leaving Deep Water: The Lives of Asian American Women at the Crossroads of Two Cultures.* New York: Dutton, 1998.

Chow, Esther Ngan-Ling. "Asian American Women at Work." In *Women of Color in U.S. Society.* Maxine Baca Zinn and Bonnie Thornton Dill, eds. Philadelphia: Temple University Press, 1994, pp. 203–227.

Clements, Marcelle. *The Improvised Woman: Single Women Reinventing Single Life.* New York: W. W. Norton, 1999.

Cose, Ellis. *The Rage of a Privileged Class: Why Are Middle-Class Blacks Angry? Why Should America Care?* New York: HarperCollins, 1995.

Cowan, Philip, and Carolyn Pape Cowan. "New Families: Modern Couples as New Pioneers." In *All Our Families: New Policies for a New Century.* Mary Ann Mason, Arlene Skolnick, and Stephen D. Sugarman, eds. New York: Oxford University Press, 1998, pp. 169–192.

Crichton, Sarah. "Will It Be Real Life—or Corporate Life." *Newsweek,* December 25, 1995/January 1, 1996, p. 122.

Crittenden, Danielle. "Yes, Motherhood Lowers Pay." *The New York Times,* August 22, 1995, p. A11.

Crosby, Faye J. *Juggling: The Unexpected Advantages of Balancing Career and Home for Women and Their Families.* New York: Free Press, 1991.

Curiel, Jonathan, and Tanya Schevitz. "New Role for Moms—Family Chauffeur: Errands, Shuttling Kids Falls to Women." *San Francisco Chronicle,* May 6, 1999, p. A21.

DaCosta, Kim. "Marriage and Motherhood: A New Perspective on Commitment, Sacrifice and Self-Development." Unpublished master's thesis. University of California at Berkeley, 1995.

Darnton, Nina. "Mommy vs. Mommy." *Newsweek,* June 4, 1990, p. 64.

Davis, Marcia D. "Defining Our Future." *Emerge,* March 1997, p. 38.

de Beauvoir, Simone. *The Second Sex.* Translated and edited by H. M. Parshley, with an introduction by Deirdre Bair. New York: Alfred A. Knopf, 1952; reprint, New York: Vintage Books, 1989.

Delbanco, Andrew. "Consuming Passions." *The New York Times Book Review*, January 19, 1997, p. 8.

Dickerson, Debra. "She's Gotta Have It: The Search for Black Men." *The New Republic*, May 6, 1996, p. 12.

Dockett, Lauren, and Kristin Beck. *Facing 30: Women Talk about Constructing a Real Life and Other Scary Rites of Passage.* Oakland: New Harbinger Publications, 1998.

Dorman, Leslie. "Sexual Regrets." *Glamour*, May 1996, p. 218.

Douglass, Marcia, and Lisa Douglass. *Are We Having Fun Yet?: The Intelligent Women's Guide to Sex.* New York: Hyperion, 1997.

Dowrick, Stephanie, and Sibyl Grundberg, eds. *Why Children? Eighteen Women Write Openly and Movingly About One of the Most Important Decisions They Will Ever Face: To Have or Not to Have Children.* London: The Women's Press, 1980.

Dreifus, Claudia. "Ms. Behavin' Again." *Modern Maturity*, May–June 1999, p. 50.

Dreyfous, Leslie. "Children: To Have or Have Not." *San Francisco Chronicle*, March 20, 1991, p. B3.

Edwards, Audrey, and Craig K. Polite. *Children of the Dream: The Psychology of Black Success.* New York: Doubleday, 1992.

Eichenbaum, Luise, and Susie Orbach. *Between Women: Love, Envy and Competition in Women's Friendships.* New York: Viking, 1988.

Etaugh, Claire. "Women in the Middle and Later Years." In *Psychology of Women: A Handbook of Issues and Theories*, Florence L. Denmark and Michele A. Paludi, eds. Westport, Conn.: Greenwood Press, 1993, pp. 213–246.

Etter-Lewis, Gwendolyn. *My Soul Is My Own: Oral Narratives of African American Women in the Professions.* New York: Routledge, 1993.

Eyer, Diane. *Mother Guilt: How Our Culture Blames Mothers for What's Wrong with Society.* New York: Times Books, 1995.

Faludi, Susan. *Backlash: The Undeclared War Against American Women.* London: Vintage, 1993.

The Families and Work Institute. "Executive Summary." *The 1997 National Study on the Changing Workforce.* New York: The Families and Work Institute, 1997. On-line. Available: http://www.familiesandwork.org/summary/nscw.pdf, p.6.

———. *Women: The New Providers* (Whirlpool Foundation Study, Part One). New York: The Families and Work Institute, 1995. On-line. Available: http://www.whirlpool-corp.com/whr/ics/foundation/NewProviders1.pdf.

Feagin, Joe R., and Melvin P. Sikes. *Living with Racism: The Black Middle-Class Experience.* Boston: Beacon Press, 1994.

Fein, Ellen, and Sherrie Schneider. *The Rules.* New York: Warner Books, 1995.

Fitzgerald, Mark. "Survey: D.C. Women Equal in Newsroom, Not Out." *Editor & Publisher Magazine*, November 2, 1996, p. 15.

"14 Reasons for Men to Be Nervous." *Glamour*, September 1996, p. 168.

Freking, Beth. "Men Find It's Tough to Be a Stay-at-Home Dad." Minneapolis *Star Tribune*, July 15, 1996, p. E3.

Friday, Nancy. *Women on Top: How Real Life Has Changed Women's Sexual Fantasies.* London: Arrow, 1993.

Friedan, Betty. *The Second Stage.* New York: Laurel, 1991.

Gaines, Patrice. "Different Paths, Common Ground." *Emerge*, March 1997, p. 32.

Galinsky, Ellen. "Do Working Parents Make the Grade?" *Newsweek*, August 30, 1999, p. 52.

Gerson, Kathleen. *Hard Choices: How Women Decide about Work, Career, and Motherhood.* Berkeley: University of California Press, 1985.

Giddings, Paula. *When and Where I Enter: The Impact of Black Women on Race and Sex in America.* New York: Bantam Books, 1988.

Gilligan, Carol. *In a Different Voice: Psychological Theory and Women's Development.* Cambridge, Mass.: Harvard University Press, 1982.

Glaser, Jeff. "Study Finds Women Gaining in Pay, Education, Entrepreneurship." *The Washington Post,* July 27, 1996, p. F1.

Golden, Marita, and Susan Richards Shreve, eds. *Skin Deep: Black Women & White Women Write About Race.* New York: Nan A. Talese/Doubleday, 1995.

Goode, Erica. "New Study Finds Middle Age Is Prime of Life." *The New York Times,* February 16, 1999, p. D6.

Griffin, Katherine. "Childless by Choice." *Health,* March/April 1996, p. 99.

———. "What I Do for Love." *Working Woman,* December 1998, p. 38.

Grimsley, Kristin Downey. "From the Top: The Women's View." *The Washington Post,* February 28, 1996, p.C1.

Gross, Jane. "Divorced, Middle-Aged and Happy: Women, Especially, Adjust to the 90's." *The New York Times,* December 7, 1992, p. A14.

Hannon, Kerry. "A Woman's Special Dilemma; Leaving The Workforce for Seven Years Will Cut Your Benefits." *U.S. News & World Report,* June 13, 1994, p. 93.

Hammonds, Keith H. "He Said, She Said." *Business Week,* August 3, 1998, p. 62.

Hardesty, Sarah, and Nehama Jacobs. *Success and Betrayal: The Crisis of Women in Corporate America.* New York: Franklin Watts, 1986.

Heilbrun, Carolyn G. *Reinventing Womanhood.* New York: W. W. Norton, 1979.

———. *Writing a Woman's Life.* New York: W. W. Norton, 1988.

Helson, Ravenna. "The Self in Middle Age." In *Multiple Paths of Midlife Development,* Margie E. Lachman and Jacquelyn Boone James, eds. Chicago: University of Chicago, 1997.

Hewlitt, Sylvia Ann. *A Lesser Life: The Myth of Women's Liberation in America.* New York: William Morrow, 1986.

Heyn, Dalma. *The Erotic Silence of the American Wife.* New York: Turtle Bay Books, 1992.

———. *Marriage Shock: The Transformation of Women into Wives.* New York: Villard, 1997.

Hochschild, Arlie Russell. *The Time Bind: When Work Becomes Home & Home Becomes Work.* New York: Metropolitan Books, 1997.

———. "There's No Place Like Work." *The New York Times Magazine,* April 20, 1997, p. 48.

Holding, Reynolds. "Women in Law: Status Report on the Glass Ceiling." *San Francisco Chronicle,* April 11, 1999, p. A6.

Hontz, Jenny. "More Than Meets the Eye in Tarses-Bashing." *Daily Variety,* July 23, 1997, p. 15.

hooks, bell. *Black Looks: Race and Representation.* Boston: South End Press, 1992.

———. *Talking Back: Thinking Feminist, Thinking Black.* Boston: South End Press, 1989.

Houppert, Karen. "The Parent Trapped." *Newsday,* January 24, 1999, p. B13.

Ireland, Mardy S. *Reconceiving Women: Separating Motherhood from Female Identity.* New York: Guilford Press, 1993.

Jacobs, Deborah L. "Back from the Mommy Track." *The New York Times,* October 9, 1994, p. F1.

Jacoby, Susan. "I Wish I Liked Sex More." *Glamour,* October 1996, p. 230.

Jamieson, Kathleen Hall. *Beyond the Double Bind: Women and Leadership.* New York: Oxford University Press, 1995.

Jones, Charisse. "Living Single." *Essence,* May 1994, p. 138.

Kaganoff, Penny, and Susan Spano, eds. *Women on Divorce: A Bedside Companion.* New York: Harcourt Brace Jovanovich, 1995.

Kaltreider, Nancy, ed. *Dilemmas of a Double Life.* Northvale, N.J.: Jason Aronson, Inc., 1997.

Kantrowitz, Barbara, and Pat Wingert. "The Science of a Good Marriage." *Newsweek,* April 19, 1999, p. 52.

Knapp, Caroline. "The Merry Recluse." *Salon.* On-line. Available: http://www.salon-magazine.com/mwt/feature/1998/07/cov_27feature.html, July 27, 1998.

Korn/Ferry International. "Diversity in the Executive Suites: Good News and Bad News." On-line. Available: http://www.kornferry.com/diversit.htm, November, 1997.

Krotz, Joanna L. "Why Can't a Woman Be Paid Like a Man?" *Working Woman,* July–August 1999, p. 42.

Kurtz, Howard. "Bosses' Words Irk Journalists; Newspaper Executives' Comments Seen As Disparaging Women." *The Washington Post,* May 21, 1998, p. C1.

Lang, Susan S. *Women Without Children: The Reasons, the Rewards, the Regrets.* New York: Pharos Books, 1991.

Laumann, Edward O., John H. Gagnon, Robert T. Michael, and Stuart Michaels. *The Social Organization of Sexuality: Sexual Practices in the United States.* Chicago: University of Chicago Press, 1994.

Lawlor, Julia. "Goodbye to the Job. Hello to the Shock." *The New York Times,* October 12, 1997, p. BU11.

Levenson, Robert W., Laura L. Carstensen, and John M. Gottman. "Emotional Behavior in Long-Term Marriage." In *Psychology and Aging,* 10, 1 (1995), pp. 140–149.

———. "Influence of Age and Gender on Affect, Physiology, and Their Interrelations: A Study of Long-Term Marriages." In *Journal of Personality and Social Psychology,* 67, 1 (1994), pp. 56–68.

———. "Long-Term Marriage: Age, Gender, and Satisfaction." In *Psychology and Aging,* 8, 2 (1993), pp. 310–313.

Levinson, Daniel J., with Judy D. Levinson. *The Seasons of a Woman's Life.* New York: Alfred A. Knopf, 1996.

Lewin, Tamar. "Men Whose Wives Work Earn Less, Studies Show." *The New York Times,* October 12, 1994, p. A1.

———. "Taming the Wild Adolescent." *The New York Times Magazine,* April 5, 1998, p. 98.

———. "Women Are Becoming Equal Providers." *The New York Times,* May 11, 1995, p. A27.

Lewis, Diane E. "Disenchanted Women Give Up Careers to Stay Home." Minneapolis *Star Tribune,* April 6, 1998, p. D7.

Lipman-Blumen, Jean, Todd Fryling, Michael C. Henderson, Christine Webster Moore, and Rachel Vecchiotti. "Women in Corporate Leadership: Reviewing a Decade's Research." Special Report. Wellesley, Mass.: Center for Research on Women, 1996.

Lorde, Audre. *Sister Outsider: Essays and Speeches.* Freedom, Cal.: The Crossing Press, 1984.

Lublin, Joann S. "Some Adult Daughters of 'Supermoms' Plan to Take Another Path." *The Wall Street Journal,* December 28, 1995, p. A1.

Ludtke, Melissa. *On Our Own: Unmarried Motherhood in America.* New York: Random House, 1997.

Lugaila, Terry A. "Marital Status and Living Arrangements: March 1997 (Update)." (Current Population Reports P20-506.) Washington, D.C.: U.S. Bureau of the Census, June 1998.

Machung, Anne. "Talking Career, Thinking Job: Gender Differences in Career and Family Expectations of Berkeley Seniors." *Feminist Studies,* 15, 1 (Spring 1989): 35–58.

Maher, Maggie. "More Women Are Calling the Shots, but They're Still Making Less Than the Guys." *Working Woman,* June 1994, p. 20.

Mahony, Rhona. *Kidding Ourselves: Breadwinning, Babies, and Bargaining Power.* New York: Basic Books, 1995.

"Marriage Rate in U.S. Drops to Record Low: Far Fewer Spouses Say They're 'Very Happy.' " *San Francisco Chronicle,* July 2, 1999, p. A1.

Marshall, Melinda M. *Good Enough Mothers Changing Expectations for Ourselves.* Princeton, N.J.: Peterson's, 1993.

Marshall, Nancy L., and Rosalind C. Barnett. "Child Care, Division of Labor, and Parental Emotional Well-Being Among Two-Earner Couples." Working Paper No. 252. Wellesley, Mass.: Center for Research on Women, 1992.

Mattes, Jane. *Single Mothers by Choice.* New York: Times Books, 1994.

May, Elaine Tyler. *Barren in the Promised Land: Childless Americans and the Pursuit of Happiness.* New York: Basic Books, 1995.

McBroom, Patricia. *The Third Sex: The New Professional Woman.* New York: Paragon House, 1992.

Miller, Jean Baker. *Toward a New Psychology of Women,* 2nd ed. Boston: Beacon Press, 1986.

Morris, Betsy. "Is Family Wrecking Your Career?" *Fortune,* March 17, 1997, p. 71.

National Association for Women in Education. "Americans Support Traditional Sex Roles More Than Those in Most Other Countries." *About Women on Campus,* Summer 1996, p. 12.

———. "Having It All? Well, Not Exactly." *About Women on Campus,* Spring 1996, p. 4.

———. "Women Less Optimistic Than Men." *About Women on Campus,* Spring 1996, p. 4.

National Center for Educational Statistics. "Postsecondary Education." *Digest of Educational Statistics.* On-line. Available: http://nces.ed.gov.pubs99/digest98/index.thml, 1999.

Neugarten, Bernice L. "Adaptation and the Life-Cycle." In *Counseling Adults,* Nancy K. Schlossberg and Alan D. Entine, eds. Monterey, Cal.: Brooks/Cole, 1977, pp. 34–45.

The 1995 Virginia Slims Opinion Poll. Storrs, Conn.: Roper Starch Worldwide, Inc., 1995.

Norment, Lynn. "Sex and the Single Woman." *Ebony,* March 1996, p. 80.

Ogden, Gina. *Women Who Love Sex.* New York: Pocket Books, 1994.

Park, Jackson. "Married . . . with Anxiety." *Elle,* July 1997, p. 68.

Parker, Gwendolyn M. *Trespassing: My Sojourn in the Halls of Privilege.* New York: Houghton Mifflin, 1997.

Passell, Peter. "Hurdles Are Still High for Women Who Want a Career and a Family." *The New York Times,* September 7, 1995, p. D2.

Peters, Joan K. *When Mothers Work: Loving Our Children Without Sacrificing Ourselves.* New York: Addison Wesley Longman, 1997.

Pogrebin, Robin. "Daughters of the Revolution." In *Next: Young American Writers on the New Generation,* Eric Liu, ed. New York: W. W. Norton, 1994, pp. 164–173.

Potuchek, Jean. "The Lives of Single Women: The Meaning of Singleness." Audiotaped lecture, Wellesley, Mass.: Center for Research on Women, 1996.

Price, David Andrew. "A Good Man Is Hard to Find." *The Wall Street Journal,* February 21, 1995, p. A26.

Ramazanoglu, Caroline, and Janet Holland. "Women's Sexuality and Men's Appropriation of Desire." In *Up Against Foucault: Explorations of Some Tensions Between Foucault and Feminism,* Caroline Ramazanoglu, ed. London: Routledge, 1993, pp. 239–264.

Rayner, Victoria L. "Many Single Women Prefer Married Men." *USA Today Magazine,* August 1996, p. 4.

Reid-Merritt, Patricia. *Sister Power: How Phenomenal Black Women Are Rising to the Top.* New York: John Wiley & Sons, 1997.

Rich, Adrienne. *Of Woman Born: Motherhood as Experience and Institution.* New York: Bantam Books, 1977.

Rich, Frank. "Hillary Clinton, R.I.P.: Hollywood Dumps the New Woman." *The New York Times,* November 29, 1995, p. A23.

Rindfuss, Ronald R., S. Philip Morgan, and Kate Offutt. "Education and the Changing Age Pattern of American Fertility: 1963–1989." *Demography,* 33, 3, (August 1996) pp. 277–290.

Roberts, Sam. "Women's Work, What's New, What Isn't." *The New York Times,* April 27, 1995, p. A12.

Roberts, Tara. "Unzipped: 5 Young Black Women Talk About Sex in the Nineties." *Essence,* August 1996, p. 68.

Robinson, Rita. *When Women Choose to Be Single.* Van Nuys, Cal.: Newcastle Publishing, 1992.

Roiphe, Anne. *Fruitful: A Real Mother in the Modern World.* New York: Houghton Mifflin Company, 1996.

Rose, Phyllis. *Parallel Lives: Five Victorian Marriages.* New York: Vintage Books, 1983.

Rubin, Lillian B. *Erotic Wars: What Happened to the Sexual Revolution?* New York: Farrar, Straus & Giroux, 1990.

———. *Intimate Strangers: Men and Women Together.* New York: Harper Colophon Books, 1983.

———. *Just Friends: The Role of Friendship in Our Lives.* New York: Harper & Row, 1985.

———. *Women of a Certain Age: The Midlife Search for Self.* Reissue. New York: Harper & Row, 1990.

Safer, Jeanne. *Beyond Motherhood: Choosing a Life Without Children.* New York: Pocket Books, 1996.

Sandroff, Ronni. "When Women Make More than Men." *Working Woman,* January 1994, p. 38.

Scarf, Maggie. *Unfinished Business: Pressure Points in the Lives of Women.* New York: Ballantine Books, 1980.

Schwartz, Felice N., with Jean Zimmerman. *Breaking with Traditional Women and Work, the New Facts of Life.* New York: Warner Books, 1992.

Schwartz, Pepper. *Peer Marriage: How Love Between Equals Really Works.* New York: The Free Press, 1994.

Scott, Kesho Yvonne. *The Habit of Surviving: Black Women's Strategies for Life.* New Brunswick, N.J.: Rutgers University Press, 1991.

Sellers, Patricia. "Women, Sex & Power." *Fortune,* August 5, 1996, p. 42.

Sheehy, Gail. *Passages.* New York: Bantam, 1976.

Shellenbarger, Sue. "Today's Young Women Are Redefining Debate About Working Moms." *The Wall Street Journal,* July 15, 1998, p. B1.

———. "Woman's Resignation from Top Pepsi Post Rekindles Debate." *The Wall Street Journal,* October 8, 1997, p. B1.

———. "Women Indicate Satisfaction with Role of Big Breadwinner." *The Wall Street Journal,* May 11, 1995, p. B1.

———. "Work & Family: Jobs and the Family Spark Political Hoopla but Few New Answers." *The Wall Street Journal,* June 26, 1996, p. B1.

Sidel, Ruth. *On Her Own: Growing Up in the Shadow of the American Dream.* New York: Viking, 1990.

Silverstein, Stuart. "Differing Views of the Executive Ceiling." *Los Angeles Times,* February 28, 1996, p. D1.

Smith, Lynn. "A Dream Denied." *Los Angeles Times*, October 12, 1994, p. E1.

Smith, Stephen. "Fear Turns to Obsession." MSNBC News. On-line. Available: http://www.msnbc.com/news/124391.asp#BODY, August 1, 1999.

Spaid, Elizabeth Levitan. "Glass Ceiling Remains Thick at Companies' Top Levels." *The Christian Science Monitor*, July 13, 1993, p. 9.

Specter, Michael. "Population Implosion Worries a Graying Europe." *The New York Times*, July 10, 1998, p. A1.

Stacey, Judith. "Gay and Lesbian Families: Queer Like Us." In *All Our Families: New Policies for a New Century*, Mary Ann Mason, Arlene Skolnick, and Stephen D. Sugarman, eds. New York: Oxford University Press, 1998, pp. 117–143.

Stock, Pamela. "Single & Loving It." *Mademoiselle*, October 1996, p. 144.

Suib Cohen, Sherry. "You Talk. He Listens. A True Story." *McCall's*, April 1999, p. 52.

Symonds, William C. "Divorce Executive Style." *Business Week*, August 3, 1998, p. 57.

Tannen, Deborah. *Talking From 9 to 5: How Women's and Men's Conversational Styles Affect Who Gets Heard, Who Gets Credit, and What Gets Done at Work*. London: Virago, 1996

Tatum, Beverly Daniel. *"Why Are All the Black Kids Sitting Together in the Cafeteria" and Other Conversations About Race.* New York: Basic Books, 1997.

Thompson, Sharon. *Going All the Way: Teenage Girls' Tales of Sex, Romance & Pregnancy.* New York: Hill and Wang, 1995.

Toufexis, Anastasia. "When the Ring Doesn't Fit . . ." *Psychology Today*, December 1996, p. 52.

Towers, Sarah. "The New Fear of Thirty." *Mirabella*, May/June 1996, p. 80.

Troester, Rosalie Riegle. "Turbulence and Tenderness: Mothers, Daughters, and 'Othermothers' in *Brown Girl, Brownstones*. In *Double Stitch: Black Women Write About Mothers & Daughters*, Patricia Bell-Scott, Beverly Guy-Sheftall, Jacqueline Jones Royster, Janet Sims-Wood, Miriam DeCosta-Willis, and Lucie Fultz, eds. Boston: Beacon Press, 1992, pp. 163–172.

U.S. Bureau of the Census. "Nearly 70 Percent of Elderly Widows Live Alone, According to U.S. Census Bureau." Press Release. Washington, D.C.: U.S. Bureau of the Census, July 1998, On-line. Available: http://www.census.gov/Press-Release/cb98-126.html.

———. *Statistical Abstract of the United States: 1998* (118th edition). Washington, D.C.: U.S. Bureau of the Census, 1998.

Vobejda, Barbara. "Children of Working Moms Get Along Just Fine." *San Francisco Chronicle*, January 28, 1999, p. A3.

Waggoner, Dianna. "For Working Women, Having It All May Mean Doing It All." *People*, September 4, 1989, p. 51.

Wallerstein, Judith, and Sandra Blakeslee. *The Good Marriage: How & Why Love Lasts.* New York: Warner Books, 1996.

———. *Second Chances: Men, Women, and Children a Decade After Divorce.* New York: Ticknor & Fields, 1989.

Walsh, Elsa. *Divided Lives: The Public and Private Struggles of Three Accomplished Women.* New York: Simon and Schuster, 1995.

Walter, Carolyn Ambler. *The Timing of Motherhood: Is Later Better?* Lexington, Mass.: Lexington Books, 1986.

Weston, Kath. *Families We Choose.* New York: Columbia University Press, 1991.

Whetstone, Muriel L. "The Working Mother's Dilemma. *Ebony*, May 1996, p. 26.

———. "Why Professional Women Should Consider Blue-Collar Men." *Ebony*, March 1994, p. 25.

Wiesendanger, Betsy. "Labors of Love," *Working Woman*. May 1999, p. 43.

Wolf, Naomi. *The Beauty Myth: How Images of Beauty Are Used Against Women.*   London: Vintage, 1991.

———. *Promiscuities: The Secret Struggle for Womanhood.* New York: Random House, 1997.

"Women Emerge in Benefits Debate." *San Francisco Chronicle,* September 13, 1999, p. A6.

"Women's Choices, Not Bias, Blamed for Lower Earnings." *Los Angeles Times,* December 15, 1995, p. 43A.

Wood, Daniel B. "Young Women Exercise Options." *The Christian Science Monitor,* May 24, 1994, p. 9.

Woodman, Sue. "On the Run from the Law." *Ms.,* November/December 1995, p. 38.

"Working Moms Relying More on Day Care, Census Says." *San Francisco Chronicle,* March 24, 1996, p. A5.

Wuetcher, Sue. "Housework Limits the Wages of Women." *Source,* Fall 1989, p. 15.

Wyatt, Gail Elizabeth. *Stolen Women: Reclaiming Our Sexuality, Taking Back Our Lives.* New York: John Wiley, 1997.

Zernike, Kate. "MIT Women Win a Fight Against Bias: In Rare Move, School Admits Discrimination." *The Boston Globe,* March 21, 1999, p. A1.

Visit the Piatkus website!

Piatkus publishes a wide range of exciting fiction and non-fiction, including books on health, mind body & spirit, sex, self-help, cookery, biography and the paranormal.

If you want to:

- read descriptions of our popular titles

- buy our books over the internet

- take advantage of our special offers

- enter our monthly competition

- learn more about your favourite Piatkus authors

visit our website at:

www.piatkus.co.uk